This book is to be returned on or before
the last date stamped below

D0766278

LIBREX

Field Guide to Butterflies and Moths of Britain and Europe

DR HELGARD REICHHOLF-RIEHM
Consultant Editors:
Dr Jeremy Thomas (Butterflies)
Barry Goater (Moths)

The Crowood Press

This edition first published in 1991 by
The Crowood Press Ltd
Gipsy Lane
Swindon
Wiltshire SN2 6DQ

British Library Cataloguing in Publication Data

Reichholf-Riehm, Helgard
    Field guide to butterflies and moths of Britain and
    Europe.
    1. Europe. Butterflies & Moths
    I. Title   II. [Die farbingen Naturfahrer Schmetterlinge.
    English]
    595.78094

ISBN 1 85223 593 4

Front cover photograph: Grayling (Paul Sterry, Nature Photographers)
Back cover photograph: Adonis Blue (Robin Bush, Nature Photographers)

Original title: *Steinbachs Naturführer: Schmetterlinge* by Dr Helgard Reichholf-
Riehm

The publishers would like to thank Iain and Ingrid Macmillan for translating the
original German text, and Dr Jeremy Thomas (butterflies) and Mr Barry Goater
(moths) for adapting the text for the English language.

Illustrations by Fritz Wendler

Phototypeset by Input Typesetting Ltd, London
Printed and bound by Times Publishing Group, Singapore

Contents

Key to the Symbols

♂	=	Male
♀	=	Female
Des	=	Description
H	=	Habitat
Dis	=	Distribution
A	=	Abundance
Fl	=	Flight
LC	=	Life cycle and/or caterpillar season
FP	=	Foodplants of the caterpillars
G	=	General
f	=	Form

Painted Lady

Preface

The purpose of this book is to introduce the reader to a selection of the butterflies and moths of Europe. Although emphasis has been laid on the more colourful day-flying butterflies and the more spectacular moths, several of the smaller and less conspicuous microlepidoptera are described and illustrated. It is thus hoped that more people will be encouraged to learn about the lives of these smaller moths and, by looking at them with a lens, to appreciate that they too are objects of great beauty. Moreover, like the larger Lepidoptera, the 'micros' are important indicators of the health of the environment, and likewise sensitive to changes in their habitats. While it is regrettable that many species are becoming rare, or have even been lost, as a result of human activity, the planting of monocultures by man has produced problems of a different kind, in which some insects have increased to such an extent that they have become pests in some crops.

Butterfly watching, as opposed to butterfly collecting, has recently become popular with many naturalists. If one of the purposes is to identify the species, then very nearly all the British butterflies and a considerable number of European species can be named accurately without handling them. Of course, they can be enjoyed and photographed even if their identity is uncertain, but if sightings are to be submitted as records proper identification is absolutely essential. It has to be accepted that with some butterflies, such as the Alpine *Erebia* species, specimens must not only be caught, but dissected, before their credentials can be established. Most of the equally interesting moths are nocturnal, and special efforts have to be made in order to encounter them. A few can be found at rest during the day, on fence posts, tree trunks, foliage or rocks or walls; some can be sighted by mounting vigil over patches of flowers at dusk and identified by their characteristic behaviour; others can be lured to artificial baits, but the majority are only seen when a bright light is exposed in their flying area. The best way of all, perhaps, is to breed the species from the egg (many female moths, taken at light, will lay freely in a small box), or to discover the early stages in the wild. In this way, the naturalist is able to gain an intimate understanding of the habits and life histories of these most fascinating of animals.

Note: The nomenclature for this volume follows P. Leraut, *Liste Systematique et Synoymique des Lepidopteres de France, Belgique et Corse* (Alexanor, Paris, 1980) updated in accordance with more recent work.

Key to the Symbols

Syntomidae and *Limacodidae*, as well as the micro-moths which include the *Pyralidae* *Pte
rophoridae*, *Tortricidae* and *Coleophoridae*, have been treated together under the same symbol. All other symbols always refer to one family of butterflies or moths.

Lycaenidae, p 60
Blues, Hairstreaks
and Coppers

Hesperiidae, p 68
Skippers

Lymantriidae, p 72
Tussocks

Arctiidae, p 78
Tigers and Footmen

Zygaenidae, p 106
Burnets and Foresters

Sphingidae, p 110
Hawkmoths

Thyatiridae, p 128
Lutestrings

Drepanidae, p 132
Hook-tips

Psychidae, p 146
Psychids

Sesiidae, p 148
Clearwings

Cossidae, p 150
Goats and Leopards

Hepialidae, p 152
Swifts and Ghosts

8

Papilionidae, p 16
Swallowtails

Pieridae, p 22
Whites and Yellows

Nymphalidae, p 32
Brush-footed Butterflies

Satyridae, p 50
Browns and Ringlets

Endrosidae, p 92
Dew Moths

Syntomidae
& Limacodidae, p 92
Syntomids and Festoons

Thaumetopoeidae, p 94
Processionary Moths

Notodontidae, p 96
Prominents

Attacidae, p 136
Silk Moths

Lasiocampidae, p 140
Eggars, Lackeys and
Lappets

Thyrididae, p 144
Thyrids

Noctuidae, p 154
Noctuids

Geometridae, p 218
Geometers

Microlepidoptera, p 248
Micro-moths

Introduction

Until recently it was calculated that there were upwards of 1.2 million different animal species in the world, over three-quarters of which were insects. Recent studies in the South American rain forests have resulted in this estimate being raised to nearly 30 million, nearly all the extra species being insects! The basic design of a body consisting of head, thorax and abdomen, with six legs and two pairs of wings, is one that is astonishingly versatile and successful. Butterflies and moths have the attributes of the generalized insect and in terms of numbers of species, rank third to the Hymenoptera (bees, wasps and ants) and Coleoptera (beetles). There are said to be more than 150,000 Lepidoptera in the world, surely a conservative figure, and of these, some 4,700 are recorded for France and Belgium, and about 2,500 in Britain.

Butterflies and moths are placed in the Order Lepidoptera. This name, translated means 'scaly-winged', for the presence of minute scales, which cover the wings like overlapping tiles, is one of the diagnostic features which distinguish these from all other insects. As in other insects, the head of a lepidopteron bears a pair of sensory antennae, club-tipped in butterflies and often serrated or feathery in moths. The paired compound eyes are also found in other insects, but the typical feeding apparatus is unique to the Lepidoptera, and consists of a long probing tongue or proboscis, which is coiled like a watch spring when not in use. Only the most primitive Lepidoptera have biting mouthparts. They feed on pollen, whereas the majority suck nectar from flowers. As such they are important pollinators, and many white, long-tubed flowers which only emit scent at night are specialized for pollination by moths. A good many moths, however, have lost their mouthparts during their evolution, and do not feed at all.

The majority of Lepidoptera use their legs for holding on, not running about, and it is only when the insect emerges from its pupa that it uses its legs for scrambling to a suitable position where it can expand its wings. Some moths are notable 'scuttlers', which run for cover when disturbed, but they are in the minority.

The two pairs of wings are attached to the second and third thoracic segments, and are coupled together so they operate in unison. The coupling structures vary in different families of Lepidoptera, but commonly there is a bristle-like frenulum on the base of the hindwing, which fits into a pocket, the retinaculum, at the base of the forewing. The females of a number of species have reduced wings, and are incapable of flight, and a few have lost them altogether. The bright colours and elaborate patterns on the wings of Lepidoptera are imparted by the individual scales, which are either pigmented or produce metallic or iridescent interference colours because of their structure.

The colours of the wings have important functions. As a rule, day-flying Lepidoptera are brightly coloured and nocturnal ones are not. The generally gaudy butterflies often use their colours in ourtship, and it has been shown recently that many butterfly 'colours' are reflections of ultra-violet light, visible to other butterflies but not to vertebrates. Adult Lepidoptera are preyed upon by many different vertebrates, notably birds

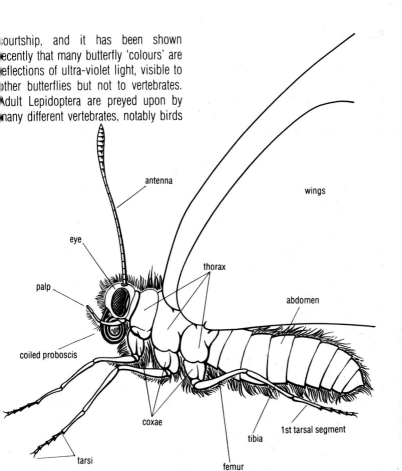

and lizards, and their colours can be used for camouflage, to confuse, or to warn.

Many moths rest in exposed sites by day, and are very difficult to detect. Some leap away when approached, revealing brightly coloured hindwings which confuse pursuers, especially when the colours disappear as the moth alights again. Eye-like markings, often very realistic, have been shown to have a deterrent effect on birds, and a brightly

coloured 'uniform' of red and black, or yellow and black, warns the attacker that the insect is distasteful. A few species mimic distasteful ones by wearing the same uniform, when in fact they are palatable.

Colour is intricately linked to a moth's or butterfly's shape and behaviour. A brightly coloured Peacock butterfly, hibernating in the dark corner of a shed, closes its wings over its back so only the blackish underside shows. Geometer

Right wing pairs

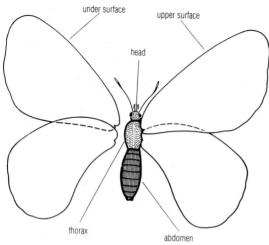

under surface
upper surface
head
thorax
abdomen

The arrangement of scales determines pattern

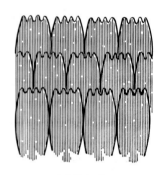

individual scales

moths, with streaks which stretch across the spread wings from tip to tip, position themselves when at rest on trees with their bodies parallel to the ground, and the streaks set vertically with the grain of bark. There is more than a lifetime's work in the painstaking observation and recording of such phenomena.

The abdomen of a butterfly or moth lacks appendages, but its colour or posture may constitute an important part of the defence mechanism. To the serious student the important structures in the abdomen are the genital organs. Those of male and female of a particular species fit together like a lock and key during pairing, and closely related species can often only be identified by examining the specific differences in the genitalia. The specimen has to be killed and dissected.

The outline of the life cycle of a butterfly or moth is known to the majority of people, but the details for many species have still to be estab-

lished. Here again lies a fruitful field for the amateur naturalist. It is often not too difficult to persuade a fertile female to lay eggs (which will differ in structure from species to species). The appearance, behaviour and foodplants of many caterpillars have yet to be discovered, and those which are known can give pleasure by being bred again. The pupal stage is that in which the animal's tissues are reorganized to form the adult insect, and pupal structure is a comparatively neglected study, especially in regard to the smaller moths.

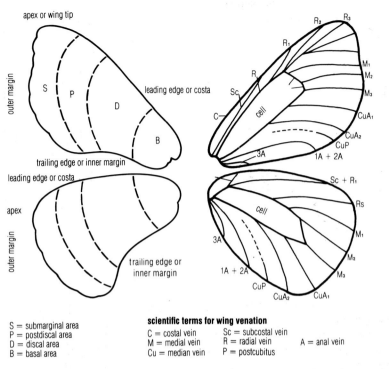

apex or wing tip

S

outer margin

leading edge or costa

S = submarginal area
P = postdiscal area

P

D

B

trailing edge or inner margin

leading edge or costa

apex

outer margin

trailing edge or inner margin

R₂   R₃
R₁
M₁
M₂
M₃

R

Sc

C

cell

CuA₁
CuA₂
CuP
1A + 2A

3A

Sc + R₁

Rs

cell

M₁

3A

M₂
M₃

1A + 2A

CuP
CuA₂   CuA₁

S = submarginal area
P = postdiscal area
D = discal area
B = basal area

scientific terms for wing venation

C = costal vein   Sc = subcostal vein
M = medial vein   R = radial vein   A = anal vein
Cu = median vein   P = postcubitus

How to look for butterflies and moths

A naturalist living in the suburbs of southern England would be fortunate to see as many as ten species of butterfly in the garden in a year. Using a moth trap with a mercury-vapour lamp, will probably produce records of about 200 species of the larger moths each season. To add to this list, it will be necessary to venture further afield.

Within their climatic zone, few species can be said to occur everywhere. This is because the great majority of lepidopterous larvae are plant feeders, and their distribution follows that of their foodplants. Plants have evolved a variety of strategies to avoid getting eaten by insects. Foremost is the production of

chemicals which are toxic or distasteful to caterpillars, and this explains why most caterpillars are found on only one or a small number of foodplants: the caterpillars in turn have evolved a metabolism to cope with such noxious substances. It is therefore important for the lepidopterist to have a working knowledge of the distribution and appearance of plants, and to be able to deduce the likelihood of a particular butterfly or moth being present in the vicinity.

Sometimes, the sight of damaged leaves can lead to the discovery of the caterpillars that are responsible. In late summer, if the tips of the shoots of young sallow bushes are seen to be

13

Egg shapes

White Admiral

Emperor

egg tower of
Map Butterfly

Black Arches

Scarce Vapourer

Canary-shouldered
Thorn

Green-veined
White

Small Heath

Scarce Swallowtail

Swallowtail

Painted Lady

Ephesia fulminea

defoliated, a search may reveal the presence of a large caterpillar of the Eyed Hawkmoth.

Many larvae of the smaller moths mine the leaves of particular species of plant, and the shape of the galleries they produce between upper and lower epidermis is characteristic. Others spin bunches of leaves together in a characteristic way, or roll them or fold them, and live within the spinning. The fruits of many species of plant harbour caterpillars in due season. Many noctuid larvae feed at night and hide in the soil by day, and an excellent way of finding many such species is to go out at night with a lantern in springtime, and search among low plants and on tree saplings with bursting buds.

The caterpillars of many moths pupate in the soil, and persistent hunting among the roots of forest trees may successfully unearth a few. However, digging for pupae around the roots of isolated trees, or under patches of specialized foodplant such as sea campion or butterbur, is more likely to be rewarding. Butterfly pupae are formed above ground, attached to vegetation, and although they are often ornate and colourful, are sometimes extraordinarily difficult to find.

It is not too difficult to see the great majority of native butterflies in a couple of seasons, given good weather and a willingness to make expeditions to find the more local species. In the first warm days of spring, hibernated Peacocks and Small Tortoiseshells are on the wing. The first butterfly to emerge is the Speckled Wood; a little later, the white butterflies emerge. May is the season for the smaller fritillaries.

High summer is the season *par excellence* for British butterflies. A visit to ancient woodland in the south should yield Silver-washed Fritillary, White Admiral, Purple Emperor and Purple Hairstreak. On heaths in August, Silver-studded Blues and Graylings are characteristic, and chalk downland is often excellent for butterflies at this time of year. County Naturalist's Trusts, local Natural History Societies and fellow entomologists are traditionally helpful to the bona fide naturalist who wishes to see the less common species.

14

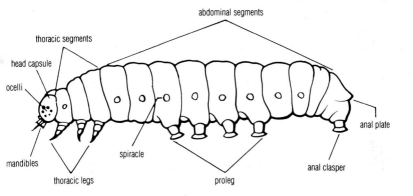

abdominal segments

thoracic segments

head capsule

ocelli

mandibles

thoracic legs

spiracle

proleg

anal plate

anal clasper

Butterfly pupa

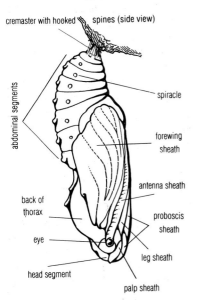

cremaster with hooked spines (side view)

abdominal segments

spiracle

forewing sheath

antenna sheath

back of thorax

proboscis sheath

eye

leg sheath

head segment

palp sheath

noctuid and geometer moths rest by day on fences, tree trunks and walls where they are often marvellously camouflaged. Many geometers hide by day among foliage, and can be dislodged by tapping bushes with a stick. In southern Europe, some moths both hide by day and hibernate in the darkest recesses of caves. They can be found, sometimes commonly, with the aid of a lantern in such gloomy haunts.

Recommended bedside reading for those who wish to know more about looking for butterflies and moths is *Practical Hints for the Field Lepidopterist* by J. W. Tutt, reprinted from the *Entomologist's Record and Journal of Variation* at the end of the last century. It is out of print, but sometimes obtainable from specialist booksellers.

Diurnal moths such as the foresters and burnets can be found easily by visiting their localities at the correct season. Moths which rest during the day and fly only at night present a different problem. The presence of many species can only be revealed by operating a light trap in their special haunts. In Britain, many

Swallowtail *Papilio machaon* L.

Description: forewing up to 3.4 cm in males. Slim body and small head characteristic of all butterflies. Antennae with small clubs at the tips. Long hairs on front legs serve as combs for grooming. Slightly arched hindwing with tail. Distinct yellow and black patterning. Swallowtails (*Papilionidae*) are extremely attractive and represent one of our most majestic butterflies.

Habitat: in Europe; open countryside ranging from coastal areas to mountains up to 2,000 m; usually frequents mountain peaks during the summer months. Also found in gardens where carrots are being cultivated. Often seen flying across summer meadows in search of wild carrot, dill, caraway and other flowers. In Britain is far more specialized and is found only on fenland.

Distribution: almost worldwide; the European races range from North Africa to the very northern part of Europe. In England this is a different subspecies (*Britannicus*) which has always been extremely local and is now confined to the Norfolk Broads.

Abundance: since the caterpillars feed on common *Compositae*, Swallowtails used to be abundant; however, changes in agriculture, rather than collecting, have brought them near to extinction in many locations.

Flight: in northern Europe – with its shorter summers – one generation develops between June and August, while in the south – with its longer and warmer summer periods – there are always two generations. In Britain there is often a small second brood, however. In North Africa there are as many as three broods with the butterflies flying from April to October.

Life expectancy is usually one or two weeks, with many dying very soon after mating and egg-laying. Food intake is only of minor importance for adults of species that do not hibernate. They need only a little nectar from flowers and dewdrops, and can often be seen on salt patches or cow pats absorbing minerals and nitrogen mixtures.

Life cycle: first generation caterpillars from May to June, second generation August to September. The caterpillar initially resembles a bird dropping being black with red warts and a large white spot on its back. Later it turns green with black rings, each of which is marked with six yellowish red dots.

Foodplants: caterpillar food is less restricted than that of other species. They feed on the leaves of various umbelliferous plants, in particular wild and cultured carrot, dill, pimpernel, caraway, and parsley (in Britain caterpillars feed exclusively on milk parsley).

General: little colour variation. In very rare cases black specimens with blue rings on the hindwings have been encountered. While the first generation tends to be pale, the second generation butterflies have a deep, dark yellow colour.

On Corsica and Sardinia the very similar Corsican Swallowtail (*Papilio hospiton* Gn.), can be found alongside the Swallowtail. Its caterpillars also feed on leaves of umbelliferous plants. It is not yet known how these two species can be separated ecologically. The same is true of the Southern Swallowtail (*Papilio alexanor* Esp.) which occurs in very small areas in the south of France, southern Italy, and southern Yugoslavia. Even within their very restricted geographical areas, these two Swallowtail species are extremely rare.

The original home of the Swallowtails is the tropics. Only a single species has managed to penetrate to the cool and temperate zones of northern Europe.

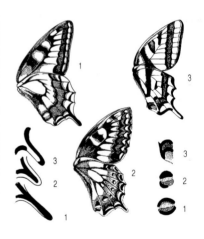

1 = *P. machaon*,   2 = *P. hospiton*,   3 = *P. alexanor*

Scarce Swallowtail *Iphiclides podalirius* L.

Description: forewings up to *c.*4 cm, with the female growing to a slightly larger size than the male. The basic colour is pale yellow, with the second generation being paler than the first. The underside of the hindwings is marked by a band filled with orange that can be easily recognized when they are at rest, but which is absent in the summer generation. The body is black and narrow, and the forehead is covered in dense hair.

Habitat: warm terrain with scrub vegetation. In mountain regions the butterflies are found on sunny slopes up to 2,000 m.

Distribution: in Europe south of 54°N. Absent in Britain.

Abundance: north of the Alps Scarce Swallowtails are rare, being restricted to a few warm areas. South of the Alps they are widespread and common especially in orchards.

Flight: north of the Alps, first generation from May to July. A second generation only in Alsace, the valley of the River Main, in lower Austria and south of the Alps, where they fly until September.

Life cycle: north of the Alps caterpillars feed from June to July, south of the Alps June to August.

Foodplants: larval diet includes blackthorn, bird cherry and cherry, also hawthorn; in the south, peach and almond trees.

General: variations are known among the Scarce Swallowtails (*I. podalirius f. inalpina*), which occur in the Alps. They are marked by broader black bands, broader and shorter wings, and shorter tails. In Spain and Portugal the form *feisthamelii* occurs, which might even represent a species on its own.

Southern Festoon *Zerynthia polyxena* L. Schiff.

Description: male's forewing up to 2.6 cm; female's 2.8 cm. The Southern Festoon can hardly be confused with any other species because of its characteristic shape and colouring. The basic colour is yellow, with black bands and a scattering of red dots which are absent in some individuals. Both sexes have the same colouring.

Habitat: warm, sunny and dry slopes up to 1,000 m.

Distribution: only found in isolated pockets because of its very specific ecological requirements. Most northerly distribution is in lower Austria and Moravia. From here it penetrates far into the southern areas of the Balkan Peninsula, into the European part of Turkey, and into southern Russia.

Abundance: never in large numbers and now faced with extinction in many places since its foodplant is becoming increasingly scarce.

Flight: end of April to May in one generation.

Life cycle: caterpillars feed from May to July, depending on altitude.

Foodplants: caterpillars feed only on the leaves of birthwort.

General: birthwort and the Southern Festoon survive together in only a few southern valleys of the Alps, and thus need strict protection, for this butterfly is one of Europe's more beautiful butterflies. A similar species, Spanish Festoon (*T. rumina* L), which can be recognized by the distribution of its red dots, occurs in the south of France, Spain, Portugal and North Africa. Its general appearance, behaviour and habitat requirements are identical to those of the Southern Festoon.

Apollo *Parnassius apollo* L.

Description: forewings up to 3 cm. Great variability in distribution of the characteristic black dots and rings filled with red or yellow. Although there is no problem in identifying the Apollo, no two individuals seem identical. Numerous sub-species have been described, and nearly every Alpine valley in which Apollos occur seems to produce its own individual pattern. Since distribution is only in isolated pockets, there is little chance for the butterflies to mix.

Habitat: valleys up to 2,000 m, also at subalpine levels, but only local distribution; prefers limestone.

Distribution: subalpine and Alpine regions in Norway, Sweden, Finland, western Russia and especially in Moravia, the Alps, Apennines, Dalmatia, the south of France, Pyrenees, central Spain, Andalusia, Sicily, Carpathian Mountains, and northern Greece. Not found in the British Isles.

Abundance: can occur in fairly large numbers locally. Some populations have disappeared, presumably because of over-collecting. Strict protection is necessary for the surviving populations. The Apollo has been protected by law for a long time, but this is of little use if its habitat comes increasingly under pressure.

Flight: relatively long period, from June to August.

Life cycle: the caterpillars generally hibernate; occasionally the fully developed caterpillars hibernate in their egg-sack and do not emerge until spring when they feed from April to June.

Foodplants: caterpillars can feed only on *Sedum* species, the best-known of which is white stonecrop.

Clouded Apollo *Parnassius mnemosyne* L.

Description: forewings 2.6–3 cm. This close relative to the Apollo is much less imposing; its markings are only black and white and it does not reach the size of the Apollo whose numerous species and forms are described further on under this entry.

Habitat: widely distributed in lowland, subalpine, and Alpine regions up to 1,500 m. Prefers meadows bordering on mixed woodlands, and mountain slopes on deciduous woodlands.

Distribution: in central Europe to 65°N. Absent only in Britain, Denmark, and the Iberian Peninsula. Even within its area it is rare and occurs in isolated pockets.

Abundance: can occur in large numbers locally. The few known populations are strictly protected and sites are often kept secret.

Flight: May to mid-July, only one generation.

Life cycle: caterpillar April to May or, if the caterpillar hibernates, August to June.

Foodplants: Clouded Apollo depends strictly on *Corydalis* which flourishes only under special conditions; therefore the butterfly is restricted to these habitats.

General: the Clouded Apollo occurs in many subspecies. For example in central Europe there is *batavus* Fr. near Regensburg/Kehlheim, *ariovistus* Fr. in southern Württemberg and the Swabian Jura, *hercynianus* in the Harz Mountains, and *hassicus* Pag. in Hesse. Similarly, numerous different subspecies can be found in Alpine valleys and the various isolated areas of distribution in Yugoslavia and Greece. The Clouded Apollo is protected by law. The few places where it occurs should be spared from changes in cultivation.

Swallowtails

Description: with fore-wings of 3.3 cm, the Large White is one of the largest representatives of its family, making it easily recognizable even in flight; it also has very distinctive black dots and dark areas. The female can be indentified by her yellow undersides which are even more marked in the second generation.

Habitat: the Large White is a highly mobile butterfly which can be found anywhere – in nature reserves and large cities, in corn and cabbage fields. Like a number of other Whites, the Large White has benefited from agriculture. Occurs in mountains up to 2,000 m.

Distribution: in Europe up to 62°N, but rarer in the north than the south. Common throughout Britain.

Abundance: one of the commonest of all butter-flies, with population explosions in some years. Many millions move south in large flocks to North Africa, where other populations of the Large White occur. The first generation produces few individuals, while the second and third generations produce large numbers. In years of abundance numerous caterpillars are parasitized by the ichneumon fly (*Apanteles glomeratus*), occasionally to such an extent that local populations are virtually wiped out. However, these are quickly replaced by newcomers from other areas.

Flight: there are two to three generations. The first flies from mid-April to the beginning of June, the second from mid-July to the end of August, and the third – which occurs only in favourable years – from September to October.

Life cycle: first generation caterpillars from August to October, second generation June to July, and third generation in September. The pupa hibernates. The yellow, lightly spun larval cocoons of the ichneumon fly are occasionally found next to the caterpillars and pupae.

Foodplants: since the favourite diet of the caterpillars is cabbage, and other domestic brassicas, attempts have been made to control the situation using pesticides. However, studies have shown that the natural enemies are more affected by these poisons than the target species, with the result that even more Large (and Small) Whites survive in fields that have been sprayed. Despite local, short-term reductions in numbers resulting from pest control, the Large White has remained very common. The traditional foodplants of the Large White are the crucifers, including wild mustard, and wild radish.

General: no different races occur within this very common and widely distributed migratory species. Before cabbage cultivation began on a large scale, it was presumably far less frequent, but the virtual paradise created for the caterpillars from Roman times onward, probably caused the large population that exists today.

Monocultures always favour certain species and thus create pests. The Large White has remained one of the few butterflies whose survival is no matter for concern. However, it is not only the Large White that benefits from this increase in numbers; its predators benefit too, since they progress in a very similar cycle, following the stages of their host with a time delay of perhaps a few weeks. Apart from the ichneumon fly, the most important enemy is a granulosis virus. Also important is the fungus *Entomophtora sphaerosperma*, which peaks at the end of the population explosion of the Large White. Since these enemies have a considerable effect, it is unusual for the Large White to increase its population significantly in two consecutive years.

Whites & Yellows

emerging butterfly

23

Small White *Pieris rapae* L.

Description: forewings up to 3 cm. As the name implies, this is a smaller relative of the Large White and displays similar colouration.

Habitat: common and widely distributed, it occurs in open countryside and gardens. Ranges from coastal to mountain regions up to 2,000 m, also over mountain passes.

Distribution: All over Europe including Britain up to 62°N. Individual butterflies are also found further north.

Abundance: common everywhere; occasional population explosions, as in the case of the Large White.

Flight: two to three generations have regularly been observed. The third generation is often incomplete. First generation butterflies fly from April to May, second generation from July to August, the third from September to October. The butterflies from the different generations differ in the development of the dark markings and the degree of scaling.

Life cycle: first generation caterpillars active from September to October, second generation in July, the third in September. The caterpillars are dull green with pale sides and a pale stripe.

Foodplants: caterpillars feed on the leaves of cruciferous plants, and also on wild mignonette, rock-cress, wild garlic, and plants of the cabbage family. They prefer the 'heart' of the cabbage while the caterpillars of the Large White (*P. brassicae*) eat their way through the cabbage from the outside to the centre.

General: flight is slow and fluttery like that of all Whites.

Green-veined White *Pieris napi* L.

Description: forewings up to 2.5 cm. Spring and summer generations differ in size and colouring. Sexes also differ in colouring, with the most obvious differences relating to colour intensity, degree of scaling, and size of the black spot on the outer margin of the forewing. The summer generation is distinctly larger, reaching a forewing length of 2.5 cm.

Habitat: open countryside, preferably damp places, woodland meadows or hillsides with scrub. In mountain regions up to 2,000 m.

Distribution: all over Europe, including Britain, except the highest polar and mountain regions.

Abundance: not a threatened species: in general occurs frequently and is easy to find.

Flight: three generations have been observed, with the third generation occurring only in warm, sunny years and often incomplete. First generation flies from May to June, second generation from mid-June to August, the third in September. Active Green-veined Whites are only very rarely found as late as October.

Life cycle: first generation caterpillars from August to September, second in June, the third in August. The caterpillar is dull green with small dots and black hairs on its upper side, and has black spiracles with yellow borders.

Foodplants: caterpillars feed on various cruciferous plants, such as rape, cuckoo flower, watercress, towercress, rock-cress, wild garlic, and all plants of the cabbage family.

General: several colour variations of this butterfly are known, for example a yellow variety, *f. flava*. In the south, males can reach the size of a Small White becoming easily confused with the latter.

Black-veined White *Aporia crataegi* L.

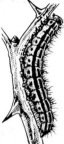

Description: one of the largest butterflies of this family, with forewings reaching almost 3.5 cm. Can be distinguished from the more or less similar-sized Large White by its dark veins. The wings appear almost transparent, especially in the females.

Habitat: everywhere in open countryside, meadows, and gardens. Used to be particularly common in orchards where it could reach pest proportions. Extinct in many places for unknown reasons. Now found almost exclusively in less intensively cultivated areas or nature reserves in the northern half of Europe, but one of the commonest and most widespread species in the south.

Distribution: all over Europe up to 62°N. Extinct in Britain, and absent from Sardinia, and Corsica.

Particularly abundant in North Africa, Morocco, an Algeria.

Abundance: used to be very common, bu modern fruit-growing methods caused extensiv reduction in numbers. Can suddenly occur in larg numbers and disappear just as quickly. Causes c these sudden increases are not yet known.

Flight: from May to beginning of July in on generation.

Life cycle: caterpillars from August to June. The assemble to build a communal nest for hibernatior The ash-grey caterpillar has two broad, orange-re stripes along its back. The pupa is a greenish yellow with black dots, and is attached to leaves c branches with threads.

Foodplants: hawthorn, but also likes cherry an other fruit trees. Also found on mountain-ash, bir cherry, and birch. The Black-veined White differ: from the other European Whites in its choice c food plants.

Bath White *Pontia daplidice* L.

Description: forewings nearly 2.5 cm. Typical White with prominent veins and black spots. Since there are some other very similar species, only an expert can reliably identify the Bath White.

Habitat: usually in lowlands, occasionally in hilly regions. North of the Alps only in warm, dry places; in mountain regions up to 2,000 m.

Distribution: despite its occurrence all over Europe up to 60°N, it has only established itself permanently in very warm places; more abundant south of the Alps. A strong migratory species which flies to North Africa in the autumn. Most northern European populations depend on migrants from the south. Pupae do not survive severe winters. A very occasional migrant to Britain.

Abundance: its European range is restricte because of its preference for warm regions; no large populations seem to be well established anywhere Despite this, mass migrations can occur in some years. Drastic population fluctuations are normal.

Flight: the Bath White occurs in two generations the first is from April to June, the second July tc August.

Life cycle: the first-generation caterpillars can be found from August to September, the second ir June. The caterpillar is grey-green with two yellow stripes running along each side of its body, anc with small black raised dots.

Foodplants: apart from wild mignonette, the caterpillars also feed on hedge mustard, tower-cress, alison, and other cruciferous plants.

General: the Bath White is a vagrant species tha migrates over a wide range.

Description: striking, bright yellow butterfly with forewings up to 3 cm. The sexes differ in colouring – only the male displays the bright yellow wings with the four orange-red dots, one on each wing. The female is much paler but is also marked with the dots. At first glance the female in flight can be confused with a White. Note characteristic wing shape.

Habitat: virtually everywhere – in gardens, open woodlands, heathlands, meadows, and mountains up to 2,000 m.

Distribution: Europe, North Africa and temperate regions of Asia, to Siberia. In Europe it is absent only from extreme north of England, Scandinavia, and Crete.

Abundance: Widely distributed but usually found in low numbers. However, tens or hundreds of adults may gather in late summer in sunny woodland areas.

Life Cycle: the Brimstone's cycle differs from other butterflies. It is on the wing for an unusually long time – beginning in July – and has one of the longest life expectancies of any butterfly, surviving until the following spring. In order to conserve energy wisely during this long period, the Brimstone takes numerous rests. After a few days of activity it becomes torpid for several weeks, before resuming activity when weather conditions are favourable. The days on the wing are spent feeding on nectar to build up a sufficient store of energy.

In spring the courtship flight can be observed, with the female flying ahead, followed by the male at a steady distance, as though he were being towed by an invisible thread. Mating occurs when the first buds emerge on buckthorn and alder buckthorn, where the female deposits her eggs. A sticky substance helps them to adhere to the food plant.

The small caterpillars hatch in June. They are dull green with paler sides and a pale, nearly white stripe along the length of the body just above the legs. Such counter shading (dark on top, pale below) gives excellent camouflage, which is vital for concealing the caterpillar from the sharp eyes of songbirds.

In July, after approximately four weeks, the caterpillars pupate. The length of the caterpillar stage depends on the weather: if it is cold and wet, the caterpillars eat little and so delay their development. Warm, dry days speed up their growth-rate and shorten the caterpillar stage.

Foodplants: Brimstone caterpillars feed exclusively on the leaves of buckthorn (*Rhamnus frangula*), from which the Brimstone derives its Latin name.

General: a single species throughout Europe with only slight variations. However in the south, forewing lengths of *f. meridionalis* can be up to 3.3 cm. It is not clear whether this is a form or a proper subspecies. An ecological adaptation seems likely to have occurred since its habitat is shared by the Cleopatra (*Gonepteryx cleopatra* L), without doubt a competitor of the Brimstone. To coexist they keep out of each other's way.

The closely related Cleopatra is extremely easy to confuse with other species. It is restricted to southern Europe where it is widespread and common. Apart from its longevity, the Brimstone possesses another astonishing ability: it hibernates without protection near to the ground or in dry leaves, and can survive temperatures far below zero without any risk. In contrast, it suffers more during mild winters since its energy consumption rises with the higher temperatures and therefore uses up its reserves more quickly. The Brimstone's resistance to cold can be attributed to the properties of its body fluid, a mixture of water, protein, and salts.

Whites & Yellows

29

Orange-tip *Anthocharis cardamines* L.

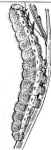

Des: ♂ forewing 2.5 cm, with bright orange patch in the apical area of forewing. This marking is absent in ♀, which is of an almost uniform pale brownish-yellow. **H:** flower meadows, up to 2,000 m. **Dis:** Europe up to Arctic Circle. Common throughout Britain except in Scotland, where local. **A:** once very common, but now scarcer. **Fl:** beginning of April to June. **LC:** June to July. **FP:** Cuckoo flower. The small green caterpillar is difficult to spot – *see* page 278.

Wood White *Leptidea sinapis* L.

Des: forewing 2.5 cm, inconspicuous colouring. The black patch in the apical area on the upperside of the forewing is more distinct in the summer generation. **H:** woodland margins, prefers limestone, also in meadows, mountains up to 2,000 m. **Dis:** all over Europe up to, and just occasionally beyond, 66°N. **A:** locally widespread but not scarce within its range, sometimes even abundant on mainland Europe. Rare in England but locally common in Ireland. **Fl:** two generations May to mid-June, and mid-July to August. **LC:** first from August to September, second February. **FP:** birdsfoot trefoil, meadow vetchling, clovers.

Moorland Clouded Yellow
Colias palaeno L.

Des: forewing up to 3 cm. Sulphur yellow, sometimes pale, with orange-red fringes. ♀ paler. **H:** upland moors and other very damp areas in central Europe; lowland moorland in the north. **Dis:** isolated pockets in central Europe, widespread in Scandinavia and Finland but not Britain. **A:** rare in central Europe, common in the north. **Fl:** June to July. One generation. **LC:** August to May. Caterpillar hibernates. **FP:** bog whortleberry. **G:** once widespread, but loss of moorlands has resulted in reduced habitat.

Danube Clouded Yellow
Colias myrmidone Esp.

Des: forewing 2.5 cm. Deep orange-yellow colouring. ♀ orange-yellow or greenish-white. **H:** a species of the steppes, it occurs on dry, sunny slopes, rarely in meadows. **Dis:** eastern Europe, in the west to Austria and in the Jura near Regensburg in Bavaria. Not in Britain. **A:** rare, but occasionally in larger numbers. **Fl:** two generations, May/June, and July/August. **FP:** broom.

Clouded Yellow *Colias crocea* Geoff.

Des: Forewing 2.8 cm. Similar to Danube Clouded Yellow. **H:** likes lowland and hilly areas, up to 2,000 m. **Dis:** over Europe up to 60°N. Migratory, reaching southern England almost every year, but only occasionally abundantly throughout Britain. **A:** very variable. **Fl:** first generation end of May to end of June, the second between end of July and beginning of August. Rarely a third generation in October. **LC:** June to July, and September. **FP:** sainfoin, birdsfoot trefoil, lucerne.

Pale Clouded Yellow *Colias hyale* L.

Des: forewing 2.5 cm. Its colouring makes it hard to overlook, but only experts can distinguish it from its twin species Berger's Clouded Yellow (*Colias australis* Vrty). **H:** everywhere in lowlands of central Europe on dry bare slopes. Up to 2,000 m. **Dis:** Europe up to 65°N; a rare migrant to Britain. Absent from Mediterranean region where *C. australis* occurs in its place. **A:** common, not endangered. **Fl:** two generations – first mid-May to June, second mid-July to October. In favourable years a third, incomplete generation can occur. **LC:** first generation from September to April, second June to July. **FP:** lucerne, birdsfoot trefoil, horseshoe vetch – *see* page 274, 278.

Description: while the male's forewing can reach 3 cm, the female's is usually larger. The four large, blue-flecked eye-spots, one on each wing, are so conspicuous that the Peacock cannot be confused with any other species. Basic colour brown to reddish. One of Europe's best-known butterflies. No other forms or races are known.

Habitat: everywhere up to 2,500 m. Peacocks can be encountered in city centres, gardens and parks, flower meadows and bushy terrain, and woodland clearings.

Distribution: throughout Europe up to 60°N. On all larger Mediterranean islands with the exception of Crete. Common in England, Wales, and Ireland, but local in Scotland and a scarce migrant over the rest of that country. Absent from the extreme north and from North Africa.

Abundance: A common butterfly, especially in wooded regions and a visitor to many gardens. Although occasional autumn and spring migrations have been observed, the Peacock is not a true migratory butterfly. Migration takes place more frequently in Finland between the southern and the northern populations of that country. The distribution of these populations fluctuates from year to year, and depends on the weather of the previous summer and autumn. In warm years the range moves north, while during cold years it has to move south. The weather is also an important factor in the Peacock's numbers.

Flight: There are two generations in the south and in warm areas. Single brooded in Britain. The first generation is on the wing from the end of June to mid-July, the second from August to May. The butterfly hibernates in sheltered places, such as cracks in wood, in roof spaces and old hay lofts.

Life cycle: caterpillar first generation from May t? June, the second from July to August. In th? northern part of their range only one generatio? occurs. The caterpillar is black, finely spotted wit? white, and has black spikes. The pupa is a ligh? greyish-green with two rows of shiny spikes an? several metal-coloured patches. Peacock caterpil? lars are a communal species, with up to 150 cater? pillars living in one nettlebed until pupation. Up t? 10,000 caterpillars have been collected in a ver? small area. The caterpillars begin to disperse onl? after the final moult and pupate out of sight. Th? main predators of the caterpillars are the two fl? species *Sturmia bella* and *Phryxe vulgaris* whic? can inflict considerable losses on the caterpilla? populations.

Foodplants: stinging nettle, and, if need be, wil? hop. The caterpillars feed communally, stripping the leaves down to the veins before moving on t? the next leaf. Then they proceed to the next nettle? Caterpillars recognize the correct foodplant by thei? sense of touch, and never climb on to the wrong? plant.

General: anyone wishing to attract Peacocks int? their garden should grow a patch of stinging nettles. The butterflies will lay their eggs on them? enabling observers to watch the full life-cycle o? this beautiful species. The newly emerged butter? flies like to settle on the flowers of a Buddleia? where they can be seen at close quarters flashing? their eye-spots. When they fold their wings, the? black-brown undersides resemble a dried-up nettle? leaf. The sudden opening of the wings and flashing? of the eye-spots has a deterrent effect on possible? predators, giving the Peacock butterfly vital moments in which to escape. This deterrent is not effective in the case of the species' two main enemies, the parasitic flies and ichneumon flies, since they feed on the caterpillars.

Brush-footed Butterflies

33

Small Tortoiseshell *Aglais urticae* L.

Description: forewings up to 2.5 cm. The Small Tortoiseshell is distinguished from the Painted Lady and the Comma by its wing shape and by a distinct row of dots along the outer margin of both fore- and hindwings. These dots are framed by black crescents and filled with blue. They give the butterfly a very attractive appearance since they contrast with the orange wings.

Habitat: everywhere in open countryside, often found in gardens, woodland margins, and on waste ground. In mountains up to 3,000 m.

Distribution: throughout Britain and Europe to the North Cape. Probably the only butterfly that occurs in large numbers across Europe.

Abundance: not only does the Small Tortoiseshell cover a vast range, but it can also be found in large numbers everywhere, from cities to the countryside. One of the first to appear in spring.

Flight: in southern Europe, the first butterflies emerge as early as February, but not until May in the north. Normally two generations occur, the first from mid-June to mid-July, the second from August to May. The butterflies hibernate in their native countries, usually well concealed in cracks in wood, in attics, old hay-lofts, and behind walls.

Life cycle: caterpillar first generation May to June, second generation July to August, but one generation only in Scotland and in Europe. The caterpillars are dark to black and have a double yellowish line along the sides of their bodies. They live communally in stinging nettles.

Foodplants: depends on the availability of stinging nettles (*Urtica dioica*), hence its Latin name *urticae*.

General: together with the Large and Small Whites, and the Peacock, this is one of the commonest central European butterflies, and is particularly abundant in Britain.

Large Tortoiseshell *Nymphalis polychloros* L.

Description: forewings just over 3 cm. Upper side a conspicuous orange colour with black markings. It is not always easily distinguished from a number of other species. Of the similar species, only the Small Tortoiseshell and the Comma are common. With experience it is possible to distinguish these two species from the rare Large Tortoiseshell by their flight pattern, but it is always safer to examine the markings and wing shape of the settled butterfly.

Habitat: widespread and can be found in most areas, though it prefers woodland areas of scrub, and mountains up to 1,500 m.

Distribution: throughout Europe, and common in the south. Possibly extinct in England. Occasionally found in northern Germany and southern Scandinavia as a migrant. Now absent from much of north-east Europe, as well as Crete.

Abundance: the past few decades have seen a dramatic decline in the numbers of this species in the northern half of Europe. This is an utter mystery that baffles scientists throughout the continent. Whereas in the past the Large Tortoiseshell was regarded as a pest by fruit growers, it is now very rare in many northern European countries.

Flight: July to May. Butterfly hibernates in cracks in wood, and also likes old barns and tunnels. May cover large distances.

Life cycle: Caterpillars out in May to July. They live in a communal web. Usually several feed on the same branch, moving on when it is stripped bare. They are therefore very conspicuous, but hardly any will eat them. They are well protected by the numerous spines along their bodies and are unpalatable to most birds. However, they are particularly vulnerable to infestation by parasites, which kill vast numbers.

Foodplants: willows, poplars, elms.

Brush-footed Butterflies

Red Admiral *Vanessa atalanta* L.

Description: forewing 2.5–3 cm. The Red Admiral's most eye-catching features are a bright-red band on a dark-coloured background and the white apical patches on the forewings.
Habitat: very widely distributed, ranging from sea coasts to mountains up to 2,000 m. It is seen particularly frequently in the autumn in orchards where it sucks the juice from rotting pears, plums or apples using its proboscis.
Distribution: throughout Europe up to 62°N. In warmer years, individual butterflies fly to the Arctic Circle. The butterflies are very sensitive to cold, hence populations north of the Alps move to the warm south in the autumn and do not return until the following spring. They are true migrants, and colonize Britain every spring.
Abundance: fortunately the Red Admiral is still one of the more common of our native butterflies and can be found almost every summer, even in city centres.

Flight: the Red Admiral arrives in central and then northern and western Europe in May, and at higher altitudes or in cold years in June. One or two generations then follow, which may overlap. Normally the first period of flight is from July to August, the second from September to October. The butterflies leave in the last few warm days of autumn.
Life cycle: first generation June to July, second generation August to September. The colour of the caterpillar can range from black to green and yellowy-brown, but it always has a yellow line along each side and yellow spines. The caterpillars are solitary, living in bag-like shelters which they make out of stinging nettle leaves. This is also where they pupate. Their colouring and solitary behaviour make them easy to distinguish from the caterpillars of the Peacock and the Small Tortoiseshell.
Foodplants: stinging nettles, occasionally thistles.

Painted Lady *Vanessa cardui* L.

Description: forewing almost 3 cm. Both sexes are of the same colour.
Habitat: anywhere where there are stinging nettles and thistles. In mountains up to over 2,000 m.
Distribution: throughout Europe, but the butterflies can hibernate only in southern Europe or, more usually, in North Africa, and migrate to areas north of the Alps every year. Sometimes vast swarms fly far into the north, reaching the north of England or even Iceland.
Abundance: one of the commonest European butterflies, it can be observed in varying numbers from year to year in all kinds of habitats where thistles grow.

Flight: from May to June the Painted Lady migrates into areas north of the Alps; the exact timing of this influx depends on weather conditions. Usually two generations emerge, the first in July and August, the second in August and September. In good years there can be three generations. Since the migration is spread over a long period, butterflies born in the area often fly alongside new arrivals, thus causing a merging of the generations. It is difficult to distinguish between the different generations, particularly in the south.
Life cycle: first generation caterpillars from June to July, second in August and September. Even here times overlap, since the caterpillar seasons depend heavily on the influx of the butterflies.
Foodplants: thistles, also burdock, occasionally stinging nettles, coltsfoot.

Camberwell Beauty *Nymphalus antiopa* L.

Description: one of the largest butterflies in Europe with fore-wings of 3.5 cm. Dark brown colouring with broad cream-coloured marginal borders. Cannot be confused with any other species.

Habitat: gardens and parks, areas of scrub, light woodland, woodland edges, meadows, ridges and clearings. Also warm valleys, up to 2,000 m.

Distribution: widespread throughout Europe to the North Cape, but absent from the southern part of Spain, Greece, the Mediterranean islands and Scandinavia. It is a rare visitor to Britain where the butterfly has been known to breed.

Abundance: at one time it was common everywhere in mainland Europe, but after the Second World War the populations crashed for reasons which are not yet understood. Numbers have remained low but surprisingly constant, in some parts of Europe, but fluctuate wildly elsewhere. Fortunately, still a common and widespread species in many parts of Europe.

Flight: end of July to following June, with hibernation in winter.

Life cycle: caterpillars June to July. The black caterpillars have a row of rusty red patches on the back. Defensive spines occur on both sides of each body segment.

Foodplants: birch, aspen, sallow and elm. Smaller and medium-sized trees are preferred.

General: in the vast distribution range, which covers almost all of Europe, temperate Asia and North America, there are no separate races or variations. The lighter margin, sometimes seen in spring, is usually a scale defect, but sometimes the result of paling during hibernation. It is not attributable to a separate spring or autumn form.

Two-tailed Pasha *Charaxes jasius* L.

Description: very large and striking butterfly with a wing of over 4 cm. The dark brown of the upper side of the forewing is bordered by a broad pale yellow band which continues, edged with black, on to the hindwings. When the butterfly is at rest, four blue spots and the two tails are evident on the hindwing. These features, together with the striking size (a female can have a wingspan of up to 10 cm), make it easy to identify and hard to overlook.

Habitat: on warm coastal areas up to 500 m. Also parks and damp woodlands.

Distribution: above the eastern Mediterranean coasts of Greece, Yugoslavia and eastern Italy, including the large islands. It is rarer to the west of this area. Occurs in small numbers in Spain and Portugal.

Abundance: common in main distribution area, otherwise in small numbers.

Flight: two broods, May to June and August to September.

Life cycle: first generation caterpillars from September to April, second June to July. The caterpillar hibernates on evergreen plants. It is bright green dotted with numerous minute yellow spots. The head has four skin prongs, the two middle ones bearing red tips. The back has two large green patches.

Foodplants: strawberry tree, which is common in the Mediterranean.

General: the male generally sits on the tip of a strawberry tree branch, waiting for a passing female. Since butterflies have relatively poor eyesight, it often mistakenly chases after other flying insects.

Comma *Polygonia c-album* L.

Description: forewing 2.5 cm. Looks like a 'frayed' Small Tortoiseshell. It differs from the latter in the distribution and extent of the black markings on the upperside of the wings, and in the jagged wing outline. Takes its name from the comma-like marking on the underside of the hindwing.

Habitat: woodland margins and clearings, terrain with scrub-cover, in meadows and gardens, in mountains up to 2,000 m, as well as in valleys.

Distribution: throughout Europe up to 66°N. Also on many Mediterranean islands.

Abundance: can be locally abundant, particularly in damp woodland meadows. Declined from local abundance to near extinction in England in the early 19th century, but increased throughout this century and is now as common as ever.

Flight: normally two generations in central Europe, one in the north. The first from end of June to en of July, the second mid-August to beginning c June. The second generation develops only par tially. In mountains and the north there is only on generation because of the short summers at hig altitudes. As early as August the butterflies retrea to their hibernacula.

Life cycle: first generation caterpillars from Ma to June, the second from July to August. Th caterpillar is a bizarre shape with a large white patch along the rear part of its back.

Foodplants: Comma caterpillars can be found or stinging nettles, elm, and, especially wild hop; ir gardens on red and black currants and on goose-berry.

General: apart from our native Comma butterfly the Southern Comma (*Polygonia egea* Cr.) occurs in the eastern Mediterranean. This species car be distinguished by the comma pattern on the underwing which is smaller and looks more like the letter 'y'.

Map Butterfly *Araschnia levana* L.

Description: forewing just under 2 cm. Occurs in two forms – termed seasonal dimorphism – the spring, and summer form. The spring form (first generation) has yellow-orange upperwings with black patches, while the underside has a white grid pattern on a contrasting orange background (the 'map'). The summer form (*f. prorsa*), with its black background colour and white bands, looks completely different, even if the yellow and orange patches are reminiscent of the spring form.

Habitat: widely distributed in meadows and damp woodlands. Prefers shaded and semi-shaded areas, and hilly country, but not above 1,000 m.

Distribution: main distribution area is temperate Europe. It occurs in a broad band ranging from France, through central Europe and central Asia down to Japan. The Map Butterfly is absent from the North Sea coast, England, Ireland, Denmark (only locally), Scandinavia and Finland, as well as from wide areas of Spain, Portugal, Italy, Yugoslavia and Greece. However, it has spread remarkably well through Europe in the 1980s.

Abundance: still very common in places, but usually only local distribution.

Flight: two generations, the first from the end of April to mid-June, the second mid-July to August. Very rarely a third incomplete generation occurs.

Life cycle: first generation caterpillar from August to September, the second June to July. The pupa hibernates. The caterpillar is a rich black-brown with numerous spines of the same colour.

Foodplants: stinging nettles, especially those growing under shrub cover.

spring form

41

Poplar Admiral *Limenitis populi* L.

Pupa – see page 279

Description: one of the largest and most magnificent of European butterflies, with a forewing of nearly 4 cm. Upperwings dark with white, sometimes almost brownish patches in discal and postdiscal areas, and orange-red and black submarginal markings. Underwings orange-red with white and blue-grey markings. The female grows to a larger size than the male, with more conspicuous white bands on the hindwings.

Habitat: in forest paths and woodland margins in hilly areas and in mountain valleys, also in pastures; up to 1,500 m.

Distribution: France, central and eastern Europe, up to 64°N. Absent from western France, the lowlands of northern Germany, Britain, Spain and Portugal; it has not yet been recorded in Italy, Greece, or the Mediterranean islands.

Abundance: a highly endangered species in many European countries.

Flight: June to July in one generation.

Life cycle: August to May. The caterpillars hibernate in the tips of aspen leaves in small webs. In August they stop feeding and move to their hibernacula where they spend the winter, usually in small groups. Pupation takes place in the following spring on top of the leaves. The caterpillar is green and has paler sides with dark spots. A fairly long pair of spiny projections serves as defence against predators such as songbirds. The butterflies suffer more from wet, cold weather than from their natural enemies.

Foodplants: caterpillars live on aspen. The scarcity of the Poplar Admiral can be linked to the decline in the aspen.

General: to ensure the survival of this species, sufficient areas of aspen habitat must be preserved.

White Admiral *Limenitis camilla* L.

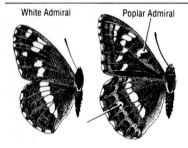

White Admiral　　　Poplar Admiral

Description: forewing 3 cm. Upperwings black and white, undersides many-coloured. Can be distinguished from the Southern White Admiral (*L. reducta*) by two rows of black spots, against one.

Habitat: White and Southern White Admiral occur in damp meadows and light deciduous woodlands. In mountains up to the tree-line.

Distribution: the two species slightly overlap in France, central Europe, Italy, Yugoslavia and eastern Europe. But the Southern White Admiral is really a southern species and the White Admiral is common in central Europe. *L. comilla* is locally common in woods in southern England, where it has extended its range in the last 40 years.

Abundance: large populations can still be found locally in central Europe. Its relative *L. reducta* is very rare north of the Alps.

Flight: mid-June to mid-August in one generation, the same as *L. reducta*.

Life cycle: from August to beginning of June. The caterpillars hibernate in a web when very small. They are green and armed with brown-red spines.

Foodplants: honeysuckle and snowberry.

♀

Purple Emperor *Apatura iris* L.

Description: forewing 2.8–3.3 cm. All Emperors are characterized by the iridescent blue on the uppersides of their wings. The notched outline of their hindwings adds to their exotic appearance. There are two species, the Purple and the Lesser Purple Emperor (*Apatura ilia*). The Purple Emperor only has two orange-framed ocelli on the hindwings, while the Lesser Purple Emperor has one ocellus on each of its four wings. The females of both species exhibit these ocelli, but lack the iridescence.

Habitat: woodlands, deciduous mixed woodlands from sea level to 1,000 m. Prerequisite for its occurrence is the presence of willow.

Distribution: up to 60°N. Absent from central and northern England, from Wales, Scotland, Ireland, Scandinavia and southern Europe.

Abundance: locally widespread and more common than is generally apparent. Can be watched more frequently in favourable years. Easily attracted to ground level, being partial to dung.

Flight: one generation from mid-June to mid-August. This heat-loving species likes to come out during the hot hours in the middle of the day. In the early morning the butterflies sit motionlessly at their resting sites.

Life cycle: from August to June. The caterpillar hibernates. It is green with yellow dots and pale stripes along the sides.

Foodplants: various types of willow, especially goat willow, eared sallow, and common sallow.

General: the iridescence is not caused by blue pigments but represents a structural phenomenon resulting from a partial reflection of the blue wavelength of light. The iridescent effect is produced by tiny air pockets in the butterfly's scales.

Lesser Purple Emperor *Apatura ilia* Schiff.

Description: forewing 3.2–3.5 cm. Similar to Purple Emperor, but can be distinguished by the two additional ocelli on the uppersides of the forewings, and by the absence of a tooth-shaped projection within the white band on the hindwing. The female is larger and is not iridescent. The inner white markings are often filled with yellow. Both forms, the white and the yellow, occur alongside each other and mix freely.

Habitat: woodland margins, clearings in deciduous woodlands on limestone, woodland brooks, sunny mountain valleys, and especially in light damp woodlands with willows, poplars and aspen.

Distribution: very common in the heavily wooded areas of central Europe, and France; absent from northern Germany, Britain, and Scandinavia. In the east ranges far into Asia, in the south to central Italy

and northern Greece; absent from Mediterranean islands. Restricted distribution in Spain and Portugal.

Abundance: the Lesser Purple Emperor is under strict protection in some parts of Europe. However, the main threat to these butterflies is not direct persecution but the destruction of their habitats.

Flight: from July to beginning of August in one generation; therefore much shorter period than for the Purple Emperor.

Life cycle: August to June. For caterpillar phase see Purple Emperor.

Foodplants: aspen, also other poplars and willows.

General: apart from the basic form of the Lesser Purple Emperor, the form f. *clytie* is also known, in which the inner white markings are filled with yellow-orange. In some areas this variety is more common. After the second moult the caterpillar hibernates on poplar branches.

♂   ♀

Brush-footed Butterflies

♂

Silver-washed Fritillary *Argynnis paphia* L.

Pupa – see page 275

Description: with a forewing of 3.5 cm, the Silver-washed Fritillary is one of the largest fritillaries. Its upperwings are bright orange-brown with a pattern of black dots and streaks. The wing undersides are marked by silvery-white bands and wing margins from which the butterfly derives its name. The female occurs in two forms: one is similar to the male, the other is darker with a green tinge.

Habitat: prefers clearings and woodland margins in hilly countryside, and sunny meadows in mountain valleys up to 1,000 m.

Distribution: nearly all of Europe up to 63°N. Absent from southern Spain and Crete.

Abundance: not rare. Usually abundent in wooded parts of central and southern Europe. Locally common in southern British woods, especially in Wales.

Flight: the butterflies are on the wing from the end of June to mid-September in one generation.

Life cycle: the caterpillars hatch in September and hibernate when very small, sometimes as completely developed caterpillars within their eggshell. When fully grown the caterpillar has an attractive appearance – along the back of the velvety-black body runs a broad yellow band subdivided by many fine black lines. The sides are scattered with yellow dots. Particularly eye-catching are the very long dark-yellow spines on the first segment of the caterpillar's body.

Foodplants: caterpillars of the Silver-washed Fritillary feed on violets. (*V. riviniana* and *V. pulustris*) In contrast to other caterpillars they move away from their food plant.

General: there is a dark greenish form of the female *valezina*, which is locally known in central southern England and many pockets on the continent. Otherwise, no variation throughout its range. *Valezina* females are less attractive to males than the normal coloured Silver-washed Fritillaries, but are eventually mated.

Dark Green Fritillary *Argynnis aglaja* L.

Pupa – see page 274

Description: with a forewing of 3 cm, the Dark Green Fritillary is distinctly smaller than the similar Silver-washed Fritillary. It lacks the latter's silver bands on the hindwings which are yellow or sometimes verging on green, with silver patches which have a mother-of-pearl sheen. The females are paler.

Habitat: in their habitat requirements the two species are very different. Whereas the Silver-washed Fritillary is strictly a woodland species, the Dark Green is almost exclusively found in grassland.

Distribution: throughout Europe, ranging nearly to the North Cape. Absent from Mediterranean islands, with the exception of Sicily. Very local in British rough grassland; commonest along the coast.

Abundance: similar to the Silver-washed Fritillary. In suitable habitat it can be observed every year, but the numbers do fluctuate.

Flight: one generation with a long flight period from mid-June to mid-August.

Life cycle: August to June. The caterpillars of the Dark Green Fritillary and the Silver-washed Fritillary are easier to distinguish than the butterflies themselves. The Dark Green Fritillary caterpillars are dark with two parallel white lines running along the back. Their sides are marked by red dots and small patches. The defensive spines and the head are black.

Foodplants: mostly violets (Viola, *V. palustris*, *V. tricolor* and others). The caterpillar hibernates when very small and does not start feeding and growing until the following spring. It remains hidden during the day, sometimes at some distance from the food plant. Active at night.

Queen of Spain Fritillary
Issoria lathonia L.

Des: forewing 2–2.2 cm. Medium-sized, dark suffusions on upperside of hindwings. **H:** dry grassland, slopes, clearings, fallow areas. **Dis:** throughout central and southern Europe. Very local in the north, though a rare visitor to Britain. **A:** used to be much more frequent in the past. **Fl:** two generations, from April to May, and July to mid-September. **LC:** first from September to April, then June to July. Caterpillar hibernates. **FP:** violets, wild pansy.

Scarce Fritillary *Euphydryas maturna*
L. Caterpillar – see page 274

Des: forewing 2.1–2.4 cm. Species is difficult to identify and occurs only in a limited area of Europe. **H:** the species depends on the occurrence of ash and can be found in damp valleys and mixed deciduous woodlands. **Dis:** locally in France, central Europe, Hungary, also in northern Germany and southern Scandinavia, but not Britain. **A:** not common. **Fl:** end of May to beginning of July. **LC:** July to May, caterpillar hibernates. **FP:** caterpillars feed on ash in the autumn and change to low-growing plants in the spring.

Small Pearl-bordered Fritillary
Clossiana selene Schiff.

Des: forewing 1.8–2 cm. **H:** wet meadows, damp slopes, fallow ground, pastures, open woods and woodland margins. **Dis:** widely across Europe, but largely absent from Mediterranean region and eastern half of Britain. Absent from Ireland. **A:** common locally. **Fl:** two generations, first, end of May to beginning of July, second, end of July to mid-September. **LC:** from September to May, second July. Caterpillar hibernates. **FP:** all violet species.

Pearl-bordered Fritillary
Clossiana euphrosyne L.

Des: forewing 2–2.2 cm. Black markings on forewings. Central silver patch on underside of hindwings. **H:** woodland margins, clearings, and clear-felled areas. **Dis:** widely across Europe, to the North Cape. **A:** has declined over the last few decades. Extinct in most of eastern England. **Fl:** mid-May to mid-July. **LC:** July to May. Caterpillar hibernates. **FP:** violets, especially dog violet.

Glanville Fritillary *Melitaea cinxia* L.

Des: forewing 1.5–2 cm. Wing uppersides with dark markings, sometimes faded. Underside of forewings yellow ochre with few markings; pale apex. **H:** flower meadows, damp meadow valleys, woodland margins. **Dis:** found across Europe, up to 2,000 m. In Britain, only on the Channel Islands and Isle of Wight on south-facing cliffs. **Fl:** end of May to beginning of July. **LC:** July to May. Caterpillar hibernates. **FP:** ribwort plantain.

Knapweed Fritillary
Melitaea phoebe Schiff.

Des: forewing 2.1 cm. Undersides characteristic. Uppersides with lively black pattern. **H:** sunny places on slopes, particularly limestone. **Dis:** foothills of the Alps and southern Europe, except Iberian peninsula. **A:** one of the commonest fritillaries of the Mediterranean, abundant in many meadows. **Fl:** June. **LC:** July to May. Caterpillar hibernates. **FP:** knapweed, *Cirsium lanceolatum*, and saw-wort.

Marbled White *Melanargia galathea* L.

Description: forewing 2.6–2.8 cm. All four wings carry on their upperside a distinct chequered black and white pattern. The female wing undersides are paler than the male's and have a yellowish tinge.

Habitat: on dry slopes, woodland meadows, clearings in hilly countryside, but also in mountains up to nearly 2,000 m.

Distribution: over a wide range in Europe to southern England. Largely absent from the north German plains, and from Denmark, Scandinavia, Finland, southern Spain, Italy, Portugal and southern France, where the Marbled White is replaced by very similar forms. The Marbled White is much commoner in central Europe than in the north.

Abundance: in suitable habitats, such as the warm, dry grasslands of central Europe. The Marbled White is often the most abundant Brown of the year.

Flight: end of June to August in one generation. The Marbled White is the archetypal summer butterfly being particularly active around noon on hot summer days.

Life cycle: September to June. The caterpillar hibernates. It is a greenish, sometimes sandy colour with several pale stripes along the body. It is armed with short, dense hair and a pair of short points at the tail, which are characteristic of the whole family.

Foodplants: the caterpillars only feed at night on soft grasses, such as cat's-tail and *holcus*-species; when young they depend on red fescue. They spend the day in the grass and amongst roots, hiding from predators, particularly songbirds.

General: this very variable species has developed a number of local forms.

Ringlet *Aphantopus hyperantus* L.

Description: forewing 2.5 cm. Medium- to dark-brown butterfly with dark-centred, pale-ringed small ocelli which are quite faded on the upper sides of the wings, but much more conspicuous on the undersides. Exact colouring and number of ocelli can vary greatly. The ocelli on the wing undersides also carry a central white dot which enchances the effect of the pale rings.

Habitat: various. Found almost exclusively in damp grassland habitats, in flower meadows, light woodlands, on woodland margins, in hilly countryside, and in mountains up to 1,500 m.

Distribution: Europe, but absent from northern England though locally common in Scotland. In Scandinavia hardly any records beyond 64°N. It is absent from the Iberian Peninsula south of the Pyrenees, but can be observed regularly in the Pyrenees themselves. Absent from Italy, Greece, and the Mediterranean islands.

Abundance: reasonably common. Each summer the Ringlet can be watched in suitable places, occuring locally in large numbers. A typical characteristic is the Ringlet's slow and measured flight. On landing it closes its wings, so that the ocelli on the underside of the hindwings are easily visible.

Flight: mid-June to August in one generation.

Life cycle: September to May. The caterpillar hibernates. Its colour is an inconspicuous grey-brown with a darker central stripe.

Foodplants: after hatching in the autumn the caterpillars eat only a little, since the supply of fresh, succulent grasses declines from September onwards. They resume their activity in the following year when soft grasses such as *holcus*, *milium*, *poa* and *carex* show new growth. The caterpillars feed at night.

Browns & Ringlets

♀   ♂

Woodland Grayling *Hipparchia fagi* Scop.

Characteristics: attracts attention because of its forewing of 4 cm, and colouring. The dark wings are marked with a pale band with one or two distinct ocelli. The pattern on the underside has richer contrasts since the band is less suffused and nearly white. As is the case with most butterflies the female is larger than the male and can also be recognized by the yellowish colouring of the pale band.

Habitat: clearings and edges in warm deciduous woodlands, dry meadows, up to 1,000 m.

Distribution: ranges from the Pyrenees towards the west and the north, but not beyond 52°N. Also found in France and central Europe, but to the north of the Alps only on 'warm islands', such as the Kaiserstuhl and the Palatinate. In the south it can t found in Italy and the Balkan Peninsula. Abse from Britain.

Abundance: the Woodland Grayling is commc in many wooded parts of central Europe.

Flight: mid-July to mid-August in one generatio Although large size makes these butterflies cо spicuous in flight, their habit of sitting on tre trunks, wings completely closed, makes them d ficult to spot when at rest. The bark pattern с the underside of the hindwings is a very effecti camouflage.

Life cycle: September to July. The caterpilla hibernate amongst leaves, making a little chambe for themselves by shaking movements of the bodies. They are pale and have thin stripes.

Foodplants: the caterpillars feed on soft grasse such as *bromus*, *lolium* and, in particular, *holcι* species. They are active at night.

Rock Grayling *Hipparchia alcyone* Schiff.

Description: with a forewing of 3.5 cm it does not quite reach the size of the Woodland Grayling. However, since there is an overlap in dimensions between the two species, size alone is not a determining factor in distinguishing these two similar species. Even the large bands on the upper- and undersides, or the ocelli, are not always reliable features. Definite identification is often only possible by examination of the genitalia by an expert. Sometimes the location of the butterfly can aid identification, although here again the range of the two species largely overlaps.

Habitat: while the Woodland Grayling spends most of its time in deciduous woodland clearings, the Rock Grayling prefers felled areas in pinewoods. It also likes dry, sandy grounds. In the south it is restricted to hilly and mountainous areas up to 1,500 m.

Distribution: its range extends without interruption from southern France across the Alpine state and southern Germany, to eastern Europe. Her especially in the east, the Rock Grayling occui further north than the Woodland Grayling. On th Iberian Peninsula and in Italy, the Rock Graylir tends to occur in more isolated mountain popu lations.

Abundance: locally common like its close rela tive, the Woodland Grayling.

Flight: July to August. The butterflies rest on tre trunks, well camouflaged by the bark pattern on th undersides of their wings.

Life cycle: September to June. The caterpilla hibernates. It is similar to the caterpillar of th Woodland Grayling, but has much more colourf markings. The caterpillars are active at night ar hide amongst vegetation during the day.

Foodplants: hard grasses, especially *brachyp dium*.

53

Grayling *Hipparchia semele* L.

Des: forewing 2.4–2.8 cm. Dark wings with a yellow to dark-suffused, often broken band; one or two ocelli on each wing. **H:** warm, sandy places ranging from the sea coast to 2,000 m. **Dis:** throughout Europe to southern Scandinavia. Very local in dry grassland in Britain; also numerous on lowland heaths and the coast. **A:** not frequent. **Fl:** July to September. **LC:** September to July. Caterpillar hibernates. **FP:** dry grasses. Not over-particular in its choice of food.

Dryad *Minois dryas* Scop.

Des: forewing 3 cm. Characteristic eye-spots. **H:** moorland meadows, warm, damp slopes with springs, and boggy woodland meadows. **Dis:** small population pockets in northern Spain, France, central and eastern Europe. Absent in Britain. **A:** rare. **Fl:** July to August. Characteristically bouncy flight. One generation. **LC:** September to June. Caterpillar hibernates. **FP:** purple moor-grass, etc.

False Grayling
Arethusana arethusa Schiff.

Des: brown butterfly with orange band on the uppersides of both pairs of wings, with a dark round patch in the apical area of the forewing. Forewing just under 2.5 cm. ♀ larger than ♂, also has more distinct eye-spots (two on the forewing). **H:** warm, dry slopes on limestone. **Dis:** only local distribution in Spain, Portugal, southern and central France, Italy and eastern Europe. In central Europe only in Alsace and in Baden. **A:** rare. **Fl:** July to September. **LC:** September to June. Caterpillar hibernates. **FP:** grasses.

The Hermit *Chazara briseis* L.

Des: brownish-white. **Dis:** pa of Spain, France, the Alpi countries, central Europe, rar ing eastwards. Present throug out Italy, the Balkan Penins and Greece. Absent in Britain. rare, can be seen rather mc frequently in good years. **Fl:** e of July to beginning of Augu **LC:** September to June. Caterp lar hibernates. **FP:** hard grass in particular *festuca* (Shee Fescue) and *sesleria* species.

Great Banded Grayling
Brintesia circe F.

Des: dark-brown butterfly with white band which merges ir white patches on the forewir Forewing tends to exce 3.5 cm. **H:** dry woodland me dows, clearings in deciduo woodlands, less frequently in w pastures. Up to 1,500 m. **Di** Spain, southern and cent France, very rare north of t Alps. **A:** locally common in ce tral and southern Europe. **F** July to August. **LC:** September to June. Caterpil hibernates. **FP:** grasses.

Alpine Grayling *Oeneis glacialis* Moll.

Des: light-coloured, beige butterfly with bands a eye-spots. Forewing just under 3 cm. **H:** being Alpine form, it occurs on steep rocky slopes 2,000–3,000 m. **Dis:** restricted to high altitudes the Alps. **Fl:** June to August in one generation **L** August to July. Caterpillar hibernates well hidden the ground. **FP:** various grasses, above all t forms of sheep's fescue, typical of Alpine regior **G:** by living in a very restricted habitat, this ra butterfly has proved that sensitive species c adapt to extreme conditions.

♀

55

Arran Brown *Erebia ligea* L.

Des: forewing 2.4–2.8 cm. One of the Brown Butterflies that occurs in many variations in Europe and is difficult to identify. **H:** in subalpine regions and foothills of central and southern Europe, and in Scandinavia: wet meadows, damp woodlands. **Dis:** central, southern, and eastern Europe, but despite name not Britain. **A:** frequent to sporadic. **Fl:** July to mid-August. **LC:** September to July. Newly hatched caterpillars hibernate, nearly fully grown caterpillars hibernate a second time. **FP:** woodland grasses.

Almond-eyed Ringlet *Erebia alberganus* Prun.

Des: forewing c. 2 cm. Dark brown with orange band which is subdivided into small patches by the dark veins. Each patch has in its centre a dark spot of varying size with a white dot in the middle. The forewing pattern continues on the hindwings. **H:** Alpine species; on grassland. **Dis:** only in central and southern Alps, absent in the northern region. Local populations also in the Apennines; up to 1,800m. **A:** isolated populations; locally common. **Fl:** end of June to August. **LC:** August to May. Caterpillar hibernates. **FP:** various grasses, especially *Poa*.

Woodland Ringlet *Erebia medusa* Schiff.

Des: forewing 2–2.2 cm. Eye-spots not integrated into continuous band. The two top ones are larger. **H:** damp valleys, woodland meadows, clearings, clear-felled areas. **Dis:** from France through central Europe to the east. Absent from Britain, northern Germany, north-west Europe, and parts of southern Europe. **A:** frequent. **Fl:** mid-May to June. **LC:** July to April. Caterpillar hibernates. **FP:** numerous grasses.

Silky Ringlet *Erebia gorge* Hb.

Des: forewing 1.7–2 cm. One of the numerous Brown Butterflies that is difficult to identify. This can sometimes only be achieved by examining the genitals. **H:** dry areas 1,600–3,000 m. Prefers scree and other areas with sparse vegetation. **Dis:** like most of its relatives, the Silky Ringlet is found only in very restricted habitats – the Pyrenees, Alps, Carpathian Mountains, Apennines, and other mountain ranges. **A:** locally common, but absent elsewhere. **Fl:** June to August. **LC:** August to May. Caterpillar hibernates. **FP:** various Alpine grasses.

Meadow Brown *Maniola jurtina* L.

Des: forewing 2.2–2.6 cm. Male with a small eye-spot on black background. ♀ larger, with reddish-brown band. **H:** woodland edges, meadows, parks. **Dis:** throughout Europe to 62°N. In the south to North Africa and on the Mediterranean islands. Probably the most widespread and abundant butterfly in Britain. Also common throughout northern half of Europe. **A:** frequent. **Fl:** June to August. **LC:** September to May. Caterpillar hibernates. **FP:** grasses, in particular *Poa pratensis*.

Gatekeeper *Pyronia tithonus* L.

Des: forewing 1.6–2 cm. Ocelli with two white dots in centre. Male with reddish-brown patches on wing, female paler and somewhat larger. **H:** damp and dry meadows, mixed deciduous woodlands, heather. **Dis:** widely distributed across Europe, up to 52°N. Very common in southern half of England. **A:** one of the most abundant species throughout central Europe. **Fl:** July to August. **LC:** September to June. Caterpillar hibernates. **FP:** grasses.

Small Heath
Coenonympha pamphilus L.

Des: forewing c. 1.5 cm. Undersides of hindwings marked by faded whitish bands along paler outer margin and darker inner part. **H:** meadow valleys, woodland clearings; also along sea coast. **Dis:** common all dry grassland habitats in Britain. Also throughout Europe to northern Scandinavia. **A:** common everywhere but seldom in large numbers. **Fl:** Up to three generations: first in May, second in July, third: end of August to September. **LC:** first – August to April, second – June, third – August. **FP:** grasses.

Scarce Heath Coenonympha hero L.

Des: forewing 1.5–1.8 cm Uppersides brown. Uppersides c hindwings with three to fou blind, reddish-brown eye-spots **H:** hilly areas, especially damp places, also mixed deciduou woodland. **Dis:** ranging from central France through centra Germany into the East. **A:** sever decline in numbers and very rar and localized throughout it range. One of the most endang ered butterflies in Europe. **Fl:** end of May to begin ning of July. **LC:** July to May. Caterpillar hiber nates. **FP:** grasses.

Speckled Wood Pararge aegeria L.

Des: forewing 2–2.2 cm. Dark brown, pale patches on wing uppersides: three eye-spots on hindwings, one apical eye-spot on forewing. **H:** deciduous and coniferous woodland, clearings, forest glades. **Dis:** throughout Europe, up to 1,000 m. **A:** frequent, declining in some parts of Europe, but has spread and increased throughout Britain in the past 40 years. **Fl:** two generations: mid-April to mid-June, July to mid-September. **LC:** first September to April, second June. Both caterpillar and chrysalis hibernate. **FP:** wild grasses.

Wall Brown Lasiommata megera L.

Des: forewing 1–2.6 cm Orange-brown with dark-brown jagged line pattern; on forewing black apical ocellus with white centre. Three to four ocelli or hindwing. **H:** light woodlands areas with shrub cover, also ir mountains. **Dis:** widely distributed across Europe, including Britain. **A:** regular. **Fl:** two generations: first May to June second July to October. **LC:** first September to May, second July. Caterpillar hiber nates. **FP:** wild grasses.

Large Wall Brown
Lasiommata maera L.

Des: forewing 2.2–2.8 cm. Brown, with paler wing apex which carries a white-centred black eye-spot and, adjacent to it, a much smaller dot. Hindwings marked by two medium-sized, and one small ocellus on orange background. **H:** light woodlands, hilly areas. **Dis:** very widely distributed in Europe, up to 2,000, but not in Britain. **A:** not frequent everywhere. **Fl:** June to July. **LC:** August to May. Caterpillar hibernates. **FP:** wild grasses.

Woodland Brown
Lopinga achine Scop.

Des: forewing 2.4–2.8 cm. Dark brown, with dark-filled, yellow and orange ringed eye-spots on both fore- and hindwings. Eye-spots are oval and close together. **H:** hilly areas in old mixed deciduous woodland where there is good under-storey. **Dis:** throughout Europe, but absent in the north and south. Main distribution areas: France, central and eastern Europe. Absent in Britain. Its total distribution area extends beyond the temperate zones of Eurasia to Japan. In mountains up to 1,000 m. **A:** exceedingly rare over most of its range. **Fl:** mid-June to July. **LC:** August to May. Caterpillar hibernates. **FP:** woodland grasses.

♀

Large Blue *Maculinea arion* L.

Description: forewing 1.4–2cm. The *Lycaenidae* form a large family, comprising over a hundred species in Europe alone. All the species are small, some very small. The males are generally more colourful than the females. Colours range from deep blue to green, red and brown. The females are usually dark, brown or grey.

Identification usually relies on examination of wing undersides which are more diagnostic than the uppersides. In many cases identification can be carried out only by expert genital examination. The Large Blue is an exception in that its identification in central and western Europe poses no problems: it is distinguished by its bright blue upper wings with deep black spots which may however vary considerably. A black band runs along the outer margins of the uppersides.

Habitat: dry areas with short grass cover.
Distribution: widely distributed but very local in central and southern Europe. Extinct in most of northern Europe, including Britain, where it has recently been reintroduced.
Abundance: used to be very common. Has disappeared from many areas over the past few years owing to intensive farming practices in meadows and lack of grazing in unfertilized fields.
Flight: June to July in one generation.
Life cycle: August to May. The caterpillar hibernates in nests of the red ant (*Myrmica sabuleti*).
Foodplants: the young caterpillars feed on thyme. At a later stage they move into ants' nests where they feed on larvae, often devouring an entire nest. The ants drink secretions produced by abdominal glands of the caterpillars.

Brown Hairstreak *Thecla betulae* L.

Description: forewing c. 2 cm. Male smaller than female. Upperwings dark brown with kidney-shaped orange patch which is faint in the male or even absent altogether. Both sexes are bright golden orange-brown colour on the underside, marked with two black and white lines on each wing. The hindwings have the characteristic tail which gives this group its name.
Habitat: prefers parks, hedgerows, woodland margins, bushes beside streams, and mountain slopes up to 1,000 m. It does not mind stony ground as long as it supports wild fruit trees such as blackthorn, and other species of *Prunus.*
Distribution: central Europe including alpine countries, Denmark, southern Scandinavia and southern Finland, northern Italy, Balkan Peninsula, and eastern Europe. In the west to the Pyrenees, but no longer found on the Iberian Peninsula. In England and Wales very local, and only in the south. In Ireland only in the Burren.
Abundance: wide distribution area, but never found in large numbers.
Flight: end of July to September in one extended generation. The Brown Hairstreak is a loner. It is a very attractive butterfly when seen at close quarters. However, some experience is needed in spotting it because of its habit of covering short distances in fast flight and then hiding skilfully amongst leaves. Unlike many other species, the female Brown Hairstreak does not attach small egg parcels to the food plant, but cements each egg individually to a twig where it remains over winter.
Life cycle: the small caterpillars hatch in May. Four to six weeks later they are ready to pupate.
Foodplants: despite the Latin name, the caterpillars never feed on birch, but exclusively use *Prunus* species, especially blackthorn and plum.

Green Hairstreak *Callophrys rubi* L.

Des: its green wing undersides make it unmistakable. Forewing 1.6–1.8 cm. **H:** dry heath and rough grassland areas, sunny pine forests. **Dis:** throughout Europe including Britain (but usually local) to eastern Asia. Very closely related species are found in North America. **A:** frequent. **Fl:** mid-April to June. **LC:** May to August. Second generations are believed to occur in warm areas. **FP:** broom, gorse, laburnum, bramble, and bilberry. **G:** the commonest of the hairstreaks. Unlike other species in its family, it feeds on a large variety of plants.

Ilex Hairstreak *Nordmannia ilicis* Esp.

Des: forewing only 1.8 cm. Wing uppersides inconspicuous, can be identified by a row of small red, black-bordered dots on the undersides of the hindwings. **H:** light, bushy vegetation with oaks. **Dis:** central, western, and southern Europe. **A:** common in wooded areas of Central Europe. Absent in Britain. **Fl:** end of June to beginning of August in one generation. **LC:** May to June. Caterpillars hibernate within the egg. **FP:** oak leaves.

Purple Hairstreak *Thecla quercus* L.

Des: dark butterfly with large areas of deep, iridescent blue on its forewings which measure only 1.5 cm. The wing undersides are marked by a white, slightly jagged line. **H:** in oak woodlands, but also in parks with old oak trees, from the lowlands to 1,500 m. **Dis:** widely distributed all over Europe as far as 60°N. In Britain, common throughout lowland England, rare elsewhere. **A:** common to abundant in most oak woods of central Europe. **Fl:** mid-June to August in one extended generation. **LC:** May to June. In the summer the caterpillars develop inside the eggs, but they do not hatch until the following spring when the oak trees come into leaf.

Small Copper *Lycaena phlaeas* L.

Des: forewing 1.5 cm, ♀ larger than ♂. Dark margin with irregularly distributed black dots, which are bordered by white on the paler undersides of the forewings. **H:** anywhere up to 2,000 m. **Dis:** throughout Europe including Britain, to the North Cape. **A:** frequent. **Fl:** two or three generations, first May to end of June, second mid-July to August. **LC:** first September to April, second June to July. **FP:** sorrel, dock, and knotgrass.

Large Copper *Lycaena dispar* Haw.

Des: forewing 2 cm. Wing uppersides bright red (*f. rutilus*). In the case of *f. batava* the forewings are marked by only one black dot each, and the hindwings by a black margin. The ♀s are distinctly darker with numerous black dots on the forewings, and a dark patch on the hindwings. **H:** wet meadows and fens. **Dis:** *F. rutilus* occurs in isolated pockets in central Europe, but is somewhat commoner in south-eastern Europe. Extinct in Britain, but subsequently reintroduced. **A:** variable, but usually scarce to very rare. **Fl:** June to mid-August. **LC:** August to May. Caterpillar hibernates. **FP:** various types of dock, especially great water dock.

Scarce Copper *Heodes virgaureae* L.

Des: forewing 1.7–2.0 cm. Precise identification difficult since this species shows considerable variations and there are a number of similar species. Wing uppersides bright orange without any markings. Undersides orange with scattered black dots. **H:** damp meadows, fens, also woodland edges; up to 1,500 m. **Dis:** Europe, but only in isolated pockets in the west. Absent from Britain, and large parts of the Iberian Peninsula. **A:** common in the past, but now scarce in some places. **Fl:** mid-June to August. **LC:** April to June. The caterpillar hibernates, fully developed, inside the egg. **FP:** sorrel and dock.

♂   ♂   63

Short-tailed Blue
Everes argiades Pall.

Des: forewing 1–1.5 cm. ♀ larger than ♂. Latter is bright blue with fine, black dots along margin of hindwing; ♀ dark to blackish, dots along hindwing margin just visible. Hindwings of both sexes have slight tail tips at the margin. **H:** dry areas of scree, woodland margins, woodland paths. **Dis:** occurs throughout the temperate zones of Europe, also in North America. **A:** not common everywhere, a rare British visitor. **Fl:** two generations, first May to June, second mid-July to August. **LC:** first September to April, second June to July, caterpillar hibernates. **FP:** clover species, lucerne, and medick.

Holly Blue Celastrina argiolus L.

Des: forewing 1.3–1.6 cm. ♂ smaller than ♀, uniformly blue. ♂ with brown wing margin apart from that blue. **H:** slopes, woodland margins, clearings and water meadows. **Dis:** widely throughout Europe, up to and above 1,000 m. **A:** common in south of England. Often abundant. **Fl:** two generations, first mid-April to mid-June, second July to August. **LC:** first August to September, second June. Pupa hibernates. **FP** flowers of holly, ivy, gorse, alder buckthorn, and other shrubs.

Scarce Large Blue
Maculinea teleius Bergstr.

Des: one of the larger Blues, with a forewing length of c. 2 cm. It is characterized by the broad, dark wing margins and several black spots (clearly visible in the photograph). The dark margins are broader in ♀s, and the black spots more conspicuous in ♂'s. **H:** damp meadows in valleys and mountainous areas. **Dis:** southern central Europe to Japan. **A:** one of the rarest and most endangered butterflies in the world. **Fl:** end of June to mid-August. **LC:** summer to spring; caterpillar lives in Red ants' nests. **FP:** great burnet for first three weeks, Red ants' nests for next nine months.

Chequered Blue
Scolitantides orion Pall.

Des: forewing 1.3–1.5 cm. Easy to identify. **H:** stony areas, scree, hot dry slopes. **D:** heat-loving species. **Dis:** found mainly in southern Alpine valleys up to c.1,300 m.; also widely distributed on the Balkan Peninsula. Isolated occurrences in southern Scandinavia and southern Finland. **A:** occurs in isolated pockets and is therefore usually rare. **Fl:** two generations, first May to mid-June, second mid-July to August. **LC:** first August to September, second June to July. Caterpillar hibernates. **FP:** restricted to various types of stonecrop (Sedum). **G:** in Scandinavia these butterflies are of a more intense blue.

Silver-studded Blue Plebejus argus L.

Des: forewing 1.1–1.5 cm. **H:** areas with heather or sandy ground. **Dis:** very widely distributed across all of central Europe. Very local in southern England, but absent in Scotland and Ireland. Sardinia and Elba are the only Mediterranean islands on which it occurs. **A:** usually frequent, but declining. **Fl:** mid-June to mid-August. **LC:** April to June. Egg overwinters. **FP:** birdsfoot trefoil, restharrow, other clover species, heather. Caterpillars live communally with large numbers of black ants.

Idas Blue Lycaeides idas L.

Des: forewing c.1.5 cm. **H:** heather areas, woodland meadows and margins. **Dis:** in mountains up to and above 2,500 m. Absent in Britain. **A:** occurs regularly but is less frequent than in the past. **Fl:** mid-June to mid-August. Sometimes second generation. **LC:** May to June. Egg overwinters. **FP:** clover species, also broom, laburnum. Lives in symbiosis with ants. Fewer ants may have caused decline of this species.

♀

Blues, Hairstreaks & Coppers

♂ above ♀

♂

65

Brown Argus *Aricia agestis* Schiff.

Des: no blue on wings! Forewing 1.5 cm. Difficult to distinguish from *A. artaxerxes*. **H:** dry grassland, heaths, along road sides, and sunny slopes of chalky hills up to 1,000 m. **Dis:** Europe up to 56°N. In southern England and southern Scandinavia only local. **A:** locally frequent, but usually rare or absent. **Fl:** two generations, first May to June, second mid-July to beginning of August. **LC:** first September to May, second June to July. **FP:** meadow cranesbill, common storksbill, and rockrose.

Damon Blue
Agrodiaetus damon Schiff.

Des: forewing 1.5–1.7 cm. ♀ slightly smaller than ♂. Greeny-blue colour on wing upsides. Not very conspicuous. **H:** on sunny hill slopes with chalky soil, woodland margins, road verges, and lush, extensively cultivated fallow land. **Dis:** scattered populations in Europe, not in Britain. The form occurring in the Alps exhibits even brighter colouring. **A:** locally common. **FP:** sainfoin. Like most *lycaenida* the Damon Blue is usually attended by ants.

Adonis Blue *Lysandra bellargus* Rott.

Des: forewing 1.6–1.8 cm. Identification very difficult since many similar species exist. Distinct sex dimorphism: the ♂ is bright blue while the ♀ is usually an inconspicuous brown colour, occasionally with a blueish tinge. **H:** chalky hilly country on dry to sandy ground with sparse vegetation. **Dis:** throughout Europe to 55°N. **A:** commoner in the past, today fairly scarce. **Fl:** two generations, first May to June, second August to September. **LC:** September to May, second July. **FP:** horseshoe vetch.

Mazarine Blue
Cyaniris semiargus Rott.

Des: forewing just under 2 c ♂ dark voilet with black marg ♀ uniformly brown. Undersic of both sexes brown. **H:** flow meadows, edges of paths, clea ings, woodland margins, up 2,500 m. **Dis:** much of cent and eastern Europe, but extinct Britain and Holland. **A:** consid ably smaller numbers than in past. **Fl:** June to August in o or two generations. **LC:** Augr to July. Caterpillar hibernates. **FP:** kidney vet clover, etc.

Chalkhill Blue *Lysandra coridon* Poda

Des: very similar to the Damon Blue, but distinc larger. Forewing 1.6–1.8 cm. The ♀ has bro wing upsides marked by a row of ocelli alo the outer margin of both fore- and hindwings. W upsides of ♂ are greeny blue. **H:** dry, wa slopes, clear-felled areas, field edges, road verg preferably on chalky soil. **Dis:** Europe, absent fr north and extreme south. Locally common on ch of southern England. **A:** has become scarce. June to August in one generation. **LC:** April June. The fully developed caterpillar hiberna within the egg amongst leaf litter. **FP:** horsesh vetch.

Common Blue
Polyommatus icarus Rott.

Des: forewing 1.2–1.5 c Undersides marked by yell patches along margins a numerous black, white-borde dots. **Dis:** by far the common blue in Britain. Also fou throughout Europe to the No Cape, and on all Mediterrane islands, up to 2,000 **A:** common. **Fl:** Two to th generations, first May to Ju second July to September. **L** first September to May, second June to July. **F** restharrow, clover, birdsfoot trefoil, many ot leguminosae.

Blues, Hairstreaks & Coppers

♀ above ♂ ♂ above ♂

Silver-spotted Skipper *Hesperia comma* L.

Description: Skippers are actually more closely related to the micro-moths than to the butterflies, although they share with the latter their diurnal lifestyle. The broad head with widely separated antennae suggests that they are zoologically close to the *Thyrididae* family. Some Skippers have the ability to conceal their scent scales by forming a pouch with the apex of their forewings. These sex-brands are found only on males and are used to attract females by emission of species-specific scents. Another characteristic of the Skippers is their unusual antennae which end in a club with a short pointed hook, known as the apiculus. This organ has specifically evolved to receive scent signals.

With a forewing of 1.5 cm, the Silver-spotted Skipper is a relatively small, but typical representative of its family in Europe. Its golden-brown colour and the pattern of white dots also make it inconspicuous. Its flight – fluttering restlessly from flower to flower – appears very nervous. The male bears a comma marking on the upperside of its forewings. This is absent in the female, which is of a darker colour and whose forewings are marked by larger, whiter patches.

Habitat: widely distributed on calcareous soils, ranging from the sea-coast to mountains over 2,500 m. Found in nearly all types of habitat on warm summer days, in flower meadows, on field edges or abandoned gravel pits and woodland clearings. It usually prefers chalky soils.

Distribution: throughout Europe. Ranges in the north as far as southern England, where it is very rare, southern Scandinavia and southern Finland. Not yet recorded on the Mediterranean islands.

Abundance: one of the most common butterflies in central and southern Europe.

Flight: mid-June to August in one generation.

Life cycle: April to June. The eggs are laid i August, but do not hatch until the following spring The almost naked or slightly hairy caterpillars sta feeding immediately. One characteristic feature i the dark, round, large head which is distinctly offse from the body and marked by a triangle on th forehead and two brown lines. The last two seg ments of the body underside are marked by tw white patches. The caterpillars live on the groun where they spin a kind of protective tube- or tent like shelter from which they emerge to feed o various grasses.

Foodplants: virtually all Skipper caterpillars fee on wild grasses and herbs, often those we regard a weeds and treat with herbicides. This has led t Skippers becoming rare in some areas. The Silver spotted Skipper feeds exclusively on sheep's fescu throughout Europe.

General: it is very difficult to distinguish th Silver-spotted Skipper from the Large Skippe (*Ochlodes venatus*), see page 70, by their uppe wings. The males of both species bear a distin comma marking on the forewing, made up of scen scales (see top photograph). However, the comm remains flat and uniformly black, while in the Si ver-spotted Skipper it protrudes above the win surface and often bears a shiny silvery dividing lin in the centre. The yellow wing markings are mo distinct and the antennal clubs shorter and broade However their undersides are very different, that the Silver-spotted Skipper has a distinctly gree background. This species is not only widely distr buted and common in central Europe, but can b found in North America and Asia.

Skippers

Silver-spotted Skippers (*Hesperia comma*) mating

Grizzled Skipper *Pyrgus malvae* L.

Des: typical pattern. Forewing just under 1.5 cm. **H:** anywhere, most frequent in hilly areas, ranging from the coast up to 2,000 m. **Dis:** nearly all over Europe up to 65°N. **A:** common, though declining in southern England. **Fl:** end of April to June in one generation. **LC:** August to September. Pupa hibernates in web on the ground. **FP:** mallow, wild strawberry, cinquefoil, and a wide variety of other species.

Dingy Skipper *Erynnis tages* L.

Des: small, forewing just under 1.5 cm. Brow with a band of fine white dots along margin of bot fore- and hindwings. **H:** widely distributed. Like sunny, dry slopes with sparse vegetation. **Dis** throughout Europe. In the north this specie reaches northern England, Ireland and norther Scandinavia, but it is always local and occurs on in small numbers. **A:** fairly common in its ow habitat, but much rarer in intensively farmed area **Fl:** two generations: first end of April to beginnin of June, second: July to August. **LC:** first: Septem ber to April, second: June to July. **FP:** birdsfo trefoil, scorpion vetch, medick, horseshoe vetch and a wide variety of other species.

Chequered Skipper
Carterocephalus palaemon Pall.

Des: forewing 1.5 cm. Marked by a series of different-sized orange-yellow spots on dark-brown wings. ♀ greyer than ♂ with yellow patches. **H:** butterfly of temperate zones. Occurs particularly in wooded areas, also flower meadows, on scrubby hillsides, and moorland meadows. **Dis:** France, central, eastern and south-eastern Europe. Absent from southern Europe, Wales and Ireland. Extinct in England, but very local in Scotland. **A:** distributed in isolated populations, therefore only locally common. **Fl:** mid-May to June in one generation. **LC:** July to May. Caterpillar hibernates. **FP:** wild grasses.

Lulworth Skipper
Thymelicus acteon Rott.

Des: forewing 1.3 cm. Golden brown with fade yellow strokes and spots. **H:** warmth-loving spec ies. South-facing slopes, meadows with scru cover, woodland margins. More common on chalk soils. **Dis:** Europe only as far as 48°N. Absent fro northern Germany. Occurs in Denmark only in ve favourable years, possibly extinct in Netherland Locally abundant in south-eastern Dorset, Englan Absent from Sardinia and Corsica. **A:** can be abur dant locally, but is generally rare. **Fl:** July August in one generation. **LC:** September to Jun Caterpillar hibernates in grass stems. **FP:** t grass.

Large Skipper
Ochlodes venatum Bremer and Grey

Des: forewing 1.7 cm. Dark brown with pale yellow-brown patches and spots, undersides with a greenish tinge. **H:** meadows, hillsides, woodland edges, parks. **Dis:** Europe. Absent from Ireland, Scotland and from Scandinavia above 56°N. In the south it is absent from Sardinia, Corsica and Crete. **A:** common, but difficult for non-experts to identify in flight as it is very similar to many other species. **Fl:** long flight period from end of May to mid-August in one generation. **LC:** September to May. Caterpillar hibernates. **FP:** wild grasses.

Small Skipper
Adopaea sylvestris Poda.

Des: forewing 1.5 cm. Brow ochre with dark sex-bran Undersides paler. **H:** widely di tributed, ranging from lowlanc up to 2,000 m. **Dis:** Europ Absent from Scandinavia, Fir land, Ireland. In the south ever where except Sardinia, Corsic and Crete. **A:** one of the com monest of the skippers. **Fl:** Jur to August in one generation. **L** August to May. Caterpillar hibe nates. **FP:** wild grasses.

71

Black Arches *Lymantria monacha* L.

Description: forewing 1.8–2.7 cm, males distinctly smaller than most females. Ground colour white, with numerous broad, black, jagged bands and dots. Hindwings are beige with black dots along margin. Completely or partially melanotic, that is, black forms occur sporadically, but much less commonly in Britain than in parts of Continental Europe.

Habitat: in Britain, in mixed woodland where the principal foodplant is oak. On the Continent shows a strong preference for spruce and pine forests, especially those of uniform size and age, as in commercial forests.

Distribution: Europe, including southern half of England and Wales. In the north, extends to central Sweden and southern Finland.

Abundance: fairly common to common in southern England, very local in Wales. On the Continent, populations fluctuate considerably, often in cycles of three to five years, with peaks of great abundance.

Flight: July to beginning of September in one generation.

Life cycle: up to 300 eggs per female are laid in crevices of bark on the lower parts of tree trunks where they overwinter. In Britain, the eggs seem to be laid singly, or in small groups, but on the Continent, batches of up to 100 are stated to occur. The larvae hatch in spring, remaining together for a short time before dispersing. They do this by climbing to the tops of the trees and spinning a silk thread enabling them to 'parachute' on the breeze to other trees, a strategy employed by various woodland species in which the female is wingless or sluggish. Interestingly this dispersal activity occurs only when the wind is light – in strong winds the small caterpillars hold on tightly and do not spin threads. This behaviour, well known on the Continent, does not seem to have been observed in Britain, and may occur only when the species reaches high density. Caterpillar season late April to June. Pupa brown with metallic gloss and covering of short, stiff bristles; formed in a slight cocoon in crevices of bark.

Foodplants: polyphagous on many tree species. In Britain, almost exclusively on oak, but on the Continent chiefly on spruce and pine; in such forests it may cause severe defoliation.

General: in Europe there have been several occasions in the last 150 years when populations have reached plague proportions and caused severe damage in plantations of spruce and pine. Such numbers seem only to be attained as a result of monoculture forestry policy. As the cycle builds up, slight damage is caused in the first year, serious damage in the second year, and in the third complete defoliation resulting in the tree's death. Per caterpillar is said to consume about 1,000 pine needles and to damage as many more. Once a spruce has lost 70% of its needles it inevitably dies; a pine can suffer up to 90% loss. Seriously damaged trees may subsequently die from other causes, such as attack by other pests, disease or unfavourable weather conditions. In susceptible forests numbers of egg-batches are monitored each year, and estimates made of numbers of natural enemies such as birds, and parasites like ichneumon flies which normally keep the population in check.

Tussocks

Pale Tussock *Elkneria pudibunda* L.

Des: forewing ♂ c.2 cm, ♀ c.3 cm. ♂ usually darker with more contrasting wing pattern and strongly feathered antennae; ♀ light grey with two or three dark crosslines. **H:** mixed woodlands, parks, old gardens. **Dis:** throughout temperate Europe including most of England and Wales; local in Ireland, absent from Scotland. **A:** often common in deciduous woodland. **Fl:** May and June. **LC:** caterpillars hairy, green, yellow, pink or blackish; July to October. **FP:** polyphagous, mostly on trees such as beech, birch, oak.

Black V Moth *Arctornis l-nigrum* Müll.
Caterpillar – see page 274

Des: forewing 1.9–2.5 cm. Sexes similar. Pale green, quickly fading to white, with distinct black L-mark in centre of forewing. Antennae of ♂ feathered. **H:** mixed deciduous woodlands in sunny situations, wooded hillsides, and valleys. **Dis:** temperate Europe; scarce immigrant to Britain, established in Essex for a few years. **Fl:** mid-June to early August. **LC:** caterpillar from September to May, hibernating when small in a thin cocoon amongst foliage. **FP:** polyphagous on deciduous trees such as elm, lime, oak, beech, often on well-grown trees.

Gipsy Moth *Lymantria dispar* L.

Des: forewing ♂ 2.0 cm, ♀ over 3 cm. Male dark medium-brown with black, jagged crosslines and patches along wing margin. Female creamy white with weak brownish crosslines. Variable. **H:** mixed deciduous woodland, holm oak forest and scrub. **Dis:** southern and central Europe, to central Sweden and southern Finland. Extinct as a breeding species in Britain. **A:** usually common, with population explosions, when larvae can cause great damage. **Fl:** July and August. **LC:** caterpillars feed from May to July. **FP:** deciduous trees of many kinds.

Scarce Vapourer
Orgyia recens Hübn.

Des: forewing of ♂ c.15 cm. Wing uppersides of ♂ dark brown, forewings variegated with black, white and orange markings, with conspicuous kidney-shaped white patch in angle of wing. ♀ flightless, with wings reduced to mere stumps and body enlarged to accommodate eggs. **H:** woodlands and hedgerows. **Dis:** temperate Europe to 2,000 m; extremely local and decreasing in England. **Fl:** June and July, and August to September, in two generations. **LC:** after pairing, egg mass deposited on cocoon from which ♀ emerged. Larvae in May, and July to August, first generation having hibernated as small larvae. **FP:** polyphagous on deciduous trees and shrubs. *Note:* vapourer moths are diurnal; in Britain, the lighter brown Common Vapourer, *O. antiqua* L is much commoner.

White Satin *Leucoma salicis* L.

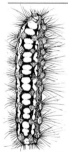

Des: forewing 2.0–2.6 cm, distinctly more robust than the otherwise similar Black V Moth, with glossy white, unmarked wings. **H:** poplar plantations and avenues, along streams and rivers, and in parks. **Dis:** throughout most of Europe, including England. **A:** locally common. **Fl:** June and July. **LC:** the newly hatched caterpillars hibernate when small, and feed up in May and June. **FP:** poplars and willows.

Ocneria detrita Esp.

Des: forewing 1.5 cm, ♀ slightly larger than ♂. Dark reddish-brown with black dusting and blurred dark markings on forewings. **H:** heathland on sandy soils, wooded limestone hills in warm, sunny locations. **Dis:** central and southern Europe, absent from Britain. **A:** rare and local. **Fl:** June and July. **LC:** eggs laid in clusters on underside of a leaf; caterpillar from August to May, hibernating. **FP:** foliage of lower branches of scrub oak, never in higher tree tops.

Yellow-tail *Euproctis similis* Fuessl.

winter cocoon

Des: forewing 1.5–2.2 cm. Female distinctly larger than male, with simple antennae, more robust abdomen, and lacking black marks on forewing. Both sexes with conspicuous tuft of yellow hair-scales at tip of abdomen; in the similar Brown-tail (*E. chrysorrhoea*), the hair-scales are dark chocolate-brown and extend further up the abdomen in the male.

Habitat: gardens, open parkland, light deciduous woodland, orchards, and hedgerows. Active from dusk into the night and frequently attracted to light.

Distribution: Europe, to central Scandinavia and southern Finland; common in England and Wales.

Abundance: often common and sometimes a minor pest in orchards.

Flight: June to August.

Life cycle: eggs laid in a batch on twigs, covered by hair-scales from the tip of the abdomen of the female. The young larvae disperse and feed until the second instar, when they hibernate in winter cocoons spun in crevices of bark or amongst dead leaves. They feed up the following spring until May. Their black-and-white coloration and densely hairy bodies evidently protect them against the majority of predators, and they feed exposed and conspicuously by day. Their hairs may cause minor skin irritation (*urticaria*), but nothing like as severe as that caused by the larvae of the Brown-tail.

Foodplants: various species of deciduous trees and shrubs, such as poplar, willow, oak, cherry, apple, and plum. Hawthorn is a favoured foodplant in Britain.

Brown-tail *Euproctis chrysorrhoea* L.

Description: very similar to the Yellow-tail. In the male, the forewing is usually unmarked, and the brown hair-scales extend from the tip almost to the base of the abdomen. In the female, the abdominal hair-tuft is much more massive than in the Yellow-tail.

Habitat: in similar places to those utilized by the Yellow-tail in mainland Europe, but in Britain more or less strictly confined to coastal localities.

Distribution: widespread in Europe to central Sweden and southern Finland, but only in southeast England.

Abundance: fairly common to common in Europe. In Britain, periodic population explosions occur, when the species becomes excessively abundant in its restricted localities and spreads inland. At such times, severe discomfort may be suffered by local people from urtication caused by airborne hair from the caterpillars.

Flight: late June to early August.

Life cycle: eggs are laid in batches covered by hair-scales from the tip of the abdomen of the female. Caterpillars hatch in late summer and spin a communal web of coarse grey silk in which they spend the winter. In spring they emerge, disperse gradually, and feed up by early June.

Foodplants: oak, but also various fruit trees such as cherry, plum, apple, and pear. In Britain, blackthorn is the usual foodplant.

♂

Tussocks

Garden Tiger *Arctia caja* L.

Description: forewing 2.5–3.5 cm. Forewings with irregular, meandering, and highly variable brown-and-white pattern; hindwings bright red (occasionally yellow), with large, round, bluish-black spots. The Garden Tiger is a good example of a species showing aposematic or warning coloration. Predators such as birds discover that such colourful insects are highly unpalatable and rapidly learn to leave them alone.

Habitat: prefers damp places such as river valleys, but also occurs commonly on farmland and in gardens and parks. The species has adapted well to human environmental changes – cultivation and urbanization.

Distribution: throughout Europe to Lapland in the north, and in mountains up to 2,000 m. Widespread in Britain to the Outer Hebrides.

Abundance: usually fairly common, in some years abundant. Comes freely to light, but late at night.

Flight: July and August.

Life cycle: eggs laid in large batches on undersides of leaves of herbaceous plants. Caterpillars hatch in early autumn, hibernate, and feed up the following spring until May. Though they feed chiefly at night, they are often encountered by day running across paths and are the familiar 'woolly bears' of countrymen. The pupa is in a firm silken cocoon spun at ground level.

Foodplants: polyphagous on many herbaceous plants such as dandelion, deadnettle, stinging nettle, comfrey, and forget-me-not, and on small shrubs such as bramble and heather. Waste ground and neglected corners of gardens and farmyards are readily colonized.

General: although extreme variations are rare in the wild, this species has been the subject of intensive selective breeding in the laboratory, and many extraordinary forms have been reared. It has been found possible to induce continuous breeding, with up to three generations per year in these conditions, rearing the larvae on a diet of cabbage.

There are several other species of tiger moth which occur in Europe, some of which are mentioned here:

Pericallia matronula L. The largest European species with forewing of some 4 cm. The forewings are brown with a series of cream-coloured spots along the leading edge, and the hindwings are orange-yellow with blue-black spots. Used to be more widespread in Europe and Asia, but its range has contracted in recent years and is now extinct in many places. It has never occurred in Britain. It occurs chiefly in the foothills of mountains; the caterpillar, which hibernates twice, feeds on a variety of plants including hawkweeds, bilberry, honeysuckle, ash, hazel, and oak.

The **Cream-spot Tiger** (*Arctia villica* L.) occurs throughout central and southern Europe. The race found in southern England and northern France is distinguished as sub-species *britannica* Oberthür. The caterpillar feeds on such common plants as dandelion, deadnettle and yarrow; even so, the species has become rare in parts of central Europe.

Scarlet Tiger *Callimorpha dominula* L.

Description: forewing 2.2–2.7 cm. Uppersides of forewings glossy blackish-brown with white and yellow spots. Hindwings dark red (occasionally yellow) with black spots. Unlike the majority of tiger moths, this species and the next have well-developed mouthparts and freely imbibe nectar from flowers such as hemp agrimony.

Habitat: characteristically a species of marshes and damp river valleys, but some British colonies occur on dry roadsides and sea cliffs.

Distribution: found locally throughout Europe, including southern England and west Wales, extending northwards to central Sweden and southern Finland.

Abundance: usually common where it occurs, and often seen flying by day.

Flight: mid-June to July.

Life cycle: caterpillar from August to late May; hibernates.

dominula   quadripunctaria

Foodplants: chiefly comfrey and stinging nettle in Britain, but also on forget-me-not, deadnettle, honeysuckle, raspberry, and even oak.

General: has been the subject of intensive experimental breeding, and much is now known about the way in which the more extreme colour variants are inherited, all of which are extremely rare in the wild.

Jersey Tiger *Euplagia quadripunctaria* Poda

Description: forewing 2.6–2.8 cm. Forewing uppersides blackish brown with yellow oblique stripes. Hindwings red (sometimes yellow) marked with two black spots and an irregularly shaped black patch. Easily identified when seen at rest, but in flight could be mistaken for a butterfly.

Habitat: limestone hills and valleys with rocky ravines, often near water: in Britain – lanes, banks and hedgerows near the sea in its restricted range.

Distribution: southern Europe to central Germany; in Britain restricted to the coast of south Devon and the Channel Isles, where it is common.

Abundance: locally common through its range.

Flight: late July and August. The moths are active during the day and also come to light.

Life Cycle: caterpillars from September to June; they hibernate when quite small, but in captivity can be induced to continue feeding slowly throughout the winter.

Foodplants: polyphagous on a variety of herbaceous plants including dandelion, deadnettle, stinging nettle, and forget-me-not; also on hazel and raspberry after hibernation.

General: in parts of southern Europe this species aestivates gregariously in enormous numbers: the most famous locality where this occurs is in the 'Valley of Butterflies' on the island of Rhodes.

pupa

Cinnabar *Tyria jacobaea* L.

Description: forewing length 1.7–2.0 cm. Forewings blackish with a long red stripe along the leading edge of the wing, and two red spots along the outer margin. Hindwings red with a narrow black border.

Habitat: dry fields and hillsides, sometimes in quarries, open parts of woods and sand dunes.

Distribution: widespread across Europe to central Sweden (scarce). Widespread in Britain and Ireland, but more restricted to coastal localities in the north of its range.

Abundance: locally common, rarer in northern Europe, and the south; associated particularly with north-south running Alpine valleys, to 1,600 m.

Flight: May to July in one generation, readily disturbed by day and coming to light late at night.

Life cycle: the easily-recognized yellow-and-black banded caterpillars feed up in late summer and the winter is spent as a pupa. The caterpillars feed gregariously and conspicuously, and are highly distasteful to potential predators.

Foodplants: in Britain, almost solely on common ragwort, but occasionally on groundsel and Oxford ragwort. On the Continent, also reported on colts foot and butterbur. Sometimes they are so abundant that all the available foodplant has been eaten before the caterpillars reach full growth in which case many starve and the population crashes the following year.

Clouded Buff *Diacrisia sannio* L.

Description: the species shows strong sexual dimorphism. Forewing just under 2.3 cm, males larger than females. Forewings of male are yellow with red central spot, hindwings creamy white with dark border and central spot. The narrower-winged, plumper-bodied female is warm orange with a dark mark on each forewing, and hindwings heavily suffused with black. At one time it was thought to be a different species.

Habitat: heaths and moors, dry calcareous downland and clearings in woods on well-drained soils; on the Continent, up to 2,400 m.

Distribution: widely distributed but local in Europe as far as 68°N. Local through most of Britain except the outer Scottish isles.

Abundance: numbers have decreased locally and some colonies rendered extinct through loss of habitat.

Flight: June and July. In mainland Europe, there is sometimes a second generation of smaller individuals in late July and August. The male is easily disturbed by day, but the sluggish female is seldom encountered, even at night. Males come to light shortly before dawn.

Life cycle: the caterpillar occurs from late July to May and hibernates when small, rarely feeding up quickly to produce a second generation. It is nocturnal.

Foodplants: polyphagous on herbaceous plants including heather, bedstraw, plantain, dandelion and stinging nettle.

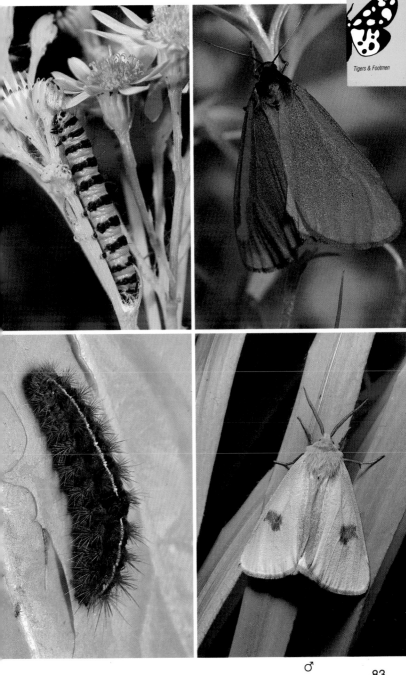

♂

Rhyparia purpurata L.

Des: forewing about 2.3 cm. Forewings rich yellow with a scattering of small brown spots. Hindwings bright red with black spots. Sexes similar, but ♂ has feather antennae. **H:** meadows and dry grassland, hillsides, and woodland clearings. **Dis:** not British; occurs particularly south of the Alps, but extends into NE France. On the German Red List but not endangered elsewhere. **A:** common in southern Europe, rare in the north of its range. **Fl:** mid-June and July. **LC:** caterpillar from August to June, hibernating when small. **FP:** bedstraw, mugwort, heather, and other herbaceous plants.

Phragmatobia caesarea Goeze

Des: forewing 1.5–1.8 cm. Wings blackish, rather thinly scaled, with prominent black veins and conspicuous yellow patch along inner margin of hindwings. Abdomen orange-yellow with series of black dorsal dots. **H:** dry, sunny, open woodland and grassy slopes. **Dis:** central and southern Europe. Absent from Britain. **A:** locally common, but very rare in northern Germany. **Fl:** late May to July, sometimes a second generation in August. **LC:** caterpillars in July and August; second generation in September. Winter spent as a pupa in a greyish-black cocoon in soil or in a crevice among rocks. **FP:** polyphagous on low plants including plantain, speedwell, bedstraw, and sandwort.

Speckled Footman
Coscinia cribraria L.

Des: forewing length 1.5–2.0 cm. ♀ narrower-winged and thicker-bodied than ♂. Several different races occur which differ in size and in the amount of black marking on the forewings. The British sub-species *bivittata* South is a particularly well-marked form. **H:** warm, well-drained localities from high in the Alps to dunes at sea level on the Baltic coast, and heather moors in southern England. **A:** locally common; extremely local in mid-southern England where it has lost habitats through heath fires and to development. **Fl:** June to August, later in north of its range. Can be disturbed by day and flies naturally at night. **LC:** caterpillar from August to June, hibernating. **FP:** polyphagous on heathland grasses and herbaceous plants.

Muslin Moth *Diaphora mendica* Clerck

Des: forewing 1.5–1.8 cm. ♂ grey-brown w small black spots, ♀ a little larger, snowy-wh with scattering of small black spots. In Irela (sub-species *rustica* Hübn.), many of the ♂ a white like the ♀, but can always be distinguish by the feathered antennae. **H:** open woodlar moorland, parks and gardens. **Dis:** widely dist buted in temperate Europe including Englar Wales, and Ireland, very local in Scotland. **A:** fair common: ♀ occasionally seen on the wing by d ♂ fly late at night and come freely to light. ■ mid-May to early July in one generation. L caterpillars in July and August. Winter spent as pupa in a grey cocoon spun at ground level. F plants including dandelion, deadnettle, and dock.

Feathered Footman *Spiris striata* L.

Des: forewing 1.5–2.2 cm. Forewing upperw. yellow with conspicuous yellow longitudinal st pes. Hindwing orange with black border or all da as in the specimen illustrated. **H:** dry, warm slop with sparse vegetation. **Dis:** throughout Europ local. Absent from many parts of southern Germa and unrecorded in Britain for many years. **A:** pop lation endangered in some areas, eg parts of Germ any, but elsewhere abundant. Flies by day. **Fl:** la May to August, one or two generations according locality. **LC:** caterpillar hibernates when sma Pupa in a grey cocoon at ground level. **FP:** pol phagous on herbaceous plants including grasses.

Hyphoraia aulica L.

Des: forewing 1.6–1.8 cm similar to ♂ but heavier-bodie and with simple antennae. For wings chocolate brown with pa yellow spots. Hindwings oran with extensive black patches. ■ dry, sunny, sandy places. **Di** local in Europe but not in Brita **A:** locally common. **Fl:** late M to early July, sometimes second generation. **LC:** caterp lar from August to April, hibe nating when small. **FP:** polyphagous, host plar include dandelion, yarrow, and hawkweeds.

♂

Buff Ermine *Spilosoma luteum* Hufn.

Description: forewing up to 2 cm. Wings creamy or yellow-buff marked on forewing by a diagonal row of dark spots, those closest to the hind margin being the largest. Abdomen bright orange-yellow marked with black. Male has comb-shaped antennae and is usually more richly coloured than female.

Habitat: widespread in open woodland, clearings, waste ground, hedgerows, parks, and gardens.

Distribution: throughout Europe to 62°N; throughout England and Wales, but mainly western in Scotland and coastal in Ireland. In European mountains to 1,800 m.

Abundance: generally common.

Flight: mid-May to July; sometimes a partial second generation. Nocturnal, and like many others of the Tiger-moth family flies late at night when it comes freely to light.

Life cycle: caterpillars reach full growth in th autumn when they are often seen hurrying acros roads in search of a pupation site. Winter is spe as a pupa in a cocoon of brown silk on the ground.

Foodplants: polyphagous on many herbaceou plants including dandelion, plantain and deadnettl also bramble and raspberry; one of the few specie to thrive on elder.

General: although variation is usually mino spectacular forms in which the wings are heavil marked with black, leaving only the veins pale, hav been bred and occasionally occur in the wild Apparently the Buff Ermine is less distasteful t predators than the closely related White Ermine; has been suggested it gains some protection b mimicking that species.

White Ermine *Spilosoma lubricipeda* L.

Description: forewing length c. 2 cm. White with scattering of black dots on forewings and a few spots on the hindwings which form a broken marginal band. Abdomen orange and black, exposed in aposematic display when the moth is disturbed. In Scottish populations there is a tendency for the forewings to be cream-coloured or buff.

Habitat: woodland margins, scrubland, old gravel pits, waste ground, dunes, etc.

Distribution: throughout Europe to 64°N. In the Alps to 1,600 m.

Abundance: common almost everywhere, but not a pest species.

Flight: May to July, occasionally a partial second generation in August.

Life cycle: larva in autumn. Another species c 'woolly bear' which is frequently encountered trav elling at high speed in search of a place to pupate As in the preceding species, winter is spent as pupa.

General: the Water Ermine (*S. urticae* Esp.) is another species which occurs in marshy ground i south-east England. It resembles the White Ermine but the markings are confined to two small spots towards the leading edge of the forewing. The American Fall Webworm (*Hyphantria cunea* Drury) a potential pest species, has become established in parts of western Europe but has not so far reached Britain.

87

Ruby Tiger *Phragmatobia fuliginosa* L.

Description: forewing 1.5–1.8 cm. Forewings dark cinnamon-brown with a small dark dot in the centre. Hindwings dark red, variably marked with black. Abdomen red and black – yet another example of warning colouration which is such a common feature of the tiger moth family.

Habitat: meadows, pastures, woodland margins, heaths and wasteland. In mountains up to 3,000 m.

Distribution: throughout Europe. In Britain, it extends to the Orkneys and Outer Hebrides and to western Ireland. The small, dark Scottish race is sub-species *borealis* STDGR.

Abundance: numbers fluctuate from year to year but usually common.

Flight: first generation from mid-April to early June; second generation, which is usually the more common, in July and August. Chiefly nocturnal, but sometimes flies in sunshine.

Life cycle: first generation larvae in June and July. Second generation larvae hibernate when fully grown and pupate in spring after sunning themselves for a few days. On moors, the cocoon generally spun amongst the upper stems of heather, elsewhere in cracks and crevices in tree trunks and fences, or on the ground.

Foodplants: stinging nettles, deadnettle, dandelion, dock and other herbaceous plants.

Wood Tiger *Parasemia plantaginis* L.

Description: forewing up to 2 cm. Marked with a pattern of cream-coloured spots and streaks. Hindwing typically orange with two radiating black streaks and a pattern of black blotches around the margin. Females usually darker than males. In northern Britain a proportion of the males have hindwings in which the ground colour is white (*ab. hospita* Schiff.) In some localities in the Alps the species is extraordinarily variable – the forewing pattern may be more extensive or greatly reduced, and the hindwings are sometimes almost or completely black.

Habitat: calcareous downland, open woodland, moors and meadows, ascending high into the mountains.

Abundance: locally common; in southern Britain has decreased through loss of downland habitat.

Flight: June to mid-July in one generation. Males fly by day. Females are sluggish and seldom if ever take wing.

Life cycle: Caterpillars hibernate when young and feed up in the spring. They may often be found basking in the spring sunshine.

Foodplants: polyphagous on small downland or heathland plants including violet, dandelion, groundsel and plantain.

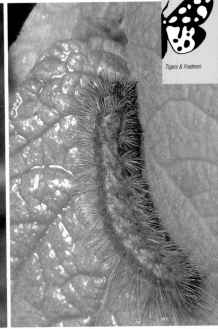

Tigers & Footmen

♀

Rosy Footman
Miltochrista miniata Forst.

Des: forewing just under 1.3 cm. Bright rose-tinted yellow forewings with fine black 'scribble'. Hindwings unmarked, pale pinkish cream coloured. **H:** a woodland species which favours old, unpolluted woods and those growing in damp areas. **Dis:** Europe to southern Scandinavia. In Britain, only in southern half of England and Wales, and in south-east Ireland. **A:** locally common. **Fl:** lichens, especially *Peltigera canina*. In captivity can be reared on withered leaves.

Four-dotted Footman
Cybosia mesomella L.

Des: forewing 1.4–1.8 cm. Forewings greyish white with a faint yellowish hue in the ♂, richer creamy yellow in the ♀, each wing marked with two widely-spaced small black dots. Hindwings darker than forewings, which is an unusual feature among moths. **H:** open woodland, moors and heaths, and young plantations. **Dis:** through Europe to 64°N and widespread in England and Wales. More local in Scotland and absent from Ireland. **A:** moderately common. **Fl:** June and July. **LC:** lichens growing on the ground or amongst heather. Said also to feed on leafy liverworts, and in captivity will accept withered leaves of sallow.

Four-spotted Footman
Lithosia quadra L.

Des: largest European footman moth; forewing 2 cm or more. Sexually dimorphic, ♂ with buff forewing, darker towards tip but without markings, ♀ with yellow forewings adorned by two round blackish spots. **H:** well-established woodland, sometimes in parks and orchards. Also migratory. **Dis:** through much of Europe. Native in some of the old woodlands. **A:** native populations fluctuate greatly in numbers, in mainland Europe and Britain. **Fl:** July and August. **LC:** caterpillars hibernate when small and feed up in spring and early summer. Pupae in loose cocoons under bark or moss on tree trunks. **FP:** lichens on trees, also cannibalistic, on the Continent feeds on caterpillars of the Black Arches Moth when they are abundant.

Buff Footman *Eilema depressa* Esp.

Des: forewing 1.6–1.8 cm. Though rather variable in the buff tone of the forewings, this is usually one of the easier of the *Eilema* footmen to identify. ♀ are often darker than ♂, and sometimes have particularly dark hindwings. **H:** mixed deciduous woodland where there are yews, and pinewoods. **Dis:** across Europe, more common in south. Occurs in the west of Ireland, and in west Wales and the southern half of England. **A:** one of the more local *Eilema* species in Britain, but generally common in mainland Europe. **Fl:** caterpillars from August to June, hibernating when small. **FP:** lichens and *Protococcus* growing on tree trunks and branches, especially of yew.

Common Footman
Eilema lurideola Zinck.

Des: forewing about 1.8 cm. This and the next species are very similar. When at rest, holds its wings flat though overlapping, Scarce Footman wraps wings tightly round the body in a cylinder. **H:** deciduous woodland and heaths. **Dis:** throughout Europe and UK. **A:** usually common to very abundant in suitable habitats. **Fl:** late June to mid-August. **LC:** caterpillars occur from September to June, and hibernate when small under lichens on trees. **FP:** lichens on trees and bushes, sometimes on stones; in captivity will feed on the foliage of trees and bushes such as sallow, dogwood, and oak.

Scarce Footman *Eilema complana* L.

Des: similar size to the preceding species, but forewings look narrower and costal streak reaches wing tip. **H:** mixed deciduous woodland and clearings. **Dis:** temperate Europe; UK, but absent from Scotland. **A:** often common. **Fl:** late June to August in a single generation. **LC:** larval habits similar to those of the preceding species. **FP:** lichens, withered leaves of oak and beech herbaceous plants such as knotgrass.

Orange Footman
Eilema sororcula Hübn.

Des: forewing length about 1.3 cm. Wings orange-yellow, hindwings slightly paler than forewings. Apart from its colour, can be distinguished from related species by the distinct bend about two-thirds along the leading edge of forewing. **H:** coniferous and deciduous woodland. **Dis:** scattered through Europe, up to 1,000 m. Only in southern and eastern England and in south Wales. **A:** locally common. **Fl:** May and June, earlier than related species. **LC:** unlike its congeners, the caterpillar reaches maturity by the autumn, and the winter is spent as a pupa in a flimsy cocoon on the ground, under moss. **FP:** lichens, chiefly those on oak and beech.

Dew Moth *Setina irrorella* Clerck

Des: forewing length 0.9–1.6 cm., ♀ considerably smaller, with less ample wings and plumper bodies. Orange-yellow wings with three rows of black dots across the forewings and a few near the margin of the hindwings. In the rather uncommon form *signata* Borkh. the forewing dots are joined to form a striking IVI pattern. **H:** in Europe, on dry grassland and heaths; in Britain, chiefly coastal on shingle, sand dunes and calcareous cliffs. **Dis:** Europe, commoner in the north. Up to 1,800 m in the mountains. **A:** locally common in suitable habitats. **Fl:** June to late August in one generation. **LC:** caterpillars hatch in August, hibernate when young and complete their growth in early summer. **FP:** lichens growing on exposed rocks and stones.

Nine-spotted *Syntomis phegea* L.

Des: forewing length 1.8 cm. Wings blue-black with numerous white spots; long abdomen with yellow ring. **H:** sunny slopes, clearings, abandoned gravel pits. **Dis:** isolated populations in south Europe; absent from the north, including Britain. **A:** very locally common, otherwise rare. **Fl:** June and July. **LC:** caterpillar from August to May, hibernating. **FP:** deadnettle, dandelion and other weeds of arable land.

Red-necked Footman
Atolmis rubricollis L.

Des: forewing length c. 1.5 cm. Wings and body chocolate brown, with red collar and yellow tip to abdomen. **H:** coniferous and deciduous woodlands, and plantations. **Dis:** through Europe to 62°N., but in Britain confined to the south and west, and Wales; has evidently retreated westwards during the last 50 years. Present status in Ireland uncertain. **A:** locally common; in Britain, populations subject to strong fluctuations, but generally less common than in the past. **Fl:** early May to July in one generation. Usually flies at night. Often found resting on bracken under trees during the day. **LC:** caterpillars feed up during the autumn and pupate in late October, in a cocoon under bark or moss. **FP:** lichens and *Protococcus.*

Dotted Footman *Pelosia muscerda* Hufn.

Des: forewing length 1.5 cm. Light greyish-brown with two short rows of small spots on forewings. In the closely similar but much rarer Small Dotted Footman, *P. obtusa* H.-S. the wings are more rounded and the arrangement of the spots is different. **H:** boggy moorland, damp woodlands and fen carr. **Dis:** Europe, commoner in the north. **A:** local, extremely so in Britain chiefly in the Norfolk Broads. **Fl:** June to August. **LC:** caterpillars hatch in the autumn and hibernate when young. Growth is complete in June. **FP:** lichens growing on alder and other trees in damp woods; also algae and wilted leaves.

Festoon *Apoda limacodes* Hufn.

Des: forewing length 1.1–1.3 cm; ♂ smaller and darker than ♀. Compact, thick-bodied moth; wings dark brown to yellowish brown with two oblique crosslines. **H:** oak and beech woods. **Dis:** throughout Europe; in Britain, virtually confined to southern England. **A:** common where it occurs. **Fl:** May to July. **LC:** caterpillar feeds in late summer and reaches maturity in autumn. Overwinters in its cocoon, but does not pupate until the following spring. **FP:** oak and beech.

Tigers & Footmen

Dew Moths

Syntomids & Festoons

93

Oak Processionary Moth *Thaumetopoea processionea* L.

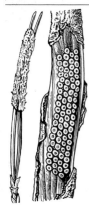

Description: male forewing length 1.3 cm, female 1.6 cm. Brownish-grey colour with more or less blurred pattern more sharply defined in male.

Habitat: Oak woods.

Distribution: most of Europe, but absent from northern German lowlands, and Britain.

Abundance: locally common, with massive population explosions in some years.

Flight: July and early August, in one generation. Males come freely to light, but females only occasionally.

Life cycle: overwinters in the egg stage. The caterpillars, which are covered with urticating hairs, live communally in a silk nest from which they disperse in procession each evening to feed on foliage in the tree canopy, returning at dawn.

Foodplant: oak.

Eastern Pine Processionary *Thaumetopoea pinivora* Treits.

Description: forewing 1.4–1.9 cm, females larger than males. In its grey colour and pattern of strong black crosslines it closely resembles the Pine Processionary (*T. pityocampa* Schiff.) which is the more common species in south-west Europe.

Habitat: pine forests, especially those growing on a light, sandy soil.

Distribution: eastern Europe, extending locally to the French Alps.

Abundance: occasional population explosions may occur, most often in monoculture pine plantations in the Baltic Sea area, but it is by no means as serious or regular a pest as *T. pityocampa*.

Flight: mid-July and August.

Life cycle: overwinters in the egg stage. Eggs are laid in a cylindrical mass around a pine needle. The caterpillars form a ball-like nest among the pine branches into which they retreat by day, coming out to feed at night. The nests of both species of pine processionary contain quantities of hairs from the bodies of the caterpillars, and severe skin rash can result from handling them. The processionary behaviour of the caterpillars has been a source of fascination and experiment. The famous French naturalist, Henri Fabre, showed that if the procession was closed to form a circle in such a way that every caterpillar had a 'leader', the procession would continue for days until exhaustion set in. He studied the larva of *T. pityocampa*, but in both species the behaviour is essentially the same. Pupa in a cocoon in the larval nest.

Foodplants: pine needles (*Pinus sylvestris* and *P. uncinata*).

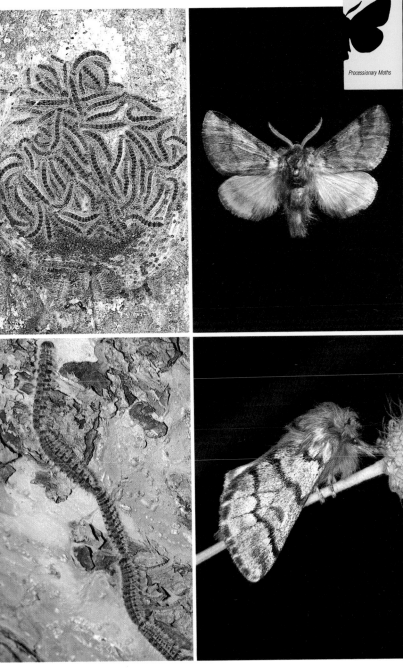

Buff-tip *Phalera bucephala* L.

Description: forewing 2.5–3.2 cm. Sexes similar but females often a little larger. When at rest, this moth bears a remarkable resemblance to a small length of broken and decaying branch, in which the cream-coloured, brown-marked thorax represents one end, and the rounded mark at the wing tip the other; the colour and pattern of the wings, wrapped tightly round the body, resemble the bark. Thus this species relies on subtle camouflage as a protection against predators.

Habitat: mixed woodland and wooded parks, heaths, meadows and river valleys.

Distribution: throughout Europe, including most of Britain and Ireland. It reaches the Arctic Circle and in mountains ascends as far as the tree line.

Abundance: though rarely seen by day, the moth comes commonly to light late at night. Colonies caterpillars are also a familiar sight.

Flight: May to July.

Life cycle: The hairy blue-black, yellow and white patterned caterpillars live communally in trees and bushes until nearly full-grown. They are apparently unpalatable to the majority of avian predators, but are recorded as having been attacked by large bugs which pierce the caterpillars with their mouthparts and suck them dry. Pupation occurs in the soil, and sometimes two winters are passed in this stage.

Foodplants: polyphagous on many species of broad-leaved tree, including oak, beech, poplar, willow, alder, and hazel.

Dusky Marbled Brown *Gluphisia crenata* Esp.

Description: one of the smaller prominents, with forewing length less than 1.5 cm. Most members of the family have a characteristic 'tooth' on the hind margin of the forewing, but in this species it is only weakly developed. The Dusky Marbled Brown is an inconspicuous species. The scales on the wings are rather loosely attached, and the moth soon becomes worn and semi-transparent.

Habitat: woods, plantations and river valleys where there are poplars.

Distribution: the typical form, in which the central area of the forewing is paler, occurs in southern Europe including south and south-west Germany, while the darker sub-species *vertunea* Derenne occurs in northern Europe, including Belgium and northern Germany. Three apparently authentic records of this sub-species have been reported in Britain.

Abundance: widespread in suitable habitat and sometimes common.

Flight: single-brooded in the north of its range in May and June, and elsewhere double-brooded, moths flying in spring and again in July and August. The moth is said to rest high in the canopy by day; at night it comes to light.

Life cycle: the hairless, green and yellow caterpillar may be found between June and September, earlier ones in the south feed up quickly and produce second generation of moths. The winter is spent as a pupa in a cocoon spun between leaves.

Foodplants: species of poplar.

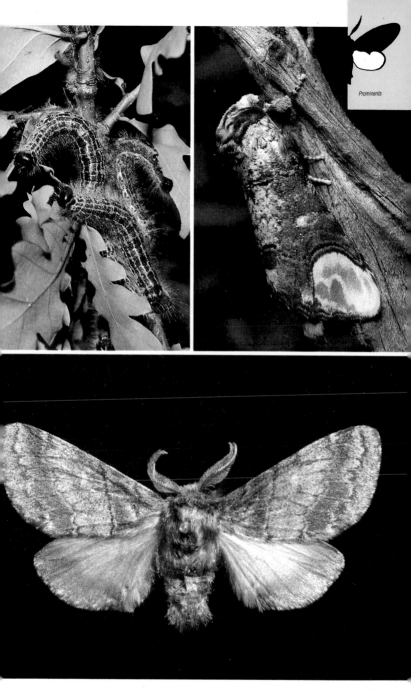

Swallow Prominent *Pheosia tremula* Clerck

1½ times
lifesize

Description: forewing 2.3–2.8 cm. The two closely related swallow prominents have a similar white-and-black pattern, and exhibit the characteristic prominent family 'tooth' on the hind margin of the forewing. They are distinguished by the markings in the hind angle of the forewing. In the Lesser Swallow Prominent, *P. gnoma* Fab., there is a narrow but distinct whitish wedge on the blackish background, which is lacking in the Swallow Prominent.

Habitat: plantations, mixed woodland, meadows and riversides where poplars grow.

Distribution: throughout Europe, extending to th Arctic Circle and to 1,600 m altitude in the Alps Throughout Britain and Ireland.

Abundance: the species has apparently increase in many areas as a result of increased planting c poplars, particularly *Populus x canadensis* Common in Britain where poplars grow.

Flight: two generations, first April to early June second late July to September. The moths ar seldom seen by day but come freely to light.

Life cycle: first generation of caterpillars in Jun and July, the second in autumn. The winter is sper as a pupa in a sub-terranean cocoon.

Foodplants: poplars, less often willows. Th Lesser Swallow Prominent on birch.

Lunar Marbled Brown *Drymonia ruficornis* Hufn.

1½ times
lifesize

Description: forewing 1.8–2.2 cm. The commonest form has the central area of the forewing whiter than in the specimen illustrated, so that the black crescent, after which the species is named, is more conspicuous. Males are distinguished by the comb-shaped antennae and paler hindwings.

Habitat: dry mixed deciduous woodland, and oak woods and scrub.

Distribution: Eurasiatic, extending to central Sweden, eastwards to Japan and south to North Africa. In Britain, locally common to central Scotland; very local in Ireland.

Abundance: usually common; comes very free to light.

Flight: April to mid-May, earlier than the majorit of prominent species.

Life cycle: the caterpillar occurs in late May an June; it rests on the under-surface of oak leaves t day, and feeds at night. The pupa overwinters in cocoon in soil under oak.

Foodplant: oak.

General: the rather similar Marbled Brown (*Dr monia dodonaea* Schiff.) – a variable species i which the outer area of the forewings is ofte predominantly white – also occurs in Britain. I southern Europe there is a third species, *D. querr* Schiff., which resembles *D. ruficornis* but has whit hindwings.

Lobster Moth *Stauropus fagi* L.

Description: one of the larger prominents, with forewing length up to 3.2 cm in females. Males tend to be rather smaller and have strongly feathered antennae. Both sexes are usually greyish-brown, with a faint pattern of pale crosslines and dots; a melanotic (black) form has become common in some areas.
Habitat: predominantly beech woods, but also in rides, clearings and along margins of mixed deciduous woodland.
Distribution: throughout Europe eastwards to Japan. Locally common in the southern half of England and Wales, and in south-west Irela where a large, pale race occurs.
Abundance: locally common.
Flight: late April to mid-July; sometimes a seco generation in August.
Life cycle: the extraordinary caterpillar (illu trated) resembles an ant when young, with disproportionately long forelegs. It is found frc June to September. The winter is spent as a pupa a cocoon spun between dead leaves on the groun
Foodplant: usually beech, but also oak, birch, a hazel.

Puss Moth *Cerura vinula* L.

Des: forewing 2.9–3.5 cm, ♀ larger than ♂, with darker hindwings and simple antennae. **H:** woods, river valleys, waste ground, moors, etc., where willows, sallows or poplars grow. **Dis:** throughout Europe to the Arctic Circle; in Lapland, the blackish sub-species *phantoma* Dalman is found. Widespread in Britain to the Orkney Is. **A:** fairly common, but decreased in parts of Britain. **Fl:** late April to early July. **LC:** the caterpillars of the puss and kitten moths are similar to the one illustrated, and all make a hard cocoon of silk and wood-fragments on a tree trunk in which the winter is spent as a pupa.

Cerura erminea Esp.

Des: resembles the Puss Moth but is whiter, a the body is strongly marked with black. **H:** dan woods and wooded river valleys where popla grow. **Dis:** Europe, but absent from Britain. considerably rarer than Puss Moth, though local fairly common. **Fl:** mid-May to early July. **LC:** for the Puss Moth. **FP:** poplar and willow.

Sallow Kitten *Furcula furcula* Clerck

Des: forewing 1.4–1.7 cm. The three central European Kitten Moths resemble one another closely. The Sallow Kitten is the smallest, is less strongly contrasting black-and-white than the Alder Kitten (*F. bicuspis* Borkh.), and the central band of the forewing is less strongly edged with black than in the largest species, the Poplar Kitten (*F. bifida* Brahm). **H:** mixed woodlands, moors, river valleys. **Dis:** Europe to China; North America. Through mainland Britain and Ireland. **A:** moderately common; rare in northern Germany. **Fl:** single-brooded in Scotland and parts of northern Europe, double-brooded in England and Wales, where it flies in May and August. **LC:** as for the Puss Moth, but where double-brooded summer pupal period is short. **FP:** chiefly sallow and willow.

Poplar Kitten *Furcula bifida* Brahm

Des: forewing 1.8–2.0 cm. Black inner margin central band of forewings nearly straight, out margin strongly angled. **H:** damp woodland a river valleys. **Dis:** throughout Europe includir England and Wales. **A:** fairly common, thou apparently rarer nowadays in Britain. **Fl:** May July in Britain, sometimes double-brooded on t Continent. **LC:** similar to that of other Puss ar Kitten Moths. Sometimes remains in pupa for tv winters. **FP:** poplar, rarely willow.

Coxcomb Prominent
Ptilodon capucina L.

Des: forewing just under 2 cm. Forewings reddish brown with particularly large 'tooth' on inner margins. **H:** mixed woodland and wooded valleys, parks. **Dis:** Europe eastwards to Japan; widespread in mainland Britain and Ireland. **A:** fairly common. **Fl:** two generations, first late April to June, second July and August. **LC:** caterpillars occur in June and July, and again in the autumn; pupa overwinters. **FP:** oak, beech, birch, hazel, and other shrubs.

Maple Prominent
Ptilodontella cucullina Schiff.

Des: forewing just under 2 cm. Shows some resemblance to the Coxcomb Prominent, but forewings are variegated with white. As in other species, the 'tooth' lobes of the forewings are pressed together when the moth is at rest, producing a hump which breaks up the symmetrical outline and adds to the effectiveness of its camouflage. **H:** mixed deciduous woodlands with maple. **Dis:** local in central and eastern Europe; in Britain virtually confined to south-east England. **A:** an uncommon species. **Fl:** May and June in one generation. **LC:** caterpillar from June to August. **FP:** maple species, especially field maple.

Iron Prominent
Notodonta dromedarius L.

Des: similar size as previous species, but darker purplish-brown in colour and lacking rounded mark at wing-tip. **H:** mixed woodlands, parks, moorland, wooded valleys. **Dis:** central and northern Europe; throughout mainland Britain and Ireland. **A:** common in suitable localities. **Fl:** usually single-brooded in Britain, but double-brooded in parts of Continental Europe, flying in May and June, and again in August. **LC:** caterpillars in summer and autumn, in one or two generations. Pupa overwinters. **FP:** birch, less often alder or hazel.

Pale Prominent *Pterostoma palpina* L.

Des: forewing 1.9–2.5 cm. The irregularities of shape produced when the moth is at rest by the closely folded wings, large 'tooth' lobes and elongated palps produce a close resemblance to a chip of wood. **H:** mixed woodlands and wooded valleys. **Dis:** throughout Europe; widespread in Britain and Ireland, commoner in the south. **A:** common. **Fl:** two generations, first late April to June, second July and August. Comes freely to light. **LC:** caterpillars in June and July and again in the autumn. **FP:** willow and poplar species.

Pebble Prominent
Eligmodonta ziczac L.

Des: forewing length c. 2 cm. Strongly patterned, the rounded mark at the tip of each forewing giving an impression of a piece of dead stick when the moth is at rest. **H:** wooded valleys, carr, woodland clearings, parks. **Dis:** Europe, up to 2,500 m; in mountains; throughout Britain to the Orkney Islands, and Ireland. **A:** often common. **Fl:** two generations over much of Europe, but single-brooded in the north. **LC:** caterpillars in June and July, and the autumn; where single brooded, in late summer. Pupa hibernates. **FP:** willow, sallow, poplar.

Three-humped Prominent
Tritophia tritophus Schiff.

Des: distinctly larger and darker than the Pebble Prominent which it resembles in having a large rounded mark at the tip of each forewing. Forewing 2.2–2.8 cm. Hindwings white, whereas in the Pebble Prominent they are greyish-brown. **H:** wooded valleys, poplar plantations, parks. **Dis:** widespread in temperate Europe, but only a very scarce immigrant to Britain. **A:** locally fairly common. **Fl:** April to August, double-brooded in the south. **LC:** caterpillars in the summer in one or two generations. Pupa overwinters. **FP:** poplar and aspen.

...colate-tip *Clostera curtula* L.

Des: the chocolate-tips form a distinct group within the prominent family. Their forewings lack the projecting 'tooth' characteristics of other members of the family; the tip of each forewing has a more or less distinct dark-brown patch; and when at rest, the tip of the abdomen is curled upwards (see illustrations). **LH:** among poplars and aspens. **Dis:** Europe, including S. England and Scotland. **A:** caterpillars seen more often than moths. **Fl:** April to June, and July and August, in two generations. **FP:** poplar and aspen.

Small Chocolate-tip
Clostera pigra Hufn.

Des: the smallest chocolate-tip. Forewing c.2 cm. Forewings dark grey-brown with chocolate-coloured tip indistinct, and faint violet suffusion. **H:** damp woodland and moors, up to 2,500 m in mountains. **Dis:** Europe and Asia; scattered through Britain and Ireland. **Fl:** two generations in early and late summer. **LC:** caterpillars in summer and autumn, living between spun leaves, as do other members of the genus. **FP:** chiefly creeping willow.

Plumed Prominent
Ptilophora plumigera Esp.

Des: forewing c.1.8 cm. ♂ with strongly plumose antennae and broader wings than ♀. Colour variable from light brown to nearly black. **H:** dry mixed woodland with mature field maple. **Dis:** Europe; in Britain virtually confined to south-eastern England. **A:** very locally common. **Fl:** late October and November over a very short period, following the first frosts. ♂ flies soon after dusk, but ♀ not until late at night. **LC:** eggs overwinter and caterpillars feed up in May and June. **FP:** field maple, sometimes sycamore.

Scarce Chocolate-tip
Clostera anachoreta F.

Des: a little larger than *C. curtula*, darker-coloured and with the dark patch at the wing-tip extending across the pale outermost crossline, and a pair of black spots below the dark patch. **H:** mixed woodland and carr. **Dis:** more limited range in Europe than Chocolate-tip, but extends further east into Asia. In Britain, temporary colonies occasionally arise in the extreme south-east. **A:** uncommon. **Fl:** two generations, first May and June, second July and August. **LC:** caterpillars in June and August. **FP:** willow and poplar.

Clostera anastomosis L.

Des: slightly larger than other chocolate-tips, markings indistinct, colour variable. **H:** river valleys, parks. **Dis:** through Europe, but absent from Britain. **A:** local, but less often seen than the other species. **Fl:** two or three overlapping generations through the summer. **LC:** early summer larvae feed up quickly and produce summer generation of moths, but autumn larvae overwinter and complete growth in spring. **FP:** poplar and willow species.

The Dragon *Harpyia milhauseri* F.

Des: forewing 2.0–2.5 cm. Forewings grey marked with black, with trace of yellow-green gloss. Hindwings white with a blackish patch. **H:** mixed deciduous woodland, cork oak and ilex forest in south Europe. **Dis:** central and southern Europe, one record from southern England. **A:** once regarded as very rare, but comes frequently to light in many parts of Europe. **Fl:** May and June. **LC:** caterpillars feed up in late summer, and spins a hard cocoon of silk and wood fragments in crevices of bark, where it is incredibly difficult to detect unless already opened by birds. Usually at a height of 1–2 m from the ground. **FP:** oak, in south Europe chiefly on evergreen oak and cork oak; rarely birch and beech.

Prominents

Six-spot Burnet *Zygaena filipendulae* L.

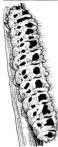

Description: burnets are an easily recognized group of day-flying moths with red and black wings and bodies, and buzzing flight. They afford another excellent example of aposematic (warning) colouration. When attacked, they often feign death and secrete a yellowish, pungent liquid from their intersegmental membranes. Their tissues also release cyanide when crushed. Predators quickly learn to associate the insects' bright colours with their high toxicity, and leave them alone. The moths themselves are immune to cyanide – their caterpillars often feed on cyanogenic plants, and the adults are unaffected by the poison in the collector's cyanide bottle.

Different species of burnet are often hard to identify because not only do certain species resemble one another closely but, being colonial and sedentary, different populations of the same species show small but constant differences from other races. Useful differentiating features are to be found in the number and position of the spots on the forewings, the width of the black border on the hindwing, and the structure of the antennae. The Six-Spot Burnet usually has six rather equal-sized spots on each forewing; the border of the hindwing is narrow. Rarely, the sixth spot is absent, sometimes two or more spots are confluent, and very rarely the red areas are replaced by orange or yellow.

Habitat: dry grassland, heaths and moors.

Distribution: Europe to 61°N and to 2,000 m altitude in the mountains.

Abundance: common through most of its range; the commonest and most widespread British burnet.

Flight: July and August.

Life cycle: caterpillar green, yellow and black, sparsely hairy. Feeds from August to June and may overwinter twice. The spindle-shaped, glossy cocoon is made high up on a grass stem.

Foodplants: species of birdsfoot trefoil.

Five-spot Burnet *Zygaena trifolii* Esp.

Description: slightly smaller than the preceding species; forewing with five spots, the third being smaller than the others. Two principal races occur: sub-species *palustrella* Verity occurs on chalk downs and the larger sub-species *decreta* Verity on boggy moorland. Both races are highly variable and show a strong tendency for the spots to become confluent.

Habitat: dry calcareous grassland and boggy moorland (see above).

Distribution: throughout central and western Europe. In Britain, both races have lost ground through habitat loss and are extinct in many places where they once thrived.

Cocoons – see illustration page 279

Abundance: strongly colonial and locally common.

Flight: June to August, sub-species *decreta* emerging later than sub-species *palustrella*.

Life cycle: caterpillars feed from late summer until May, and sometimes overwinter twice. The cocoons of sub-species *palustrella* are spun high on grass stems, those of sub-species *decreta* at ground level.

Foodplants: Sub-species *palustrella* – birdsfoot trefoil (*Lotus corniculatus*); sub-species *decreta* – marsh birdsfoot trefoil (*L. uliginosus*).

107

The Forester *Adscita statices* L.

Des: the metallic green foresters are related to burnets and even more difficult to differentiate – dissection is often necessary. **H:** *A. statices* in damp meadows, boggy moorland or dry grassland. **Dis:** throughout Europe to the Arctic Circle, including Britain and Ireland. **A:** locally common, though lost in many parts of Britain through habitat destruction. **Fl:** May to August. **LC:** young caterpillar mines leaves of sorrel, later feeding exposed. July to May; hibernates. **FP:** sorrel (*Rumex acetosa* and *R. acetosella*).

Narrow-bordered Five-spot Burnet *Zygaena lonicerae* Scheven.

Des: antennae longer and more pointed than thos of Five-spot Burnet, and wing markings much les variable. **H:** dry grassland, sunny hillsides, clear ings and waste ground – apparently more adaptabl to habitat alteration than other species. **Dis:** Europ except extreme south-west. Widespread in Englanc local in Ireland, and represented in Scotland by unique race on Skye. **Fl:** July and August. **LC** caterpillar hairier than others in the genus. Septem ber to June, sometimes overwintering twice Cocoon high on grass stem. **FP:** meadow vetch ling, red clover, and sometimes other plants of th pea family.

Zygaena transalpina Esp.

Des: another six-spotted burnet with bright scarlet-red spots and hindwings. Forewing about 1.7 cm. **H:** dry, warm, sunny hillsides with sparse vegetation, on limestone. **Dis:** isolated populations in the limestone Alps of central Europe, absent from Britain. **A:** locally common. **Fl:** June to August. **LC:** caterpillar from August to June, hibernates when small. **FP:** horseshoe vetch, crown vetch (*Coronilla*), birdsfoot trefoil. **G:** numerous local races have been given names.

Zygaena ephialtes L.

Des: forewing about 1.8 cm. A highly polymorphi species. One form resembles the Six-spot Burne but the red ring round the abdomen shows it to b *Z. ephialtes*. Another form has only the basal spot red, the others white; both five- and six-spotte forms occur. Some of the forms are widesprea others extremely local. **H:** dry, sunny limeston grassland. **Dis:** local in central Europe. Absen from Britain. **A:** local, rather uncommon. **Fl:** Jul and August. **LC:** caterpillar from September to July hibernating. **FP:** crown vetch (*Coronilla varia*).

Scotch Burnet *Zygaena exulans* Hochenw.

Des: forewing 1.3–1.5 cm. Thinly scaled, blackish with rather fuzzy pattern of five red spots and blackish-suffused red hindwings. **H:** high mountains. **Dis:** between 1,800 and 3,000 m in Alps and Pyrenees, and on one mountain in Scotland; extending to Lapland and Mongolia. **A:** locally common. **Fl:** July and August. **LC:** caterpillars usually hibernate twice or more. Cocoon delicate, ovoid, spun at ground level among roots of heather and crowberry. **FP:** in Scotland, chiefly crowberry.

Zygaena fausta L.

Des: forewing 1.2 cm. One of the smaller burne species. Scarlet spots, outlined in yellow, coalesc on a black ground colour. Hindwings, collar, an broad band on abdomen scarlet. **H:** warm lime stone hills with sparse vegetation. **Dis:** south western Europe, very local in Germany, and absen from the north. Unknown in Britain. **A:** locall common in south-west Europe. **Fl:** late May t August, depending on locality. **LC:** caterpillar fron late summer to May or June, hibernating. Pupa i an oval, white cocoon. **FP:** species of crown vetcl (*Coronilla*).

♀

Death's Head Hawkmoth *Acherontia atropos* L.

Description: with a forewing of about 6 cm and a body weight of around 7 g, the Death's Head Hawkmoth is one of Europe's largest and heaviest moths. The marbled blue-black and evidently procryptic forewings contrast strongly with the yellow, dark-banded abdomen and hindwings. It has been suggested that sudden exposure of these structures may constitute a second line of defence if the primary camouflage is penetrated by an attacker.

This moth has the curious habit of regularly raiding beehives, and the unusually short, stumpy proboscis appears to be specially adapted for taking honey. The well-known squeak the insect emits when disturbed is said to have a quietening effect on the occupants of the hive, but the role of the skull-mark on the thorax remains unknown. The flight of the Death's Head is comparatively slow and laborious compared to other hawkmoths, many of which are extremely agile.

Habitat: strongly migratory species that moves north from Africa in varying numbers every year, occasionally reaching Ireland. Migrants can appear anywhere, but the eggs are laid in fields of potatoes and on solanaceous (nightshade family) plants growing in hedgerows.

Distribution: native of Africa and the warmer parts of southern Europe, but recorded every year in varying numbers north of the Alps, and reaching Britain most years.

Abundance: numbers in Europe vary greatly from year to year. Caterpillars and pupae, once found commonly during the potato harvest, are nowadays much less often seen because crops are regularly sprayed.

Flight: the first migrants appear in May and June. They may produce locally bred offspring in August and September, which are reinforced by other waves of migrants from the south. Sometimes a third generation appears in October and November.

Life cycle: immigrant female Death's Heads lay their eggs on potato, sometimes on species of nightshade or other *Solanaceae* such as Duke of Argyll's tea plant. Caterpillars, which occur in two colour forms, green and brown, feed only at night, resting on the potato haulms during the day. Pupation occurs in a brittle earthen cocoon up to 20 cm deep in the soil. The pupae are unable to survive the European winter, and the best way to rear them is to 'force' them by keeping them in an incubator and spraying regularly with tepid water, the moths will emerge before Christmas. Recently it has been shown that bred moths can be persuaded to pair and lay eggs if they are force-fed by gently unrolling the proboscis into a solution of honey. They will drink up to 1 cm³ at a time, after which pairing and oviposition will occur if the moths are given plenty of space. Caterpillars can be fed on privet during the winter.

Foodplants: potato, woody and deadly nightshades, Duke of Argyll's tea plant, also ash and (in captivity) privet.

Hawkmoths

brown caterpillar

yellow caterpillar

111

Eyed Hawkmoth *Smerinthus ocellata* L.

Description: forewing 3.5–4.0 cm. When at rest, the forewings which in shape and colour resemble a cluster of withered leaves, completely conceal the hindwings with their enormous blue and black eye spots. If disturbed, the wings are curved downwards and the eye markings are suddenly revealed. Such behaviour has been shown experimentally to have a strong deterrent effect on the attentions of marauding predators. After the display, the moth resumes its normal resting position. This defence reaction can be provoked repeatedly by gently prodding the insect's thorax with a pencil.

Habitat: river valleys, parks, orchards and deciduous woodland.

Distribution: throughout central and northern Europe. Widespread in England and Wales, local in Ireland, but absent from Scotland.

Abundance: rarely seen by day, but often common at night; sometimes the caterpillars can be found in quantity.

Flight: May to July, sometimes a second generation in the autumn.

Life cycle: the caterpillars rest by day on the undersides of foodplant stems. They are an excellent example of countershading, in which the upper surface of the body is darker than the lower surface thus when resting upside down they are rendered invisible as a result of the play of light from above; when turned, so that their backs are facing upwards, they are highly conspicuous. Camouflage is enhanced by the presence of pale oblique stripes along the body which mimic the veins of leaves.

Pupation occurs in a weak earth cocoon in the soil. The pupa overwinters.

Foodplants: many species of sallow and willow, preferring small bushes; also apple, and sometimes plum and poplar.

General: the hawkmoths are most abundant in the tropics. There are some 850 species known worldwide, of which 23 occur in central Europe and 18 have been reliably recorded in Britain. Of these only nine are native breeding species. Many are large, some highly colourful, and the majority are fast and agile fliers which can hover motionless while feeding from flowers. They often have robust cigar-shaped bodies and long, narrow wings, the hindwings being considerably smaller than the forewings. Many rest with wings held flat and swept back, like small aircraft (see page 121). The great majority of hawkmoth caterpillars have a characteristic horn-like projection near the tip of the abdomen, and several of the most familiar ones rest with the front part of the body held up in a sphinx-like attitude (see opposite) – hence the scientific name of the family *Sphingidae*.

Many hawkmoths, and some other species of moth, are migratory, but it appears that the movements of the majority of insects, unlike those of birds, are one-way journeys. There is however some evidence of emigration southwards of the progeny of a few European butterflies, for example the Red Admiral. It is hard to obtain data for nocturnal moths, but it is generally supposed that the offspring of migrant moths perish and do not move south. The mass movements of individual Monarch butterflies in America between breeding grounds and winter quarters, followed by a return, is an example that can be compared to the migrations of many vertebrates.

mating

Poplar Hawkmoth *Laothoe populi* L.

Description: forewing length up to 4 cm. Similar in shape and behaviour to the Eyed Hawkmoth, but wing margins are more crenulated, and there are red patches at the base of the hindwings instead of eyespots. At rest, the Poplar Hawkmoth resembles a bunch of dead leaves. When disturbed, it arches its wings in the same way as the Eyed Hawkmoth, displaying the red patches. However, these seem to be less effective as a deterrent to insectivorous birds, and in years when the moths are common, many are apparently eaten.

Habitat: wooded valleys, stream and river banks, gardens, parks, and even city centres.

Distribution: throughout Europe, extending to the Arctic Circle. Throughout Britain and Ireland with the exception of the outer isles.

Abundance: one of the commonest hawkmoths in Britain as well as mainland Europe.

Flight: May to August in an extended brood, sometimes there is a partial second generation.

Life cycle: caterpillars occur from June to October, the later ones being progeny of the second generation of moths. Pupation occurs in soil around the roots of poplar trees. Sometimes one finds that moles have systematically tunnelled around the bases of these trees and nearly every pupa has gone.

Foodplants: poplars and aspen, less often willow and sallow.

Lime Hawkmoth *Mimas tiliae* L.

Description: forewing 3.0–3.5 cm. Rather smaller and narrower-winged than the two preceding species, but clearly one of the same group of hawkmoths, with strongly crenulated wing-margins. Though highly variable, especially in the development of the dark band across the forewing, its contrasting pattern of green and brown makes it easy to recognize.

Habitat: mixed deciduous woodland, but also commonly associated with avenues of lime trees in towns, parks, and old gardens.

Distribution: Europe and Asia. In Britain, chiefly in the southern half of England, and absent from Scotland and Ireland.

Abundance: moderately common, especially in urban areas. Freshly emerged moths may sometimes be found commonly in the early morning on the lower parts of lime trunks; pupae are also common in places, under limes.

Flight: May to early July in one generation.

Life cycle: eggs are laid singly or in pairs on the underside of lime leaves, or on elm or birch. Caterpillars are green with pale oblique stripes along the body, red spiracles and blue horn; just before pupation they become dark purple-brown all over. June to August. Pupation in soil at the foot of lime, elm or birch trees.

Foodplants: lime, elm and alder, sometimes birch; oak and plum have also been reported as foodplants.

General: Eyed, Poplar and Lime Hawkmoths are easy to breed in captivity and hybrids between the species have been obtained occasionally. The trick is to place a male and female of different species together in a roomy, net-lined cage on each side of which are other cages which contain females of the same species as the experimental male. The male, excited by the scent (pheromone) wafted in from these females, will sometimes pair with the female of the other species. The hybrid caterpillars which result usually grow perfectly satisfactorily; the resulting moths are intermediate in appearance between the parents but are infertile.

Privet Hawkmoth *Sphinx ligustri* L.

Description: forewing 4.5–5.2 cm; female usually larger than male. Privet, Convolvulus, and Pine Hawkmoths hold their long forewings obliquely against the sides of the body when at rest, completely concealing the body and hindwings. The Privet Hawkmoth is browner than the Convolvulus Hawk, the thorax is very dark brown, and the body and hindwings show a stronger contrast between the bands of black and pink. It rests on fence posts and tree trunks by day, but is more often seen at light sources at night.

Habitat: deciduous woodland, downland, hedgerows, and gardens.

Distribution: occurs throughout the Palaearctic Region, but in Britain is only found in England and Wales.

Abundance: in Britain common only locally, in southern and eastern England; in mainland Europe widespread but not common.

Flight: late May to July. Flowers such as honeysuckle are adapted for pollination by long-tongued nocturnal insects, e.g. the Privet Hawkmoth. The flowers start to emit their scent at dusk, and shortly afterwards the moths may be seen hovering in front of the flowers. The long proboscis is coiled like a watch-spring when not in use; when it is extended to reach the nectar at the base of the flower-tube pollen also adheres to it, and is transferred to the next flower visited.

Life cycle: the eggs are laid on the underside of a leaf, near the midrib, singly or in pairs. Caterpillars from July to September, feeding chiefly at night and resting on the underside of a stem by day. Like the other species with similar habit, they are strongly countershaded and, though large, are surprisingly difficult to detect. Pupa in a brittle cocoon in the soil.

Convolvulus Hawkmoth *Agrius convolvuli* L.

Description: forewing 4.5–5 cm. Size and build similar to Privet Hawkmoth but thorax and forewings grey, hindwing pattern less contrasting, and abdominal bands pale pink edged with white, alternating with black. The unrolled proboscis is about the same length as the body, and can reach nectar in the most long-tubed flowers such as *Nicotiana*. Beds of these flowers are a feature of many English seaside resorts; in migration years numbers of these magnificent insects may be seen hovering among them shortly after dark.

Habitat: the true home of this moth is the tropics, but migrants appear in Europe every year and may travel a long way north, even reaching Iceland.

Abundance: apart from the diurnal Humming-Bird Hawkmoth, the Convolvulus Hawk is by far the commonest migrant hawkmoth to reach Britain. It is reported every year, though numbers fluctuate enormously. Early migrants may give rise to a generation of home-bred moths in the autumn, which are often reinforced by another wave of immigrants.

Flight: early arrivals in May; the influx continues through the summer, but in Britain peak numbers are to be expected in September and October.

Life cycle: early immigrants lay their eggs on corn bindweed, and caterpillars are then found in late summer. The unmistakable pupa, which is very large, has the proboscis case free from the main body of the pupa, curled round like a jug-handle at the front end. If found, pupae can be reared by forcing (see Death's Head), but are unlikely to survive the north European winter in the wild.

Foodplants: bindweeds and *Ipomoea*, especially corn bindweed.

Hawkmoths

♀

117

Pine Hawkmoth *Hyloicus pinastri* L.

Description: forewings 3.5–4 cm, grey-brown with three conspicuous black dashes near the middle. The moth rests on pine trunks during the day and, despite its considerable size, is well camouflaged. The hindwings and abdomen are patterned as in the Privet and Convolvulus Hawks, but the colours are much less contrasting.

Habitat: woods and heathland with stands of pine.

Distribution: throughout the pine forests of Europe and north Asia; in Britain only in south eastern England, where it extended its range in the 1940s from strongholds in Dorset and Suffolk.

Abundance: generally common; became particu larly common in south-east England in the lat 1940s, but is now much less so.

Flight: May to July, April in south Europe. Fl from dusk onwards into the night and visit flower such as soapwort and honeysuckle.

Life cycle: the caterpillar, which seems highl colourful when examined in the hand, is neverthe less well-camouflaged amongst pine foliage. Feed in August and September on pine, occasionall spruce.

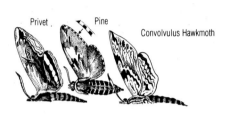

Privet   Pine   Convolvulus Hawkmoth

Spurge Hawkmoth *Hyles euphorbiae* L.

Description: forewing 2.8–3.2 cm. Hawkmoths of this genus are similar-looking, medium-sized species with olive, buff and grey forewings and hindwings patterned in red, black and white. They rest on low vegetation with wings held flat and swept back, like high-perform-ance aircraft. The Spurge Hawk illustrated is in a very unusual posture.

Habitat: dry hillsides, dunes, wood margins.

Distribution: probably the commonest hawkmoth in the Mediterranean region, whence it migrates north every year, very rarely reaching Britain. Well-established colonies also exist in central Europe.

Abundance: extremely common in south Europe but less often seen in more northerly latitudes tha formerly.

Flight: May to July; double-brooded in sout Europe.

Life cycle: caterpillars occur through the summe and autumn according to latitude. They are extremely gaudy and aposematic. Toxins calle diterpenes are obtained in the food (species o spurge) and retained in the insect's body – a strategy found in a number of other moths an butterflies. Pupa in a cocoon of silk and plan debris on the ground.

Foodplants: species of spurge, especially cypres spurge.

118

Bedstraw Hawkmoth *Hyles gallii* Rott.

Description: forewing 2.5–3.5 cm. Similar to the preceding species, but the whole of the leading edge of the forewing is olive-coloured, the broad stripe which extends across the wing from near the base to tip is pale cream-coloured, and there is less red on the hindwing.

Habitat: sunny heaths, dunes, clearings, wood margins. Caterpillars sometimes found on waste ground in cities.

Distribution: a more eastern species than the Spurge Hawk, extending to the Arctic Circle and across Asia and North America. An uncommon migrant to Britain which may establish small colonies for a number of years.

Abundance: no more than moderately common in Europe.

Flight: mid-May to September, often in two generations.

Life cycle: caterpillars are found in late summer and autumn. They are more sombre in colour than those of the Spurge Hawk, but each segment is marked by a pair of large, yellow, black-ringed spots; legs and horn red.

Foodplants: bedstraw, especially ladies' bedstraw growing on dunes, and rosebay willow-herb growing on waste ground and along wood margins.

Striped Hawkmoth *Hyles lineata* F.

Description: forewing 3–4 cm. Individuals vary considerably in size but not in colour or pattern; the female is usually larger, and has finer antennae, this being a reliable feature for distinguishing the sexes of all hawkmoths. Easily identified by the streaks of pale-coloured scales overlying the veins on the forewing.

Habitat: strongly migratory and can occur virtually anywhere, usually in reasonably open country.

Distribution: almost world-wide. The race which migrates to Europe from Africa and southern Europe is sub-species *livornica* Esp. It is the commonest *Hyles* species to reach Britain, the majority occurring in the southern counties of England, and southern Ireland.

Abundance: numbers fluctuate greatly. Usually common in south Europe and rare north of the Alps.

Spurge   Bedstraw   Striped Hawkmoth

Flight: at least two broods: moths can occur in north Europe, including Britain from March to October, peaking in August and September. Sometimes fly by day, but chiefly at night, when they visit tubular flowers such as *Nicotiana*.

Life cycle: caterpillars occur during summer and autumn; polymorphic, varying from bright green to nearly black, variously marked and patterned.

Foodplants: bedstraw, willowherb, fuchsia, dock and other herbaceous plants.

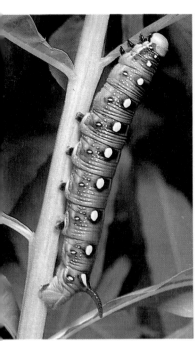

Elephant Hawkmoth *Deilephila elpenor* L.

Caterpillar – see page 276

Description: forewing 2.7–3.0 cm. Larger than the similar Small Elephant Hawkmoth, with more contrasting pattern which includes a pinkish stripe which extends to the tip of the forewing from about halfway along the trailing edge of the wing. Hindwings red with black base. Another high-performance moth which visits flowers at dusk, moving from one to another with great speed and agility. It is particularly fond of rhododendron and honeysuckle.

Habitat: woodland glades, river valleys, heathland, parks and gardens.

Distribution: throughout central Europe, including mainland Britain and Ireland.

Abundance: one of the commonest hawkmoths in England and Wales, increasing its range in Scotland.

Flight: May to July in one generation.

Life cycle: caterpillars from late June to early September; green when young, but usually dark brown or blackish in the later instars, a green form being rather rare. The second and third abdominal segments have lilac-coloured eyespots; when alarmed the caterpillar rears up and withdraws the small head and thoracic segments into the front of the abdomen which becomes swollen, producing a 'horror mask' threat display. Caterpillars rest low down on the foodplant or on the ground during the day, ascending at dusk to feed. Pupa in a cocoon of woven plant debris on the ground.

Foodplants: species of willowherb, bedstraw, sometimes balsam or grape vine.

Small Elephant Hawkmoth *Deilephila porcellus* L.

Caterpillar – see page 276

Description: forewing 1.8–2.0 cm. Smaller and with less clear-cut pattern than its congener. A broad band of red, with a jagged inner margin, extends along the outer edge of the forewing in this species, and the conspicuous oblique stripe across the wing of the Elephant Hawk is absent. The trailing edge of the Elephant Hawk's forewing is white, whereas in the Small Elephant it is the same colour as the rest of the wing.

Habitat: chiefly on dry limestone downland, and dunes.

Distribution: all over Europe; in the Alps to at least 1,800 m. Widespread in England and Wales, chiefly on the east side of Scotland, and local in Ireland.

Abundance: in parts of south Europe, much commoner than the Elephant Hawkmoth; in Britain the two species tend to occupy different biotopes, and the Small Elephant is common where it occurs.

Flight: May to July in one generation.

Life cycle: caterpillars resemble those of the Elephant Hawk, but are smaller and stumpier and with less strongly retractile head, and are usually paler in colour.

Foodplants: in Britain, chiefly ladies' bedstraw; also occasionally willowherb species, purple loosestrife and balsam.

Small
Elephant

Elephant Hawkmoth

Willowherb Hawkmoth *Proserpinus proserpina* Pall. Caterpillar – see page 27see page 27

Description: forewing 1.8–2.1 cm. Outer margins of both fore- and hindwings jagged; forewings strongly patterned in shades of dark and light green; hindwings orange with a dark border. An extremely fast and agile flier.

Habitat: sunny slopes, clearings and rides in deciduous woodland.

Distribution: southern Europe to central Germany; one record of a migrant in Sussex, England. To 1,500 m in the Alps.

Abundance: has decreased considerably in the western part of its range, but still locally not uncommon.

Flight: May and June in a single generation. Flies at early dusk and at dawn.

Life cycle: caterpillars in July and August. They hide by day and feed at night; they are olive-green with whitish sides, across which run a series of dark oblique stripes. These slope in the opposite direction to those on most hawkmoth caterpillars, with the upper end towards the front of the body. The anal horn is reduced to a small hump. The pupa overwinters and is formed in a cocoon on the ground.

Foodplants: willowherb, evening primrose.

Hummingbird Hawkmoth

Willowherb Hawkmoth

Hummingbird Hawkmoth *Macroglossum stellatarum* L.

Description: forewing 1.6–2.0 cm. A striking feature of this moth is the broad, flattened hind part of the abdomen, edged with elongated black and white scales. The forewings are light brown with narrow dark cross-lines, and the hindwings are orange-yellow.

Habitat: sunny clear-felled areas, south facing grassy slopes, heathland and wood margins.

Distribution: a native of southern Europe which migrates northwards in varying numbers every year. Sometimes common in Britain, and there is evidence that it can overwinter occasionally in south-west England.

Abundance: common in south Europe.

Flight: has been recorded in every month of the year, even in Britain. At least two generations in southern Europe. Peak numbers occur in late summer. The moth is diurnal, but occasionally occurs at light sources. These are presumably migrants. During the day the moth visits flowers such as phlox, petunia and buddleia, sometimes even in the rain. In very hot weather it tends to rest on walls and banks during the middle part of the day. Females are often observed flying along walls and banks, ovipositing on patches of bedstraw.

Life cycle: Eggs are laid singly or in pairs on bedstraw, especially ladies' bedstraw. Caterpillars are most frequent from June to August, and in the autumn. Pupa in a loose cocoon on the ground.

Foodplants: bedstraw species.

Broad-bordered Bee Hawkmoth *Hemaris fuciformis* L.

Description: forewing 1.7–2.0 cm. When freshly emerged, the wings are thinly powdered with greenish scales. These are quickly lost and the insect is clear-winged with chocolate-coloured borders which are somewhat wider than in the similar Narrow-bordered Bee Hawk. The hindwings of both species are much smaller than the forewings.

Habitat: woodland rides, including the more open parts of pine woods, and clearings. The diurnal moths congregate where there is a suitable nectar source, such as avenues of rhododendrons and woodland edges with an abundance of bugle.

Distribution: throughout Europe to 2,000 m in the Alps. In Britain, confined to England and Wales.

Abundance: sometimes common in suitable habitat. In England, the population was severely reduced about 25 years ago, evidently by heavy parasitization, but has recovered recently in parts of the south.

Flight: May and June, double-brooded in the south of its range but only exceptionally so England.

Life cycle: eggs are laid, often in pairs, on honeysuckle in open parts of woods or amongst scrub land on damp heaths. The presence of caterpillar is betrayed by pairs of round holes gnawed on either side of the midrib of honeysuckle leaves Caterpillars in July and August.

Foodplants: honeysuckle species, sometime snowberry (*Symphoricarpus racemosus*).

General: insects which wear a red-and-black yellow-and-black 'uniform' and are poisonous distasteful are recognized by predators and avoided. They are known as Müllerian mimics. The harmless, edible beehawks which mimic bees appearance and behaviour are known as Batesia mimics. This alternative survival strategy on works if the mimic is greatly outnumbered by the genuinely distasteful or dangerous species.

Oleander

Broad-bordered Bee
Hawkmoth
(not to scale)

Oleander Hawkmoth *Daphnis nerii* L.

Caterpillar – see page 27

Description: forewings are narrow with strongly curved inner margin and reach a length of 4.5–6.0 cm. Hindwings are much smaller, bluntly pointed at the hind angle. Wing colour a rich moss-green with paler pink and cream pattern. The powerful, streamlined body is similarly coloured.

Habitat: highly migratory. The natural habitat is river valleys and dried-up stream beds with oleander bushes.

Distribution: occurs througout the Palaearctic, Ethiopian and Oriental Regions, but only as an immigrant in the more northerly parts of its range.

Abundance: not uncommon in the Mediterranea region, but a very rare migrant north of the Alp and to Britain.

Flight: chiefly in May and June, and August and September in Europe.

Life cycle: the very large caterpillar is green with a white stripe along its sides and a conspicuous blue, black-ringed eye mark on each side of the second thoracic segment. Horn pale, rough and drooping. Spiracles conspicuous, black, and there are scattered whitish, dark ringed raised dots on the body above and below the lateral stripe. July September in Europe.

Foodplants: Oleander (*Nerium oleander*), sometimes lesser periwinkle.

Peach Blossom *Thyatira batis* L.

Description: forewing 1.6–1.9 cm. The lutestring moths are very similar to the noctuids in general appearance, but differences in wing venation and other features show they are unrelated. The Peach Blossom and Buff Arches are by far the most colourful of an otherwise rather drab group. The blackish-brown forewings of the Peach Blossom are weakly patterned with darker crosslines, but are also most beautifully marked with several round, pinkish-white, darker centred blotches. The hindwings, concealed when the insect is at rest, are light greyish-brown with a faint line across them.

Habitat: deciduous woodland with ground flora of bramble or raspberry, overgrown hedgerows, parks and gardens.

Distribution: throughout Europe to 64°N, and to 1,500 m in the mountains. Throughout Britain and Ireland with the exception of the outer isles.

Abundance: found in many localities, but seldom in large numbers.

Flight: late May to July. The moths come to light and are also strongly attracted to sugar bait. 'Sugaring' is a traditional method used by lepidopterists for attracting nocturnal moths. Black treacle laced with additives such as stale beer and a drop of amyl acetate, is painted in vertical strips on tree trunks or fence posts, and recently lengths of clothes line steeped in a wine and sugar concentrate and slung between bushes have been found to be efficacious.

Life cycle: eggs are laid in small clusters on bramble and raspberry leaves. The dark purplish brown caterpillars have conspicuous double-pointed humps along the back and on the hindquarters. They feed at night in August and September.

Foodplants: bramble and raspberry.

Buff Arches *Habrosyne pyritoides* Hufn.

Description: forewing 1.9–2.2 cm. The pale olive-coloured basal area of the forewings is separated from the predominantly golden-brown outer area by an oblique white crossline, and the outer area is intricately patterned with white and an elaborately meandering darker crossline. Despite the complexity of their wing patterns, both the Peach Blossom and and Buff Arches are highly invariable.

Habitat: similar to that of the Peach Blossom.

Distribution: throughout Europe to southern Scandinavia and southern Finland. Through England, Wales and Ireland.

Abundance: generally common.

Flight: late May to August in one generation.

Life cycle: similar to that of the Peach Blossom. Caterpillar is rusty or dark brown, with a black edged yellowish spot on the first abdominal segment and a smaller one on the next; double-pointed humps along the body. August and September. Pupa subterranean, in an earth cocoon.

Foodplants: bramble and raspberry.

Lutestrings

Poplar Lutestring *Tethea or* Schiff.

Description: forewing 1.8–2.0 cm. The typical lutestrings have two groups of narrow, closely set and weakly zigzag lines across the forewing, giving rise to the popular name of the family. In dark forms of the Poplar Lutestring (illustrated), the crosslines are indistinct, but the pale stigmata, depicting the figure 80, show more clearly than in the pale form. The very similar Figure of Eighty (*T. ocularis* L.) takes its name from this feature; it has fewer crosslines in the basal area of the forewing than the Poplar Lutestring.

Habitat: aspen woods, poplar plantations, river valleys, parks and gardens.

Distribution: northern and central Europe. Widespread in Britain. The Scottish and Irish races have been described as separate sub-species.

Abundance: occurs in many localities where poplar and aspens grow, even in the ravines of the Scottish Highlands and Islands; often common.

Flight: single-brooded in Britain, flying in May and June; in mainland Europe, two generations, early and late summer. The moths come to light and very freely to sugar.

Life cycle: caterpillars yellowish green with a dark dorsal line and two black spots on the front edge of the first thoracic segment. They live between spun together leaves of poplar and aspen, and pupate spun up among leaves.

Foodplants: chiefly aspen, sometimes other poplar species.

Oak Lutestring *Cymatophorima diluta* F.

Description: forewing 1.5–1.7 cm. The two fascia of closely set lines across the forewings are characteristic of the family, and show particularly clearly on the north European race, sub-species *hartwiegi* Reiss. In the typical race, which occurs southwards from southern Germany, the forewings are browner and the pattern more blurred. The Oak Lutestring differs from the Poplar Lutestring in having hairy eyes and rusty yellow antennae.

Habitat: favours warm oakwoods on light soils, but also in mixed deciduous woodland.

Distribution: south and central Europe to Asia Minor. In England, Wales and southern Scotland.

Abundance: fairly common to common in oak woodland, but rare or absent in parts of north-east Europe where the woods are predominantly pine and spruce.

Flight: early August to October. In Britain, not before the end of August.

Life cycle: eggs are deposited singly on twigs of oak, below a bud, and overwinter. The caterpillars are yellowish above and grey beneath, with a pale line along the back and yellow lateral lines. They feed in May and June, and spend the day among tightly spun oak leaves. Pupa through the summer in a cocoon spun amongst the leaves.

Foodplants: exclusively oak.

Lutestring

Pebble Hook-tip *Drepana falcataria* L.

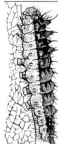

Description: forewing 1.4–2.0 cm. Most members of the hook-tip family (*Drepanidae*) have forewings characteristically hooked at the apex. This species is pale golden-brown. A black line on each forewing extends into the wing tips. One of the dots in the centre of each wing is much larger than the other, a feature which distinguishes this species from the Dusky Hook-tip (*Drepana curvatula* Borkh.). A number of wavy lines run through both fore- and hindwings, and there are two very small dots near the centre of each hindwing. The summer brood specimens are smaller than those of the first brood, and single-brooded Scottish specimens have whitish ground colour (sub-species *scotica* Byt-Salz).

Habitat: mixed woodlands, birch heath, and woodland.

Distribution: Europe to central Sweden and Finland, and southwards to mountains of Italy. Britain and Ireland.

Abundance: fairly common in suitable habitat.

Flight: up to three generations; two in south Britain, only one in Scotland. Between May and September. Moth rests on foliage by day, resembling a dead leaf, flies from dusk onwards.

Life cycle: like other members of the hook-tip family, caterpillars lack anal claspers, and hind end is held in the air. Body green, with reddish-brown back and pairs of raised warts on second to fifth body segments. Pupa overwinters.

Foodplants: chiefly birch, sometimes alder.

Chinese Character *Cilix glaucata* Scop.

Description: forewing 1.0–1.2 cm. The tips of the forewings are rounded, not hooked as in other members of the family. Wings white; the forewings marked by a dark patch on the trailing edge and a large olive-coloured oval in the middle of the wing, from which the moth's alternative English name, the Goose Egg, is derived. These patches are occasionally tinted with red.

Habitat: warm woodlands, heaths, hedgerows, and thickets.

Distribution: through Europe to southern Sweden. In Britain, extending to southern Scotland, and in Ireland.

Abundance: widespread and sometimes very common.

Flight: regularly triple-brooded in mainland Europe, and double-brooded in Britain and Ireland, between April and September.

Life cycle: the structure of the caterpillars shows the Chinese Character's affinity with the hook-tips. They are reddish brown with pairs of raised warts on the second and third thoracic segments, and a long, pointed tip to the abdomen.

Foodplants: blackthorn, plum and hawthorn, occasionally mountain ash, apple and pear.

When at rest this moth bears a remarkable resemblance to a 'pellet' type bird dropping and has been shown to be overlooked or avoided by insectivorous birds.

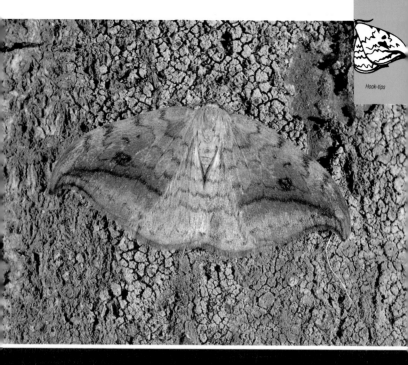

Scalloped Hook-tip *Falcaria lacertinaria* L.

Description: forewing 1.5–1.9 cm. Differs from other hook-tips in having forewings with serrated margins. The forewings are traversed by two narrow lines, nearly straight and parallel. Hindwings paler, with a small discal dot. Second brood examples are less richly marked than those of the first brood.

Habitat: birch woods and thickets. Prefers colonies of young trees.

Distribution: through much of Europe, extending to the tree limit in the north and confined to mountains in the south. Throughout Britain and Ireland, with the exception of the outer isles.

Abundance: locally common.

Flight: two generations, flying in late April to early June, and July and August. Single-brooded in Scotland. There is often a pre-dusk flight. Later, comes to light.

Life cycle: the dark brown, rugose caterpillars rest by day on the upper surfaces of leaves of the foodplants, with head and tail held high, gripping solely by means of the abdominal claspers. In this posture they appear to resemble a fragment of curled, dead birch leaf or the remains of a catkin. First brood of caterpillars in July, second in September. They pupate between spun leaves.

Foodplant: birch.

Oak Hook-tip *Drepana binaria* Hufn.

Description: forewing 1.6–2.0 cm. The dark ochre-coloured forewings are traversed by two narrow, sinuous pale lines and there are two blackish dots near the middle of the wing. Males are smaller and darker than the females, and have strongly feathered antennae. In north and central Europe can only be confused with the Barred Hook-tip (*D. cultraria* F), in which the area between the two crosslines is darkened and there is only one spot in the centre of the wing.

Habitat: oak woodland and scrub, and mixed woodland containing oak.

Distribution: central and southern Europe to southern Scandinavia. England and Wales.

Abundance: locally common.

Flight: two generations, in May and June, and July and August. Sometimes there is an afternoon flight in hot weather, around the tops of oaks.

Life cycle: caterpillars rest on upper side of oak leaves with raised fore- and hind parts. They occur in June and July, the second generation in September. Pupae from the second generation overwinter.

Foodplants: oak. Stated also to occur occasionally on beech, alder, lime, and birch.

♂

The Nail-mark *Aglia tau* L.

Description: forewing 3.0–4.2 cm. Fore- and hindwings are bright orange-brown, each with a large blue, broadly black-rimmed eye-spot with a white, nail-shaped centre. The wing margins have a darkish border. There is a marked difference between the sexes: the females are always larger and paler, and the darker wing-border is replaced by a narrow line running parallel to the margin. The eyespot is not as intensely coloured as on the male. The antennae of the male are strongly feathered; those of the female are thread-like. The body of the female is considerably more robust than that of the male, because of her need to produce eggs. The male spends most of its time and energy attracting the female.

Habitat: occurs in open light beechwoods or mixed woodland providing it contains mature beech trees.

Distribution: found in most parts of Europe as far north as 62°N. Since they occur anywhere there are beech trees their range extends well into Asia and even as far as Japan. However, this attractive moth is not found in the British Isles.

Abundance: common in beechwoods. In some years large populations may occur.

Flight: one generation in April and May, coinciding with the opening of beech buds and apple blossom. The males fly rapidly and erratically through the woods during the late morning in search of the females, which rest on stems and trunks close to the ground and emit their sexually attractive pheromone scent. The males always keep a distance from one another and a male will chase off a rival who comes too close. The females do not fly until after dark, and are then attracted to light.

Life cycle: the young caterpillars are adorned with long, branched spines which are lost after the third moult. The full-grown caterpillar is green with pale yellow stripe along each side and a yellow ring behind the head; spiracles outlined with red. Caterpillars are gregarious at first, later becoming solitary. They pupate in a flimsy cocoon amongst dead beech leaves on the ground. Caterpillars occur from May to August, and the pupa over-winters.

Foodplants: beech leaves, particularly younger tree-top foliage; occasionally oak, birch, hawthorn or apple.

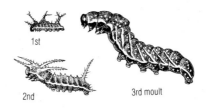

1st

2nd

3rd moult

♂

Great Peacock *Saturnia pyri* Schiff.

Great Peacock (size comparison) Emperor Moth

Description: forewing 5–7 cm. Largest European moth with regard to sheer wingspan, though the bodies of some other species are considerably heavier. Sexes alike, though the male has feathery antennae and the female's body is more robust. Grey wings have broad, whitish borders and pinkish, black-edged crosslines, but the most conspicuous feature is a large black-centred eye mark in the middle of each wing. If the illustration opposite is turned upside down, the eye markings of the hindwing appear to be set in the face of a menacing small mammal, the dark thorax forming its snout. A similar effect is produced by the 'eyes' on the forewings when the wings are fully closed. The deterrent effect is here produced by the permanent display of a 'horror mask' – a different technique from the sudden exposure of 'eyes' by an alarmed Eyed Hawkmoth.

Habitat: shrubby hillsides, woodland, orchards, parks, and large gardens.

Distribution: south European, extending northwards to southern Germany and Paris.

Abundance: sometimes sufficiently common to be a pest of orchards, but usually rather uncommon and populations appear to have declined in recent decades.

Flight: May and June. Both sexes are nocturnal, and come to light.

Life cycle: caterpillars when young are black with yellow warts, becoming grossly fleshy, greenish-yellow with bright-blue warts. Pupa in a large, bag-shaped silken cocoon amongst the branches of trees.

Foodplants: fruit trees, blackthorn, ash, etc.

Emperor Moth *Eudia pavonia* L.

Life history – see pages 272–273

Description: forewing 2.5–3.5 cm. The males are considerably smaller than females, with feathery antennae and smaller bodies. The wing-pattern is the same in both sexes, but males are reddish with orange hindwings and the females are grey. The eye-markings of the forewings are set in a clear white patch, one of several features that distinguish females of this species from the Great Peacock.

Habitat: heaths and moors, marshes, clearings, and rides in open woodland.

Distribution: throughout Europe to central Sweden and Finland, and to 2,000 m in the mountains. Through Britain and Ireland, including the Orkneys and Hebrides.

Abundance: locally common.

Flight: one generation in April and May. Males fly in the sunshine from mid-afternoon in rapid zigzag flight. Females fly shortly after dark, and during the afternoon rest on low vegetation with scent-gland extruded. Males have been shown to respond to a calling female from up to 3 km distance, showing phenomenal sensitivity to the airborne scent-gradient. As in other moths, the scent receptors are situated on the antennae.

Life cycle: eggs are laid after dark in clusters round the stems of heather and other low plants. The newly hatched caterpillars are black, and live communally for a time. Later they become bright green with black markings and with scattered pink, yellow, or blackish warts which bear stiff black bristles. It is said that people who are red-green colour blind can see these larvae on their food-plants more easily than those with normal vision. The pear-shaped cocoon is spun amongst heather or other plants. It has a valve-like double entrance, surrounded by stiff silk strands which allow the moth to escape but deny access to intruders. The pupa overwinters in this structure.

Foodplants: heather, sallow, bramble, blackthorn; in marshes, often meadowsweet.

♂

♂

December Eggar
Poecilocampa populi L.

Des: forewing 1.5–2.2 cm. Blackish-grey moth with jagged buff crosslines. ♀ larger and longer-winged than ♂. Both sexes rather thinly scaled. **H:** woodlands and gardens. **Dis:** through central and northern Europe, including much of Britain and Ireland. **LC:** caterpillars May to July. Pupation in soil in earthen cocoon. **FP:** various deciduous trees including oak, apple, plum, cherry, hawthorn, and elm.

Lackey *Malacosoma neustria* L.

Des: forewing 1.4–2.0 cm ♂ smaller than ♀ a more variable, colour ranging from pale yellowis to chestnut-brown; crosslines sometimes absent. ♀, area between crosslines often darker than rest wing. **H:** woodlands, orchards, suburban avenue **Dis:** Europe to central Sweden; Britain and Irelan but absent from Scotland. **A:** common. **Fl:** Ju and August in Britain, starting earlier in mainlar Europe. **LC:** hairy, blue-striped caterpillars li in loose communities, sometimes causing loc defoliation. Oval silk cocoons contain a sulphu like powder. Eggs overwinter, laid in tight cylinde around twigs. **FP:** many deciduous trees ar shrubs, including fruit and ornamental trees.

Small Eggar *Eriogaster lanestris* L.

Des: forewing 1.5–2.1 cm. ♀ larger than ♂ with threadlike antennae and almost spherical anal tuft of loose, grey hair-scales. Both sexes rich dark brown, with conspicuous white spot near centre of wing and pale patch at base, and narrow, wavy crossline. **H:** hedgerows, downland scrub, young plantations. **Dis:** Europe; now very local and decreased in Britain and Ireland. **A:** moths rarely seen, but larval nests frequent in some areas. **Fl:** February to April. **LC:** egg masses covered by hair scales from ♀ abdomen. Caterpillars in communal silk nests in hedges and bushes, May to July. Up to 12 winters spent in pupa. **FP:** mainly blackthorn and hawthorn in Britain.

Oak Eggar *Lasiocampa quercus* L.

Des: forewing 2.6–4.0 cm. ♂ much smaller ar darker than yellowish ♀, and with strongly feath ered antennae. **H:** open wooded country, heath and moors. **Dis:** several races throughout Europ to tree line in Alps. **Fl:** in Britain, southern 'Oa Eggar' has a one-year life cycle, and flies in Ju and August; 'Northern Eggar' has a two-year larv stage and flies in May and June of the second yea **LC:** caterpillars of 'Oak Eggar' hibernate in thir instar, and pupate in June in an oval cocoon of silk those of 'Northern Eggar' spend first winter a a small caterpillar and second as a pupa. **FP** polyphagous; commonly on heather, brambl sallow, oak or blackthorn.

Grass Eggar
Lasiocampa trifolii Schiff.

Des: forewing 2.0–3.5 cm. ♂ differs from ♀ in much smaller size and feathered antennae, but colour and pattern are the same. Different races vary in colour. In Britain, usual form is rich dark brown, but race on Romney Marsh, Kent, is light ochreous. **H:** downland, sea cliffs, heaths, shingle. **Dis:** through Europe from southern Sweden to Spain and Asia Minor. In Britain, very local in south and south-west England, south Wales and Lancashire. **A:** locally common. **Fl:** July to early September; ♂ fly with great rapidity in late after-noon and evening, ♀ become active after dark. **LC:** eggs broadcast by flying ♀ and overwinter; caterpillars feed up in spring and summer. **FP:** grasses including marram; broom, creeping willow, tree lupin, etc.

Fox Moth *Macrothylacia rubi* L.

Des: forewing 2–3 cm. ♀ large and greyer than ♂, which ha strongly feathered antennae. Bot sexes with two narrow, pal transverse lines on forewings. **H** heaths, downs, dunes and com mons. **Dis:** much of Europe including the British Isles. **A** locally common. **Fl:** mid-May t July; ♂ fly from mid-afternoon ♀ not before nightfall. **LC** caterpillars reach full growth i autumn, hibernate and pupate in spring after sun ning themselves, but without resuming feeding Difficult to rear. **FP:** weather, bramble, bilberr and other herbaceous plants.

♂ ♂ 141

Drinker *Philudoria potatoria* L.

Description: forewing 2.3–3.2 cm. Males are smaller than females and usually reddish-brown, whereas females are typically yellow-ochre. Both sexes have a whitish spot near the centre of the forewing, and an oblique dark line across the wing to the tip. The resting posture adopted by the female illustrated opposite is typical of members of the eggar family. The species is variable, and dark females and pale males occur from time to time.

Habitat: woodland rides, marshes, water meadows, ditches, and commons. Also wet moorland and bogs.

Distribution: throughout Europe, including much of Britain and Ireland. Extends northwards to central Scandinavia and Finland, and to about 1,500 m the mountains.

Abundance: locally common. Decline in so places owing to drainage of wetlands.

Flight: late June to mid-August. Both sexes fly night.

Life cycle: eggs are laid on stems of coa grasses. Caterpillars from September to Ju hibernating when small. The hairy caterpillars grey, but the golden-brown, black and white ha produce a variegated effect. There is a tuft of lo hair on the thorax and near the tip of the abdom Besides eating grass, the larvae are partial to a d of water in the form of dew or rain, and hence b the English and scientific names. Cocoon is lo and spindle-shaped, constructed of dense yell ish silk and attached low down on a grass stem.

Foodplants: common reed and other coa grasses, and large sedges.

Pine Lappet *Dendrolimus pini* L.

Description: forewing 2.5–3.5 cm. Females always larger than males. Both sexes have the same pattern as the specimen illustrated, but colour is extremely variable, from light grey with a greater or lesser admixture of brown, to dark mahogany or near black. To some extent this variability is local. The small white dot in the centre of each forewing is a constant feature.

Habitat: pine forests, particularly plantations on poor, sandy soil.

Distribution: through most of the European p forests, but absent from large areas of central G many, and from Britain. Occurs up to 1,500 m the Alps.

Abundance: numbers fluctuate greatly and n reach pest proportions in parts of northern a eastern Europe. In the south, numbers appear to more constant.

Flight: June to mid-August. Both sexes noctur and rest by day in the tops of pines.

Life cycle: caterpillars from August to June. T hibernate on the ground in their fourth instar a return to the tree-tops in spring. Serious defoliat may occur when numbers are high.

Foodplant: pine.

♀ ♂

Eggars, Lackeys & Lappets

♀

Kentish Glory *Endromis versicolora* L.

Description: only European representative of small family of moths of rather controversial affinity, perhaps related to the silkmoths. Forewing length 2.5–4 cm. Both sexes have similar pattern, but males are much smaller, with feathered antennae and wings rich reddish brown rather than predominantly white. Specimens from south Europe are particularly large, and the females are strongly suffused with pink.
Habitat: requires stands of young birches, on moors and open parts of woodland.
Distribution: chiefly northern Europe, to northern Scandinavia and Finland; in the south to the high-lands of northern Italy. Believed extinct in England but still present in the Scottish Highlands.
Abundance: occasionally common in parts of its range; extremely local in Scotland but not uncommon.
Flight: mid-March to mid-May. Males fly in the morning sunshine and also come to light; females only at night, resting conspicuously during the day on twigs of leafless birch bushes.
Life cycle: eggs laid in large batches on birch twigs. Young caterpillars densely gregarious, resembling clusters of unripe birch catkins. Later solitary, bright green, fleshy, with oblique yellow stripes on the body and red spike on hind end. They rest on the foodplant in characteristic posture with head thrown back, and are difficult to see. Pupa in a firm subterranean cocoon; may remain in this state for one to three winters.
Foodplant: birch.

Thyris fenestrella Scop.

Description: only European representative of a chiefly tropical family of some 700 species. Forewing 0.7–1.0 cm. Small, marbled brown and black moth with thinly scaled, window-like patches on both pairs of wings. Wings held half open when at rest.
Habitat: south-facing slopes amongst bushes, edges of woods, dry, sunny wasteland. Limestone hills, where clematis grows.
Distribution: southern Europe; not in Britain.
Abundance: locally common, but inconspicuous and easily overlooked.
Flight: mid-May to mid-August. Diurnal, visiting flowers of umbelliferous plants, scabious and elder.

Life cycle: caterpillar in late summer. Small, black or brown and covered with raised warts. It smells unpleasantly of bugs. Lives rolled up in a leaf of clematis, and pupates in a loose cocoon in the ground or in a hollow stem. Pupa overwinters.

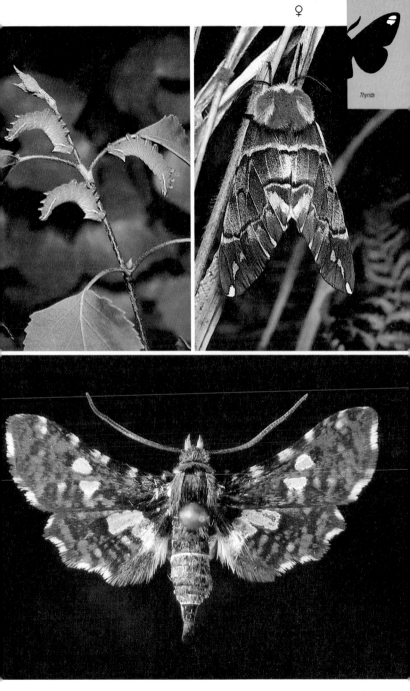

Sterrhopterix fusca Haw. (= hirsutella sensu Hübn.)

Description: there are 100 or so psychids which occur in central Europe; some are very difficult to tell apart. They tend to be small, inconspicuous species. The females are wingless. In the male of *Sterrhopterix fusca*, the forewing length is about 1 cm and the wings are unicolourous greyish brown.

Habitat: wetlands, including moors, fens, carr, wet mixed woodland, and damp pasture.

Distribution: across Europe, including England and Wales.

Abundance: very local, but one of the commoner psychids.

Flight: early June to early July. The wingless female remains in the cocoon; males fly at dusk and are attracted to the females.

Life cycle: pairing takes place through the fabric of the cocoon and eggs are laid inside the empty female pupa-case. Caterpillars hatch in four to five weeks, and construct a case of silk and fragments of dry plant material, in which they live for two years, eventually pupating in them. Males pupate near ground level, females up to 2 m above the ground. Males emerge normally, but females which lack all body appendages and have even their eyes much reduced, remain in their cocoons.

Foodplants: polyphagous, on heather, birch, sallow, hawthorn, oak, etc., and grasses.

Lepidopsyche unicolor Hufn.

Description: forewing up to 1.5 cm in males. Strongly feathered antennae; wings soft smoky brown, less transparent than in other species. Forewing distinctly longer and less rounded than in *Sterrhopterix fusca*. This is the largest of European psychid species. Female wingless.

Habitat: found in a wide range of biotopes.

Distribution: temperate Europe; widely distributed but not often noticed. Only a single dubious record from Britain.

Abundance: locally common.

Flight: June to August (males only).

Life cycle: caterpillars can be found almost throughout the year. In both sexes, the cases end with a simple tube, but male caterpillars use shorter

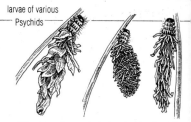

larvae of various Psychids

and broader pieces of plant material, often bits of dried leaves, whereas females use longer pieces of stem and twig.

Foodplants: polyphagous.

General: a number of other psychids can be identified by the characteristic structure of their cases (see illustrations). *Apterona crenulella* Bruand is unique in making a case which is coiled like a snail shell.

Canephora unicolor, sac of ♀ (caterpillars) *Sterrhopterix hirsutella*, sac of ♂ 147

Hornet Clearwing *Sesia apiformis* Clerck

Description: like the bee hawkmoths, clearwings are examples of Batesian mimics, none more convincing than the two hornet clearwings which not only look and behave like large wasps, but also buzz. The markings on the front of the thorax give the impression of the triangular head of a hornet, but underneath is a perfectly ordinary moth face! The Hornet Clearwing is the largest species, with forewing length 1.5–2.0 cm.

Habitat: poplar avenues, less often isolated trees, in parks, along edges of woods, and by rivers.

Distribution: Europe to central Sweden and nearly 2,000 m in the Alps. Occurs in England, parts of Wales and in the south-east of Ireland.

Abundance: locally common. The adult moth is rarely seen, but the old exit-holes at the bases of poplar trunks are often abundant.

Flight: late May to late July. The moths emerge early in the day and have usually flown by mid-morning. During an emergence, specimens can be found drying their wings low down on poplar trunks or on the grass nearby.

Life cycle: a single female lays up to 1,400 eggs in bark crevices or in old exit holes. Caterpillars tunnel in poplar wood under the bark and live for two or three years. They pupate in tough, oval cocoons just under the bark. Before making its cocoon the caterpillar cuts a 'cap' in the bark at the end of the burrow, which the moth dislodges at emergence. Capped burrows are impossible to see.

Foodplants: black poplar, sometimes other poplar species.

Dusky Clearwing *Paranthrene tabaniformis* Rott.

Description: forewing length about 1.2 cm. A medium-sized clearwing, unusual in having the forewings covered in scales. Body has four yellow bands.

Habitat: poplar plantations, aspen groves, in stream and river valleys, and damp woodland.

Distribution: local throughout Eurasia. A few British records, and possibly overlooked.

Abundance: an elusive species, seldom if ever encountered as an adult. Like many other clearwings, occurs in small colonies.

Flight: late May to early July. Diurnal.

Life cycle: caterpillars tunnel in the wood of poplars and aspens, sometimes living low down in the trunks and root systems of larger trees, sometimes in slender stems of saplings, often at first in the gall of the wood-boring beetle *Saperda*, later making a differently shaped gall of their own. The life cycle takes two years. Pupa in a tunnel below the bark which has been gnawed thin. No cocoon is made.

General: of about 50 European species of clearwing, 15 have been recorded in Britain. In one group, the caterpillars live in the trunks or stems of trees and bushes, and in the other, they inhabit the root systems of herbaceous plants such as dock, thrift, or birdsfoot trefoil. The species of the latter group are more frequent in hotter climates. Study of clearwings is a specialized and fascinating branch of lepidopterology.

The Currant Clearwing, *Synanthedon tipdiformis* Clerck, may sometimes be seen flying around currant bushes on sunny afternoons in July. The eggs are laid on pruning wounds and the caterpillars bore into the twigs but are difficult to detect. The small Red-belted Clearwing, *S. myopaeformis* Borkh., is associated with apple trees, and the caterpillars live in colonies under the bark, sometimes on a single tree in an orchard.

♀

Clearwings

Goat Moth *Cossus cossus* L.

pupa

Description: forewing 2.8–3.8 cm. Females larger than males. Large, grey moths with characteristic 'tree bark' camouflage. Though the proboscis is rudimentary and the adult moths do not feed, they occasionally appear at the sugar patches set out by entomologists. It is thought they mistake the sugar for the exudate of a wounded tree which would make a suitable site for egg-laying.

Habitat: mixed woodland, meadows and riversides where there are old willows, parks and old gardens.

Distribution: throughout Europe. Scattered through Britain and Ireland, but evidently decreased.

Abundance: still fairly common to common in parts of Europe.

Flight: late May to early August.

Life cycle: eggs laid in large masses in crevices of tree bark. Traditional trees, '*cossus*-trees', tend to be used for a number of years, and human destruction of these old, gnarled and damaged trees is thought to be a reason why this moth is less common than formerly. Caterpillars live in colonies in these trees, criss-crossing the wood with their galleries. Up to four years is spent in the caterpillar stage, and the infected tree may be killed. The full-fed caterpillar is sometimes found in the autumn wandering in search of a site for pupation. Pupa in a cocoon in rotting wood, or in soil.

Foodplants: living wood of deciduous trees, especially willow, birch, elm and ash. In captivity can be reared on raw beetroot or apples.

Leopard Moth *Zeuzera pyrina* L.

Description: forewing 2.0–3.0 cm. Female considerably larger than male, with tip of abdomen tapered and containing long extensible ovipositor. Antennae of male feathered to about half-way. Unmistakable species; thorax covered with peculiar white, woolly hair scales, and bearing six round black spots arranged in two converging rows.

Habitat: mixed woodland, orchards, parks and gardens.

Distribution: throughout Europe; in England and Wales to Yorkshire; absent from Scotland and Ireland.

Abundance: sometimes common.

Flight: early June to August. Males come freely to light, but females only rarely. The females are sometimes found resting on lawns, where they are frequently attacked by ants.

Life cycle: eggs inserted into bark crevices with the aid of the long ovipositor of female. Caterpillars burrow in wood of trunks and branches of trees and shrubs, occasionally causing sufficient damage to fruit and ornamental trees to be classed as pests. They feed for two or three years, then pupate in the larval burrow without forming a cocoon. The spiny pupa can move up and down the burrow, and protrudes half out of the exit hole when emergence takes place, a habit shared with the goat moths and clearwings.

Foodplants: the caterpillar has been recorded on about 150 different species of tree and shrub, including horse chestnut, ash, elm, lilac, and many kinds of fruit tree.

♂

Ghost Swift *Hepialus humuli* L.

Description: the swift moths are a very primitive group with a unique coupling between fore- and hindwings. The Ghost Swift is the largest European species, with forewing 2.0–3.2 cm. Males are shiny white, with dark under- sides, and females are orange with darker orange-brown mark- ings. In the Shetlands, the males are highly polymorphic, variably marked, and some are as dark as females.

Habitat: damp lowland pasture, hillsides, clear- ings in woods, parks and waste ground.

Distribution: throughout temperate Europe, extending to Lapland. Throughout Britain and Ireland to the Shetlands.

Abundance: local, but often common where occurs.

Flight: late May to mid-August. Males start to fl just before dusk, swinging in peculiar pendulatin flight just above the ground vegetation. This is sexual display, during which the males emit specific scent to which the females respond. female will fly into a group of pendulating male and pair with one of them, the couple subsequentl hanging from a grass-stem.

Life cycle: eggs are dropped into vegetatio singly from flying female. Caterpillars occur fror August to May, probably overwintering twice. The feed on roots of a variety of herbaceous plants suc as deadnettle, dock, and burdock, and may caus damage to crops such as hop and strawberry.

Foodplants: polyphagous on herbaceous roc systems.

Gold Swift *Hepialus hecta* L.

Description: forewing 1.1–1.6 cm. Female larger and duller-coloured than male, lacking the bright white or golden markings on forewings.

Habitat: heathlands, moors, clearings, and rides in woods, especially on light soils where bracken occurs.

Distribution: in temperate and northern Europe. Throughout mainland Britain and Ireland, though local. Extends eastwards right across Asia, and in mountains up to 1,500 m.

Abundance: locally common.

Flight: late May to early August. Males fly before dusk, females rather later. After dark, pairs may be found suspended from grass stems. If a mothin light is set up early in the evening, males of th and other species of swift moth will arrive freely about dusk, but soon the flight stops and the onl visitors later on are occasional females.

Life cycle: eggs broadcast by female ov bracken. Caterpillars feed in rhizomes of bracke living for two years. Pupation occurs in a cococ at the soil surface, and emergence occurs soc afterwards.

Foodplants: bracken; occasionally other he baceous plants.

Swifts & Ghosts

Square-spot Dart *Euxoa obelisca* Schiff.

Description: forewings 1.4–1.8 cm in length, brown to reddish brown. As in many noctuids, the forewings are patterned with crosslines and three spots or stigmata towards the middle of each wing – the oval or circular orbicular stigma; the kidney-shaped reniform stigma; and behind them the dart- or wedge-shaped claviform stigma. Differences between species of the genus *Euxoa* are often subtle. The absence of wedge-shaped marks in the outer region of the forewing, and the fact that the outer crossline touches the outer face of the reniform stigma are useful characters in identifying the Square-spot Dart.

There are several other continental species with which it might be confused, but the above features are sufficient to distinguish it from the much more variable White-line Dart, the only similar species occurring in Britain.

Habitat: dry heathlands, sandy waste ground, sunny hill slopes especially on chalky soil. In Britain found on sea cliffs, both basic and acidic.

Distribution: widespread in temperate Europe from the lowlands up to 3,000 m; on British sea cliffs on the south and west coasts of England and Wales, east Scotland, the Hebrides, and south Ireland.

Abundance: locally common in its British localities, and usually common on the Continent.

Flight: July to September; in Britain, flies later in the year than the White-line Dart. Moths come well to light and sugar.

Life cycle: caterpillars of this group of noctuids are known as cutworms; they spend most of their lives underground, feeding on roots, and several are important pests. The caterpillars of the different species are all rather alike, nondescript brown or grey, with dark marks along the back, and with small feet. The caterpillar of the Square-spot Dart occurs from September to June on the Continent, is said, but details of the cycle in British populations have not been worked out. It is reported to feed on low plants such as bedstraw and rock-rose.

White-line Dart *Euxoa tritici* L.

Description: forewings 1.2–1.8 cm. Similar in shape and appearance to the Square-spot Dart, but wedge-shaped black marks are normally present in the outer region of the forewings, and the outer line stands clear of the reniform stigma. It is an extremely variable species, both within and between populations, and some of the larger, paler forms can be confused with the Coast Dart. This has slightly longer and narrower forewings, and the underside markings are different. In mainland Europe, the White-line Dart can be compared with *E. aquilina* Schiff., but this has a broad pale smudge traversing the forewing behind the claviform stigma. In cases of doubt, it is necessary to refer to the structure of the genitalia.

Habitat: light soils including heaths, dunes, downland and grassy pastures, sometimes grain fields.

Abundance: in places extremely common, though it is said to have decreased in parts of mainland Europe.

Flight: late June to September; July and August in Britain. Comes abundantly to light and sugar, and to flowers such as ragwort.

Life cycle: method of hibernation in Britain remains unknown; said to overwinter as a caterpillar in Europe. Caterpillars lie buried in the soil by day and feed at night on a variety of small herbaceous plants.

Foodplants: various grasses and small herbs such as chickweed, corn spurrey and bedstraw.

Turnip Moth *Agrotis segetum* Schiff.

Description: forewing 1.5–1.8 cm, light brown to almost black, the three stigmata distinct, with claviform pale-centred. Black specimens often have a terminal line of pale dots. Dark moths are often females, but not always. The sexes can be distinguished by examining the antennae, feathered in the male, simple in females. Hindwings white, with dark veins.

Habitat: fields and open, cultivated land; British population reinforced by immigration.

Distribution: almost the whole of Europe and in the huge corn-growing areas of Russia. In mountains to over 2,000 m.

Abundance: generally common everywhere, and may be a pest in large cereal and root-crop growing areas. May also be a pest in young forestry plantations.

Flight: two generations, from May to July, and mid-August to November.

Life cycle: eggs laid in small, irregular clusters. Caterpillars are typical cutworms and almost completely subterranean. One generation feeds up quickly, in July and August, the other more slowly through the winter.

Foodplants: leaves and roots of many species herbaceous plant and garden vegetables such a turnips, carrots, and cabbages.

General: it is worth considering some of th factors which keep potential pest species und control. As a conservative estimate, a female Turn Moth may lay 1,000 eggs. If, on average, four eg per batch survive to maturity, the population w double in the next generation. The caterpilla suffer heavy mortality from insectivorous birds an small mammals; when a population starts t increase, the number of parasites such as ichneu mon wasps increases too, and larvae and pup lying in the soil are also destroyed by fungi. If th population falls below average, predators search fo other kinds of food and the numbers of parasite drop. Thus, a balance is maintained over the years By planting monoculture crops, humans encourag the build-up of pests, and it is not easy to contro them with insecticides without the risk of upsettin the natural balance.

Heart and Dart *Agrotis exclamationis* L.

Description: forewings 1.5–1.8 cm long. The ground colour varies from pale straw through shades of brown and grey to nearly black. The black claviform stigma is often the most prominent marking, but the other stigmata may also be well-defined and sometimes all the stigmata are joined to form an irregular black patch. Crosslines are often absent, but occasionally strongly developed. Many variants have been given names. Hindwings of males are white, those of females brown.

Habitat: generally distributed in grassy places, especially downland and dunes.

Distribution: all of Europe and throughout Britain and Ireland except for Orkney, Shetland and most of the Outer Hebrides. To over 2,000 m in mountains.

Abundance: one of the commonest Europea noctuids.

Flight: mid-May to early August, sometimes with small autumn generation. One of the most abundar moths to visit the sugar patch, and also common a flowers and light.

Life cycle: caterpillar a typical cutworm, but ca be distinguished from others by the particularly large, dark spiracles. Caterpillars reach maturity i the autumn, and spin weak cocoons in the soil i which they hibernate, pupating in the spring.

Foodplants: polyphagous on many wild and culti-vated herbaceous plants.

Dark Sword-grass *Agrotis ipsilon* Hufn.

Description: length of forewing 2.0–2.2 cm. Wings long and narrow, darker towards leading edge of forewing, and characterized by presence of black streak projecting beyond reniform stigma. Claviform stigma small. Hindwings pearly white with dark veins.

Habitat: open country, arable fields and gardens. Strongly migratory.

Distribution: cosmopolitan. In Europe, to 64°N. Not native in Britain, but a common immigrant species which may breed.

Abundance: numbers in north and central Europe depend on the species' breeding success further south, but in most years it is common, sometimes excessively so.

Flight: immigrants start to appear in March or even February, and continue to enter northern Europe in waves throughout the summer, reaching peak numbers in the autumn. At least two generations are involved.

Life cycle: caterpillars more or less completely subterranean and seldom seen in the wild, though they have been bred from eggs and their behaviour is known. Typical cutworms which pupate in soil in a weak cocoon.

Foodplants: polyphagous on many herbaceous plants.

Flame Shoulder *Ochropleura plecta* L.

Description: forewing 1.2–1.4 cm. Forewings rich reddish-brown with pale stripe along leading edge, small, pale-rimmed reniform and orbicular stigmata and no claviform stigma. The pale costa is sharply demarcated from the rest of the wing by a black line. Hindwings whitish.

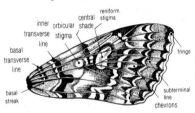

Habitat: woodland, farmland, gardens, meadows, and marshes.

Distribution: widespread in Europe, and throughout Britain to the Orkneys, and Ireland.

Abundance: one of the commonest moths in Europe.

Flight: throughout the summer and autumn, with peaks of emergence in May and June, and in August.

Life cycle: caterpillars are mottled grey and brown, with broad yellowish line along each side. They feed at night during the summer months. Pupa in soil near the surface.

General: the Flame Shoulder can only be mistaken for the very similar *O. leucogaster* Freyer which has slightly longer wings, a black mark extending beyond the reniform stigma, purer white hindwings, and a clothing of white hair-scales on the anterior part of the abdomen. It is common in south Europe, but has been recorded only once in Britain. Flame Shoulders in Spain lack an orbicular stigma and are sub-species *unimacula* Stdgr.

Dotted Rustic *Rhyacia simulans* Hufn.

Des: elongated forewings 1.6–2.2 cm. Colour varies from light brown to almost black in *f. suffusa* Tutt from parts of northern Britain. Stigmata and crosslines faint; numerous small dark dots in outer area of wings and along outer margin. **H:** grassy fields, farmland, dry hillsides, especially on light soils. **Dis:** temperate Europe and Asia; scattered through Britain to Orkneys; to 2,000 m in Alps. **A:** in Britain, subject to great fluctuation in numbers especially in the south. **Fl:** in England, June and July, followed by aestivation and reappearance in autumn; in north Britain, apparently only one flight period, in July and August. **LC:** caterpillars not found in wild; those obtained from eggs very difficult to rear successfully. **FP:** herbaceous plants.

Rhyacia helvetina Boisd.

Des: forewing length up to 2 cm. Smooth grey-brown, central area somewhat darker. Wing shape characteristic, with leading edge of forewing almost straight. **H:** Alpine meadows and grassland. **Dis:** Alps and Pyrenees; unrecorded from Britain. **A:** often common in Alps, less so in Pyrenees. **Fl:** July and August. **LC:** nocturnal caterpillars from August to June, hibernating. **FP:** grasses and small Alpine herbs.

Large Yellow Underwing *Noctua pronuba* L.

Des: narrow, elongated forewings 2.3–2.8 cm. Forewings variable in colour, but dark specimens are male and pale ones female. Hindwings yellow with narrow black border. **H:** almost anywhere including town gardens. **Dis:** throughout Europe including whole of Britain and Ireland. **A:** very common. **Fl:** May to late autumn. **LC:** caterpillars continue feeding through winter; largely subterranean, like a cutworm. **FP:** polyphagous. **G:** rests by day on ground amongst dry leaves; easily disturbed, flying off erratically and displaying bright hindwings, then crashes to ground becoming invisible until disturbed again. Combination of bright hindwings (flash colouration) and skittish behaviour is effective defence strategy against predators.

Broad-bordered Yellow Underwing *Noctua fimbriata* Schreber

Des: forewing length 2.3–2.5 cm. Forewing dark in ♂, pale in ♀ hindwings of both sexes orange yellow with broad black border nearly half width of wing. **H:** open deciduous woodland, parks, gardens. **Dis:** central Europe to 2,500 m in mountains mainland Britain and Ireland. **Fl:** June to September, aestivating. **LC:** caterpillars September to May feeding slowly through winter. **FP:** low herbs in autumn, opening buds of woodland saplings in spring, also primrose and bramble.

Lesser Broad-bordered Yellow Underwing *Noctua janthina* Schiff.

Des: forewing 1.5–1.7 cm. Head, collar and legs whitish; forewings purplish-brown, orbicular and reniform stigmata outlined white. Hindwings dark yellow with fairly broad black border. **H:** woodland, parks and gardens, river valleys and meadows. **Dis:** throughout Europe including Britain to Orkneys, and Ireland. **A:** common. **Fl:** June to September. **LC:** caterpillars September to April on dandelion, dock, primrose and many other herbs and shrubs.

True Lover's Knot *Lycophotia porphyrea* Schiff.

Des: forewing 1.2–1.5 cm. Small, reddish brown noctuid with whitish stigmata and crosslines highly procryptic amongst debris under heather. Hindwings uniform brown with whitish margin. **H:** heathland, heathy woodland, gardens with cultivated heathers. **Dis:** Europe. Britain to Shetlands, Ireland. Alps to 2,000 m. **A:** often abundant. **Fl:** June to August. **LC:** caterpillars September to May. **FP:** heathers including cultivated varieties.

161

Ingrailed Clay *Diarsia mendica* F.

Des: forewings 1.4–1.8 cm long, ochre-yellow to reddish-brown. Extremely variable; small Scottish moorland race often mauve-tinted; smallest and darkest specimens from Shetland (sub-species *thulei* Stdgr.). Amount of black between stigmata and development of crosslines varies greatly. **H:** deciduous woodland in south, moors in north Britain. **Dis:** throughout Europe; in mountains up to 2,000 m. Throughout Britain and Ireland. **A:** common. **Fl:** June to August. **LC:** caterpillar from September to May. Hibernates but easily forced. **FP:** primrose, bramble, bilberry, birch, sallow, heather, etc.

Purple Clay *Diarsia brunnea* Schiff.

Des: forewing length 1.6–2.0 cm. Dark, purplish brown or violet-red forewings, with leading edges less arched than in Ingrailed Clay; dark patch between stigmata usually present. Hindwings light brown. **H:** deciduous woodland, heaths and moors, meadows and parks. **Dis:** northern and central Europe; in Britain to the Orkneys, and Ireland. **A:** common. **Fl:** June to August, earlier on the Continent. **LC:** similar to Ingrailed Clay. Caterpillars can be induced to feed up and produce moths by Christmas. **FP:** before hibernation on dock, etc. in spring on bilberry, sallow, birch, as well as low growing herbs.

Small Square-spot *Diarsia rubi* View.

Des: forewing 1.4–1.7 cm. Reddish-brown forewings short and blunt, specimens from Scotland larger and duller-coloured. More uniformly-coloured than the Ingrailed Clay, crosslines more evenly curved. **H:** damp woodland and marshes, pasture and cultivated ground. **Dis:** in Europe, to 2000m in Alps, and throughout Britain and Ireland. **A:** common. **Fl:** two generations on Continent and in southern Britain, first in May and June, second July to September. Single-brooded in Scotland, in July and August. **LC:** caterpillars in June and July, and from autumn to April, hibernating. **FP:** various herbaceous plants such as dock and dandelion; also heather.

Fen Square-spot
Diarsia florida Schmidt

Des: forewing 1.5–1.8 cm. Very similar to the Small Square-spot, but a little larger, paler and brighter in colour. The Fen Square-spot is single brooded, flying in June and July, between the broods of the Small Square-spot. Moreover, it appears not to fly until well after midnight, whereas the Small Square-spot is on the wing from soon after dusk. There remains controversy as to whether the univoltine Scottish populations should more properly be considered to be this species rather than *D. rubi*. It seems that the Fen Square-spot is in the process of evolving into a separate species.

Great Brocade *Eurois occulta* L.

Des: long forewings 2.4–2.8 cm, grey to bluey-grey or black in colour. Large size, pale orbicular stigma, pale-rimmed reniform stigma and white-fringed dark greyish-brown hindwings good distinguishing features. **H:** boggy moorland and woodland with bilberry. **Dis:** mainly northern Europe, but occurs in Alps to nearly 2,000 m. Resident in Scotland, where mostly blackish *Ab. passetii* Th.-Mg., and immigrant to other parts of Britain and Ireland. All immigrants pale grey in colour. **A:** widespread but uncommon on Continent; Scottish population locally common. **Fl:** June to September. **LC:** caterpillars September to May, difficult to force. **FP:** chiefly bog myrtle in Scotland, but also birch, sallow, bilberry and crowberry.

Green Arches
Anaplectoides prasina Schiff.

Des: forewing length 2.0–2.5 cm. Strongly patterned forewings heavily green-tinted (fades to yellow); conspicuous pale area beyond large reniform stigma. Hindwings dark brown with pale fringe. **H:** deciduous woodland. **Dis:** Europe, commoner in north; in mountains to 1,600 m. **A:** fairly common. **LC:** caterpillars September to May, easily forced. **FP:** bilberry, birch, honeysuckle, bramble and other plants.

Setaceous Hebrew Character
Xestia c-nigrum L.

Des: forewing length c. 1.8 cm. Forewings ashy grey-brown with conspicuous and constant black-and-whitish mark between reniform stigma and first crossline. Hindwings light brown. **H:** woodland, heaths, cultivated ground and built-up areas. **Dis:** through Europe, to 1,800 m in mountains; throughout Britain and Ireland; migratory. **A:** uncommon in May and June, becoming abundant in autumn. **FL:** probably two generations, first much less common. **LC:** details of behaviour in wild remain uncertain, but up to six generations can be obtained per year in laboratory. **FP:** widely polyphagous; captive larvae reared easily on dock.

Double Square-spot
Xestia triangulum Hufn.

Des: bears a close resemblance to Triple-spotted Clay, but forewings ochreous brown without reddish or fuscous suffusion, hindwings relatively dark and underside less glossy. **H:** deciduous woodland, gardens. **Dis:** throughout Europe, including Britain to the Orkneys, Ireland. In Alps, to 2,000 m. **A:** common; in Britain far more common and widely distributed than preceding species. **Fl:** June to August. **LC:** as preceding species. **FP:** polyphagous; in spring often one of the commonest nocturnal larvae on primrose, dock, bramble, and opening buds of saplings.

Square-spotted Clay
Xestia rhomboidea Esp.

Des: forewings shorter and broader than those of congeners, dark fuscous or purplish-brown. Characterized by black quadrate mark between stigmata and especially by presence of another black rhomboidal patch between orbicular stigma and first line. **H:** deciduous woodland. **Dis:** generally distributed in Europe, but very local in Britain. **A:** locally common. **Fl:** July and August. Visits flowers or burdock inside woods. **LC:** caterpillars from September to May, hibernating when small; easily forced. **FP:** herbaceous plants.

Triple-spotted Clay
Xestia ditrapezium Schiff.

Des: forewings 1.6–2.0 cm long, and varying i colour from reddish-brown to blackish-brown. Ver similar in size, shape and pattern to Double Squa re-spot (*Xestia triangulum* Hufn.) but forewing darker, hindwing paler, and underside very muc more glossy. **H:** deciduous woodland and woo borders, parkland. **Dis:** local in Europe, includin Britain and Ireland. **A:** locally fairly common. **Fl** late June to early August. **LC:** caterpillars Septem ber to April, like others of the genus, easily forced **FP:** polyphagous; in spring, on opening buds c saplings of dogwood, birch, sallow and hazel; als honeysuckle and bramble.

Dotted Clay *Xestia baja* Schiff.

Des: forewings 1.6–2.0 cm long, brownish-red brown-grey, sometimes violet-grey. Most promi nent feature is the small, double, black spot nea the apex of forewings – the other markings are rather obscure. Hindwings light brown. **H:** mixe woodland, heaths, parks and gardens. **Dis:** throug Europe, including British Isles and Ireland. **A** moderately common. **Fl:** June to September. **LC** caterpillars from September to May; hibernate, bu easily forced. **FP:** in autumn, low plants, such a primrose and dock; in spring, bog myrtle, birch sallow, blackthorn, etc.

Square-spot Rustic
Xestia xanthographa Schiff.

Des: length of forewings 1.6–1.8 cm. Colou varies from light sandy grey to ochreous brow red-brown, or nearly black. Reniform stigma ofte pale and almost square in outline – hence name Outer line a series of separate dots. Hindwings pal with broad, broken, darkish border. **H:** woodlan edges, open grassland, pasture, dunes, downlan and meadows. **Dis:** Eurasiatic; throughout Britis Isles and Ireland. **A:** often abundant. **LC:** caterpil lars October to May. Feeds through winter, at night **FP:** chiefly grasses, but also broad-leaved her baceous plants.

165

Red Chestnut
Cerastis rubricosa Schiff.

Des: forewings 1.2–1.6 cm in length, blunt-tipped, reddish brown or violet-tinted; most conspicuous markings series of dark dots on leading edge. Hindwings brownish, with dark discal spot. **H:** mixed woodland, boggy moorland. **Dis:** through Europe, commoner in north; to 1,700 m in mountains. Britain to Orkneys; Ireland. **Fl:** March to May. Comes to sallow bloom at night. **LC:** caterpillars from May to July; pupa overwinters. **FP:** various herbaceous plants, and sallow.

White-marked
Cerastis leucographa Schiff.

Des: similar shape to preceding, but slightly smaller. Antennae of ♂ with longer pectinations than those of Red Chestnut. Forewings with conspicuously pale reniform and orbicular stigmata. **H:** deciduous woodland. **Dis:** scattered and local in Europe, mainly towards north. Likewise in scattered colonies in England and Wales. **Fl:** March to May; emerges a little later than Red Chestnut, sallows are often over before it appears. **LC:** caterpillars in June and July, seldom if ever found in wild. **FP:** in captivity, sallow, plantain; dock, bilberry and oak also recorded.

Mesogona oxalina Hübn.

Des: forewings 1.5–1.8 cm, violet-brown to yellow-brown, with two almost straight crosslines which converge strongly towards trailing edge of wings; wavy outer line broken into series of dots. Stigmata indistinct. Hindwings grey with grey fringe. **H:** valley woodlands, river and stream banks, damp hollows. **Dis:** widespread in parts of Europe, but absent from north Germany, and from Britain. In mountains, up to 2,000 m. **A:** widespread, but not common. **Fl:** August and September. **LC:** egg overwinters; caterpillars April to June. **FP:** willow, poplar, and alder.

Nutmeg *Discestra trifolii* Hufn.

Des: forewings 1.5–1.6 cm in length. Recognized by combination of light brown ground colour, rounded, pale orbicular stigma, dark mark in lower part of reniform stigma, strong 'W' shape in middle of outermost crossline and pale, dark-bordered hindwings. Several other European species are similar. **H:** fairly open country on light, well-drained soils, sea coasts, wasteland. **Dis:** throughout Europe; in Britain, commonest in south-east, but extending to Orkneys, and Ireland. In Alps to about 1,600 m. **A:** locally common. **Fl:** two generations in south of range, including southern England; single-brooded from English Midlands northwards. **LC:** one or two generations of caterpillars. Pupa overwinters. **FP:** chiefly *Chenopodiaceae*.

Grey Arches *Polia nebulosa* Hufn.

Des: forewings 2.0–2.5 cm in length. Large, grey noctuid with large, black-edged orbicular and reniform stigmata and crenulated crosslines. Shows interesting local variation: predominent form in Britain is grey; on west coast of Scotland ground colour is whitish, while dusky forms occur in woods in industrial areas. Spectacular all-black form with white fringes used to occur in north England, but now believed extinct. **H:** deciduous woodland; in mountains to 1,600 m. **A:** fairly common. **Fl:** June and July. **LC:** caterpillars hibernate when small, and feed in spring on opening buds of birch, willow, sycamore, etc., and bramble. Brown, with blackish diamond-marks along back.

The Shears *Hada nana* Hufn.

Des: forewings 1.4–1.6 cm in length; colour highly variable, from light ash-grey to dark brown; pale forked patch under orbicular stigma usually present; central area of forewings often darker; crosslines jagged. **H:** mountains, downs, dunes, moors. **Dis:** Europe to 2,500 m in mountains; Britain to Orkneys, Ireland. **Fl:** regularly double-brooded on Continent, but single-brooded, from May to July, in most of Britain. **LC:** caterpillars live in or close to ground and are nocturnal. **FP:** mostly roots, of dandelion, hawkweeds, chickweed, knotgrass, etc.

Cabbage Moth *Mamestra brassicae* L.

Des: forewing length 2.0–2.3 cm. Mottled brown forewings, orbicular stigma light brown, reniform stigma edged white on outer side, crosslines jagged, outermost whitish, with pronounced 'W'. **H:** cultivated fields, gardens. **Dis:** throughout Europe, including Britain and Ireland. **A:** common. **Fl:** has been seen in every month of the year, but chiefly in summer; two or three overlapping generations. **LC:** caterpillars occur throughout summer and autumn. **FP:** polyphagous, sometimes a pest on cultivated varieties.

Dog's Tooth *Lacanobia suasa* Schiff.

Des: forewing length 1.6–1.8 cm. Two main forms: the first more or less unicolorous, with fine, white outer line forming 'W' near middle (illustrated); and the second a light brown with well-marked stigmata, including claviform, and black, pale-edged basal streak. **H:** waste ground, low moorland and salterns. **Dis:** through Europe to 1,800 m in mountains, but a lowland species in Britain and Ireland. **A:** locally common. **Fl:** two generations, April to July and July to September. **LC:** caterpillars in summer and early autumn; overwinters as pupa. **FP:** herbaceous plants, including persicaria, dock and plantain.

Broom Moth *Ceramica pisi* L.

Des: general resemblance to two previous species but more brightly marked, reddish brown, often with violet flush; outer line irregular, expanding to form a triangular pale patch in angle of wing. **H:** widespread. **Dis:** central and northern Europe, to 2,000 m in mountains. Throughout Britain to Orkneys; Ireland. **A:** often common. **Fl:** May to July, with partial second generation in late summer. **LC:** handsome caterpillars green or brown, with yellow sides. **FP:** polyphagous; bracken, dock, persicaria, heather, sallow, etc.

Dot Moth *Melanchra persicariae* L.

Des: forewing length 1.8–2.0 cm. Forewings blue black with conspicuous white reniform stigma orbicular stigma occasionally outlined white. A form with reniform stigma darkened (*ab. unicolo* Stdgr.) is not uncommon in Europe, but i extremely rare in Britain. **H:** cultivated ground market gardens, field headlands and waste groun in preference to genuinely wild habitat. **Dis** Europe; in Britain, reaching southern Scotland an Ireland. **A:** common; in Britain, progressively les so northwards. **Fl:** end of May to August. **LC** caterpillar with pronounced hump on segment 8 varies in colour from green to dark, purplish brown **FP:** polyphagous, persicaria, lupin and young sal lows; recorded as minor pest of larch seedlings.

Bright-line Brown Eye
Lacanobia oleracea L.

Des: similar in general appearance to Dog's Tooth; aptly named, having clear white 'W marked terminal line and light-brown reniform stigma; rathe invariable. **H:** widespread. **Dis:** through Europe; in Britain to Orkneys and Ireland. **A:** common. **Fl:** two generations, early and late summer. **LC:** caterpillars in summer and autumn green and brown forms, both with pale stripe along sides. **FP:** goosefoot, orache, persicaria; a pest on tomatoes, eating out the young fruits.

Antler Moth *Cerapteryx graminis* L.

Des: forewings 1.0–1.7 cm, ♀ larger than ♂. Ground colour greyish to rich red-brown; pale orbicular and reniform stigmata; elongated claviform stigma; pale central vein branches to form characteristic 'antler' pattern. **H:** downland, meadows and moors; in mountains, to 2,000 m. **Dis:** Eurasiatic, extending to Iceland. Throughout Britain to Shetlands; Ireland. **A:** locally common to abundant in Britain, but never having spectacular population explosions that occur from time to time in parts of mainland Europe. **Fl:** June to September. **LC:** subterranean caterpillar feeds on grass roots and bases of shoots; when abundant, can be a serious pest of grasslands.

Campion *Hadena rivularis* F.

Des: forewings about 1.4 cm long, brown with violet suffusion; conspicuous orbicular and reniform stigmata set at an oblique angle to one another; pale outer crossline jagged. Hindwings light brown. **H:** meadows and pastures. **Dis:** temperate Europe to 1,600 m in foothills of mountains. Britain to Orkneys, Ireland. **A:** fairly common. **Fl:** one or two broods during the summer, according to latitude and altitude. **LC:** caterpillars of the Campion and its near relatives feed in capsules of campions, females having laid their eggs in the flowers, one per flower. Flowers are pollinated by the moth, but cost to the plant is many seeds eaten by the caterpillar. Strategy seems to work! **FP:** capsules of ragged robin (in meadows), and sea campion (on coasts), preferred by this species.

Lychnis *Hadena bicruris* Hufn.

Des: similar size and wing-pattern to Campion, but forewings slightly narrower; lacks purplish tint and orbicular and reniform stigmata do not touch its rear. **H:** stream and river banks, hedgerows, borders of woods. **Dis:** central Europe to 2,000 m throughout Britain and Ireland. **A:** common. **Fl:** two generations, early and late summer, only one in the north. **LC:** caterpillars live inside capsules of white and red campion; occur through summer. **FP:** Campion species, including sweet william.

Feathered Gothic
Tholera decimalis Poda

Des: forewing 1.6–2.2 cm. ♀ considerably larger than ♂ and with simple antennae, which in ♂ are strongly feathered. Pale-coloured stigmata with darker centres and black outlines, wavy, cream-coloured outer crossline and conspicuously pale veins. Black chevrons between veins before outer crossline. **H:** damp meadows and heaths. **Dis:** through Europe, to 2,000 m in mountains; Britain and Ireland, but local in Scotland. **A:** locally common. **Fl:** August and September. **LC:** overwinters as an egg; caterpillars March to July. **FP:** roots of grasses.

Marbled Coronet
Hadena confusa Hufn.

Des: forewings 1.5–1.7 cm long, typically marbled brownish-black and white, with round, white orbicular stigma and white patch immediately below the stigmata. In the closely-related Varied Coronet (*Hadena compta* Schiff.), the median white area extends across wings to trailing edge. Marbled Coronet varies little in mainland Europe, but extreme local races occur in parts of Britain with white markings replaced by yellow, or obliterated to produce all-dark moths. Most extreme forms in Shetlands. **H:** downs, shingle, low sea cliffs, warm hillsides. **Dis:** Eurasiatic; scattered through Britain to Shetlands, and Ireland. **A:** locally common. **Fl:** May to July; visits flowers and comes to light. **LC:** caterpillars chiefly in capsules of bladder campion and sea campion, feeding at night. Pupa in soil sometimes overwinters twice.

Hedge Rustic *Tholera cespitis* Schiff.

Des: forewing c.1.5 cm. Forewings dark, dull brown or blackish, stigmata and crosslines edged with whitish. Hindwings of male white, brown in female. **H:** meadows and pastures, heaths and moors, sea coasts, gardens. **Dis:** local in Europe in mountains to 1,600 m. Mainland Britain, Hebrides, Ireland. **A:** moderately common. **Fl:** August and September. **LC:** overwinters as an egg; caterpillars March to July. **FP:** mat-grass (*Deschampsia*) and other grasses.

Pine Beauty *Panolis flammea* Schiff.

Des: forewing 1.2–1.6 cm; variable pattern of orange, grey, red and white; pale stigmata usually well-developed, with reniform extended to a point. Hindwings dark grey-black. **H:** coniferous woodland, especially pine plantations. **Dis:** pinewoods throughout Europe, to 1,700 m in mountains; in suitable habitat through Britain and Ireland. **A:** has increased as a result of pine planting and can be a serious pest. **Fl:** March to early June. **LC:** caterpillars May to July, green, striped white and difficult to see among pine needles. **FP:** species of pine.

171

Powdered Quaker
Orthosia gracilis Schiff.

Des: forewing 1.4–1.8 cm. Typically pale whitish straw colour, slightly greyer in south Europe; in bogs containing bog myrtle in different parts of Britain extraordinary red-brown, and highly variable populations occur. Pointed tip of forewing helps distinguish Powdered Quaker from related species. **H:** low-lying ground, meadows, marshes, and bogs. **Dis:** widespread in Europe, including Britain and Ireland. **A:** locally common. **Fl:** March to May. Visits sallow catkins. Caterpillars May to July, concealed in spun leaves by day and feeding at night. Pupa overwinters. **FP:** favours sallow, meadowsweet, yellow loosestrife, purple loosestrife, and bog myrtle.

Common Quaker
Orthosis stabilis Schiff.

Des: forewing c.1.5 cm. Varies in colour from light greyish-brown to dark brown or brick-red. Stigmata palely outlined; crosslines often absent except for pale, evenly curved outer line; pale veins in marginal area. **H:** woodlands, parks, gardens. **Dis:** widespread through Europe, Britain and Ireland. In Alps to 2,000 m. **A:** common. **Fl:** March to May. **LC:** caterpillars in May and June. **FP:** sallow, oak, elm, and other deciduous trees.

Twin-spotted Quaker
Orthosia munda Schiff.

Des: same size as preceding, forewings ochreous to reddish-brown. Reniform stigma with dark lower half. Outer line with two black spots just above middle, sometimes more, occasionally none. **H:** deciduous woodland. **Dis:** widespread but local. Widespread in England and Wales, local in Scotland and Ireland. **A:** fairly common. **Fl:** March to May. **LC:** caterpillars May to July. **FP:** sallow, oak elm, aspen, preferring young or coppiced trees.

Lead-coloured Drab
Orthosia populeti F.

Des: forewings c.1.5 cm long, leaden grey, often with purplish tone, indistinct markings except for two black dots in outer crossline near wing-tip. Characteristically rounded tips. ♂ with rather strongly feathered antennae. **H:** woodlands and valleys with poplar and aspen. **Dis:** central Europe to Asia. Chiefly in southern half of England, Wales, and isolated populations in Scottish Highlands. Absent from Ireland. **A:** locally common. **Fl:** March to May. **LC:** Caterpillars between spun leaves. **FP:** chiefly aspen.

G: *Orthosia* species are among the first noctuids to emerge in spring. They have lain fully developed in pupa all winter, so can hatch as soon as weather favourable. Most species occur in abundance at sallow catkins, arriving soon after dusk.

Clouded Drab *Orthosia incerta* Hufn.

Des: forewings 1.5–1.8 cm long, extremely variable in colour from light grey through shades of brown and reddish-brown to black; lighter forms marbled darker. Reniform and orbicular stigmata pale-outlined, and pale, wavy outer line. Tip of forewing squarer than in related species. **H:** generally distributed in woodland, parks, and more open country. **Dis:** throughout Europe, to 2,000 m in mountains, Britain and Ireland. **A:** common. **Fl:** March to May. **LC:** caterpillars May and June. **FP:** on numerous trees and shrubs, especially sallow and oak.

Hebrew Character
Orthosia gothica L.

Slightly smaller than preceding species, especially towards north of its range. Forewings greyish- or reddish-brown, often with golden wash. Irregular black 'C' mark surrounding orbicular stigma is characteristic, but in *ab. gothicina* H.-S. it is same colour as rest of wing. Variable, especially in Scotland. **H:** generally distributed. **Dis:** Eurasiatic, in Europe reaching Arctic and above 2,000 m in Alps. Britain to Orkneys, Ireland. **A:** common. **Fl:** March to May. **LC:** caterpillars May and June. **FP:** polyphagous, preferring deciduous trees but also on herbaceous plants.

Brown-line Bright-eye
Mythimna conigera Schiff.

Des: forewings 1.5–1.7 cm long and pale golden-brown to brownish-orange. Dark inner crossline sharply angled, outer curved; lower part of reniform stigma contains a clear white spot. **H:** open woodland, pastures, meadows, gardens. **Dis:** Europe, to 2,000 m in mountains; most of Britain and Ireland. **A:** common. **Fl:** June to mid-August. **LC:** caterpillars hibernate when small and feed up quickly in spring. **FP:** grasses.

White-point
Mythimna albipuncta Schiff.

Des: forewing length 1.5–1.8 cm. Reddish-brown to grey with reddish tinge. Sharply-defined white dot in centre of wing (in similar Clay, *Mythimna ferrago* F., lower part of dot is blurred). **H:** woodland margins, dry slopes and pastures. Migrant to Britain, periodically established on shingle o dunes. **Dis:** Europe; apparently spreading northwards. Chiefly migratory to south and south-eas England. **A:** common in south Europe. **Fl:** April to October; in Britain mostly in autumn. **LC:** in wild apparently unknown; in captivity, can be reared ir an incubator in two to three months. **FP:** grasses.

White-speck
Mythimna unipuncta Haw.

Des: long, narrow forewing c.2 cm long, light brown to reddish brown; oblique dark line in apex of wing and small white dot in centre; hindwings rather pearly grey with dark veins. **H:** widespread; in Britain, strongly migratory and established on sheltered southern sea coasts. **Dis:** occurs nearly all over world: Army Worm of America. **Fl:** almost throughout year; in Britain, numbers peak in autumn. **LC:** continuously-brooded in many parts of world; can be reared in captivity in about seven to eight weeks. A pest in some countries, on maize, etc. **FP:** grasses, including crops.

Smoky Wainscot
Mythimna impura Hübn.

Des: forewings 1.4–1.6 cm long, pale, straw-coloured, with pale veins, and small black discal spot. Distinguished from similar Common Wainscot (*Mythimna pallens* L.) by dark edge to white vein from wing-root, presence of blackish dots in position of postmedian line and dark hindwings. **H:** meadows and marshes, other grassy places. **Dis:** Europe, Asia and North America; throughout Britain to south Shetland; Ireland. **A:** common. **Fl:** mainly single-brooded in Britain, in June and July. **LC:** caterpillars nocturnal, hibernating when small and pupating in May. **FP:** grasses.

White L Wainscot
Mythimna l-album L.

Des: forewing 1.5–1.6 cm. Pale olive-yellow with weak dark streaks and very conspicuous white L-shaped streak in centre of wing; pale diagonal stripe into apex of wing not always well-developed. ♂ has black tuft of hair-scales at base of abdomen. **H:** grassland. **Dis:** widespread; rare migrant to Britain which has recently become established along south-west coast. **A:** common. **Fl:** two generations, the autumn one is commoner. **LC:** caterpillars July, and October to May, hibernating. Easily forced. **FP:** grasses.

Bird's Wing *Dipterygia scabriuscula* L.

Des: forewing 1.5–1.7 cm. Forewings blackish-brown with indistinct markings, except for pale area in outer angle separated from rest of wing by a wavy line. Stigmata and crosslines outlined intense black. Hindwings brown. **H:** woodlands and pastures, gardens. **Dis:** Europe, to 1,500 m in mountains; Wales and southern half of England. **A:** fairly common but local. **Fl:** May to July, with occasional partial second generation. Caterpillars in autumn; winter spent as pupa. **FP:** sorrel, knotgrass, dandelion, and other herbaceous plants.

Copper Underwing and Svensson's Copper Underwing

Amphipyra pyramidea L. and
A. berbera svenssoni Fletcher

Des: European 'Copper Underwing' recently shown to be two very similar species, differing chiefly in structure of genitalia and details of markings of underside. Forewing length 2.0–2.5 cm in both species, brown, with small orbicular and reniform stigmata and dentate crosslines. Hindwings in both species copper-coloured. The specimen illustrated is probably *A. berbera svenssoni*. **H:** woodlands, parks, gardens. **Dis:** both species widespread in Europe; in Britain, both occur in England and Wales, with a few records of each from Scotland, but so far only *A. pyramidea* reported from Ireland.

The Olive *Ipimorpha subtusa* Schiff.

Des: forewing 1.2–1.4 cm, light brownish grey. The three stigmata same colour as rest of wing, but pale-outlined; two pale crosslines nearly straight, converge towards trailing edge. Similar Double Kidney (*I. retusa* L.) darker brown, forewing distinctly indented below tip, crosslines parallel. **H:** meadows, river valleys. **Dis:** Europe, chiefly in wetlands but to 1,600 m in Alps. Local in Britain and Ireland. **A:** fairly common. **Fl:** July to September. **LC:** egg overwinters. Caterpillars April and May in spun leaves. **FP:** aspen and poplars.

Brown Rustic *Rusina ferruginea* Esp.

Des: forewing c.1.5 cm. ♂ broader-winged than ♀, more strongly patterned and with strongly feathered antennae. **H:** woodland, downs, moors, parks and gardens. **Dis:** widespread in temperate Europe, to above 1,600 m in mountains. Through much of Britain and Ireland. **A:** common. **Fl:** June and July. **LC:** caterpillar overwinters nearly full-grown. **FP:** herbaceous plants such as dock.

Mouse Moth

Amphipyra tragopoginis Clerck

Des: forewing length 1.5–1.7 cm. Structure and behaviour similar to that of the copper underwings but smaller; forewings grey-brown, shiny, with three small black spots near centre of wing, two in the reniform stigma and one in the orbicular. Hindwings light greyish-brown. **H:** widespread in woods, fens and marshes, dunes, moors, parks and gardens. **Dis:** widespread in temperate Europe including Britain and Ireland. **A:** common. **Fl:** mid-July to late October. **LC:** overwinters as egg, caterpillars from April to June. **FP:** polyphagous on many herbs and shrubs.

Old Lady *Mormo maura* L.

Des: very large species, with forewing 3.0–3.8 cm. Margins of wings serrated; central area of forewing often darker than rest of wing; elaborate pattern of pale markings. **H:** woodlands and river valleys; roosts by day, often in groups, under river bridges and in houses and sheds. **Dis:** widespread in Europe including Britain and Ireland. **A:** fairly common, but evidently decreased. **Fl:** July and August. **LC:** overwinters as small caterpillar, which feeds up in spring on variety of trees and shrubs, especially blackthorn, hawthorn, and sallow.

Orache Moth *Trachea atriplicis* L.

Des: forewings c.2 cm long. Forewings brown and green, when fresh suffused purple; elongated white patch below stigmata, sometimes filled pink. Reniform and orbicular stigmata with pale outlines. **H:** damp woodlands, wooded valleys, marshes; somewhat migratory. **Dis:** temperate Europe, to 1,800 m in mountains. Extinct as a breeding species in Britain, but recently a few migrants have been recorded. **A:** fairly common in mainland Europe. **Fl:** May to October in two overlapping broods. **LC:** two generations of caterpillars in summer and autumn; overwinters as a pupa. **FP:** goosefoot orache and possibly other herbaceous plants.

Red Sword-grass
Xylena vetusta Hübn.

Des: forewings 2.5–2.8 cm long, wood-brown mixed with lighter colour; reniform stigma well developed, and black streak extends from this to outermost crossline. Hindwings brown. **H:** damp woodland, moors and bogs, waste ground. **Dis:** through Europe, including Britain and Ireland. Extends to Lapland, and to 2,000 m in mountains. **A:** commoner in north of Britain. **Fl:** August to May, moth hibernates. At rest it resembles a splinter of wood, wings pleated longitudinally. **LC:** moths pair in spring after visiting sallow bloom; many eggs laid; caterpillars May to July. **FP:** dock, yellow iris, bog myrtle, sedges, etc. Easy to rear.

Sword-grass *Xylena exsoleta* L.

Des: slightly larger than Red Sword-grass, usuall greyer, orbicular as well as reniform stigma usuall well defined. Best distinguishing mark, however ' pale straw-coloured hind tarsus in this specie (dark red-brown in Red Sword-grass). **H:** ope woodland, moors. **Dis:** through Europe, rarer i south; to 2,000 m in mountains. Decreased in Bri ain and now chiefly in north Britain and north-wes Ireland. **A:** locally common. **Fl:** September to Ma hibernating as adult. Camouflaged like Red Sword grass (see illustration) and visits ivy bloom i autumn and sallow catkins in spring. **LC:** similar t that of Red Sword-grass, but usually a difficu species to rear. **FP:** variety of herbaceous plants.

Small Angle Shades
Euplexia lucipara L.

Des: forewings 1.4–1.6 cm long; dark sienna brown with reddish or purplish sheen. Central field often black; orbicular stigma dark, usually indistinct, but reniform is bright metallic yellow. **H:** occurs in wide variety of habitats, including woodland, meadows, pastures, gardens and parks. **Dis:** throughout Europe; to 1,500 m in mountains. Britain to Orkneys, and Ireland. **A:** common. **Fl:** normally single-brooded in Britain, in June and July; occasional partial second generation. **LC:** caterpillars in August and September, on bracken, other ferns and a variety of other plants. Winter spent as a pupa.

Burren Green *Calamia tridens* Hufn.

Des: forewing length 1.6–2.0 cm. When fresh forewings are deep malachite-green, but they fac to pale green or yellowish. Small, white reniform stigma. Hindwings light grey. **H:** sunny slopes wasteland with sparse vegetation, margins of mea dows or tracks. **Dis:** widespread through tempera Europe, to 1,800 cm in mountains. Not in Britai but common in Co. Clare. **A:** fairly common. **Fl** July to September. **LC:** egg overwinters. Cate pillars May and June. **FP:** various grasses.

Dark Spectacle *Abrostola trigemina* Werneb.

Description: forewing c. 1.5 cm. Dark brown to blackish-brown; basal area pale reddish-brown; stigmata clearly outlined; first crossline strongly curved, outlining pale basal patch; outer line with S-shaped curve ñear trailing edge. Only other British species liable to be confused with Dark Spectacle is Spectacle (*Abrostola triplasia* ʟ) which is more grey-and-white, but two other very similar species occur in Europe. On front of thorax is a pale, double, dark-rimmed mark like a pair of spectacles.
Habitat: widespread, but shows a preference for damp areas.

Distribution: Eurasiatic; in mountains to 2,000 r More common in western parts of Britain, an Ireland.
Abundance: fairly common; rare in easter Britain.
Flight: regularly double-brooded on Continer but normally only one in Britain, in June and July.
Life Cycle: caterpillars variable in colour, fro green to dark brown. Overwinters as pupa.
Foodplants: stinging nettle and hop.

Angle Shades *Phlogophora meticulosa* L.

Description: forewings 2.2–2.5 cm long, straw-yellow to olive brown. The inner and outer crosslines approximate at the trailing edge of the wing, enclosing a darker-coloured triangle, which in turn contains the reniform and orbicular stigmata; these touch dorsally, forming a thick V-shaped marking. Outer margin of wing toothed. Hindwings pale with discal spot and two transverse lines. Thorax strongly crested. When at rest (see illustration), the forewings are pleated.

Habitat: widely and generally distributed; migratory.

Distribution: resident population of norther Europe reinforced annually by migration fror south. In Alps to 2,000 m. Throughout Britain t Orkneys; Ireland.

Abundance: common, sometimes exceedingly sc

Flight: in Britain, chiefly May to October, bt reported every month of year. Frequently found a rest on fences, foliage, etc. Comes freely to suga and flowers such as ivy.

Life Cycle: caterpillars can be found at any time c year, including mild winter nights. Winter caterpi lars produce spring moths which in turn produce a least one further brood during summer and autumn

Foodplants: wide variety of wild and cultivate plants: stinging nettle, dock, deadnettle, cranesbil raspberry, bindweed, willow, bracken, etc.

Staurophora celsia L.

Description: forewing 1.8–2.0 cm. Cannot possibly be confused with any other moth: forewings malachite green with irregular brown bar across middle, and other brown markings along termen. Thorax similarly marked green and brown. Hindwings light brown.

Habitat: sandy and limestone soils, in mixed coniferous and mixed deciduous woodland, particularly along margins, in rides and clearings. Also on heaths and moors, less commonly in pastures, gardens and parks.

Distribution: isolated populations in Europe and Asia; in central Europe, particularly plentiful on Lüneburg Heath, north Denmark, Mark Brander burg, rarer in Bavaria, in Alpine valleys and easter Hungary. Up to 64°N. Absent from Britain.

Abundance: local and rare, commoner towarc north of its range.

Flight: early September to early October.

Life cycle: Round, pale yellow eggs deposited ⁊ grass and overwinter. Caterpillars do not hatch unt June. They are translucent whitish-yellow, and liv in clumps of grass among the roots, where the pupate in a flimsy cocoon. Pupa has four conspicu ous spines at tip of abdomen.

Foodplants: species of grass.

181

Angle-striped Sallow
Enargia paleacea Esp.

Des: forewing c. 2 cm. Forewings yellow to orange-yellow; reniform and orbicular stigmata narrowly outlined, former with dark spot in lower half; three fine crosslines, second (antemedian) strongly angled; row of small dots along margin of wing. Hindwings whitish. **H:** mature birch woodland, heaths and moors with birch; mixed deciduous woodland. **Dis:** northern and central Europe, including England and Scotland, and west Siberia. Occasional immigrant to southern England and Wales. **A:** locally common. **Fl:** June to September. **LC:** egg overwinters. Caterpillars from late April to June, in spun leaves of birch. **FP:** silver birch and downy birch.

Dun-bar *Cosmia trapezina* L.

Des: forewings 1.4–1.6 cm long, yellowish-brown to ochre, sometimes coppery-red or even bright red; rare form blackish, or with blackish central band. Characteristic features are two crosslines, inner straight, outer bent, and dark spot in reniform stigma. Hindwings greyish. **H:** mixed deciduous woodland, parkland, even city centres where there are trees. **Dis:** Europe to Arctic Circle, including Britain and Ireland. **A:** populations fluctuate, but often common. **Fl:** June to September. **LC:** egg overwinters. Caterpillars May and June. Pupa in cocoon on ground. **FP:** broad-leaved trees. The caterpillar is also a notorious cannibal, feeding particularly on caterpillars of Winter Moth (*Operophtera brumata* L. (see page 219).

Auchmis detersa Esp.

Des: forewings 1.8–2.2 cm long, light grey, streaked darker; long black streak from wing-root and another in angle of wing. Orbicular and reniform stigmata outlined darker. **H:** warm hillsides and mountains, field verges, depending on presence of foodplant. **Dis:** widespread; in mountains to 2,000 m. Does not occur in Britain. **A:** common in south of range, rare in north. **Fl:** late June to September. **LC:** caterpillars from September to May, hibernating. **FP:** exclusively barberry (*Berberis vulgaris*).

Dingy Shears *Enargia ypsillon* Schiff.

Des: forewings c. 1.7 cm long, grey to dark greyish brown, often with mauve sheen when fresh. Orbicular and reniform stigma outlined whitish with dark area between. Claviform stigma present. Crosslines indistinct except for pale, wavy, outermost line. **H:** water meads, river and stream banks, marshes. **Dis:** temperate Europe, absent from mountains. Widespread in Britain, very local in Ireland. **A:** locally common. **Fl:** June to August. **LC:** egg overwinters. Caterpillars May and June feed at night and rest in numbers under loose bark at tree bases during day. Pupa in soil. **FP:** mainly on long-leaved species of willow, sometimes poplar.

Lunar-spotted Pinion
Cosmia pyralina Schiff.

Des: about same size as Dun-bar, but much darker brown to reddish-brown or violet-brown. Outer transverse line is edged white on outer side or leading edge of wing. Hindwings lighter brown with pale fringe. **H:** dry mixed deciduous woodland, gardens and orchards. **Dis:** central Europe, up to 1,600 m in mountains. In southern Britain only. **A:** locally common. **Fl:** June to August. **LC:** egg overwinters; caterpillars in May. **FP:** elm, wych elm, other deciduous trees including apple.

Purple Cloud
Actinotia polyodon Clerck

Des: forewings 1.3–1.5 cm, brown and creamy-brown with violet tinge; reniform stigma large and conspicuous, orbicular stigma absent. Deeply serrated outermost crossline, and other crosslines absent. **H:** warm deciduous woodland, clearings, hillsides. **Dis:** throughout central Europe extremely rare immigrant to Britain. Up to 1,500 m in mountains. **A:** local, sometimes fairly common **Fl:** May and June, second generation in south Europe. **LC:** caterpillars July and August. Pupa overwinters. **FP:** flowers and seeds of St. John's wort; milk vetch also given as a foodplant.

183

Dark Arches
Apamea monoglypha Hufn.

Des: forewing length 2.2–2.4 cm. Large, powerful species with irregular pattern on brown forewings which contrasts clearly with ground colour. Only in very dark specimens (*ab. aethiops* Tutt.) is the pattern lost. Reniform and orbicular stigmata large, latter obliquely set. Outermost crossline strongly toothed. **H:** generally distributed; on moorlands in north. **Dis:** throughout Europe, including Britain to Shetlands, Ireland. Up to above 2,500 m in mountains. **A:** common everywhere. **Fl:** June to September, sometimes small second brood into October. **LC:** caterpillar feeds from August to June; subterranean. **FP:** roots and stem bases of grasses.

Clouded-bordered Brindle
Apamea crenata Hufn.

Des: forewing length 1.6–2.0 cm. Extremely va able, but characteristic 'jizz' facilitates identi cation. May be white, lilac, grey or brown, wh usually also strongly patterned; very dark bric red (illustrated) or blackish specimens have visit pattern reduced to pale outlines of reniform a. orbicular stigmata. **H:** woodland, fens and marshe downs, heaths and moors, etc. **Dis:** throughc Europe, including Britain and Ireland. To 2,000 in mountains. **A:** common. **Fl:** May to August. **L** caterpillars from August to May; subterranean. **F** roots and stem-bases of grasses.

Rustic Shoulder-knot
Apamea sordens Hufn.

Des: forewing length 1.5–1.8 cm. Forewing ground colour light reddish-brown or ochreous-grey, somewhat mottled. Stigmata and crosslines rather faint, but wavy black basal streak is a conspicuous feature. **H:** pastures, mixed woodlands and parks. **Dis:** through Europe, to 1,500 m in mountains. Widespread in Britain and Ireland. **A:** common. **Fl:** May and June, later in parts of Europe. **LC:** caterpillar overwinters, feeding slowly. Subterranean. **FP:** wild grasses and cereals.

Marbled Minor *Oligia strigilis* L.

Des: forewings 1.1–1.3 cm. Dark brown or blac ish, often with greyish-white outer area of forewin Stigmata and crosslines well developed on pal forms but obscured in black ones. In forms w. white outer region, a constant feature is a shc black projection into the pale area from the out crossline, close to the trailing edge of the win **H:** generally distributed in grassy places. **Di** throughout Europe, to 1,500 m in mountain Widespread in England and Wales, less so in Scc land; status in Ireland uncertain. **A:** general common. **Fl:** late May to July. **LC:** caterpillar liv inside stems of robust grasses, where it probab overwinters. **FP:** grasses such as cock's foot ar reed canary grass.

Rufous Minor *Oligia versicolor* Borkh.

Des: very similar to Marbled Minor and distinguished for certain only by examination of genitalia. Very slightly smaller, frequently with clear, round, pale orbicular stigma and bright vinous-red tint. Black projection on outer crossline absent. **H:** deciduous woodland and open, grassy places such as sea cliffs. **Dis:** widely distributed. In Britain, to southern Scotland; Ireland. **A:** apparently the commonest minor in parts of central and south Europe, locally common in Britain. **Fl:** June to August. **LC:** apparrently unknown, but probably similar to that of Marbled Minor.

Tawny Marbled Minor
Oligia latruncula Schiff.

Des: very similar to the two preceding specie often dark-coloured, with distinct coppery tint outer area of forewing, but examination of genital only positive means of identification. **H:** grasslar of all kinds. **Dis:** temperate Europe to 2,000 m mountains. Widespread in Britain and Ireland. **A** common. **LC:** caterpillar full-grown in spring; feec internally. **FP:** grasses.

Common Rustic *Mesapamea secalis* L. and Lesser Common Rustic *Mesapamea didyma* Esp.

Des: forewings 1.2–1.5 cm long. The highly polymorphic species known as the Common Rustic has recently been shown to be two species, each one variable, only separable by examination of the genitalia. It appears that several of the forms, or 'morphs', occur in both species. A third species has also been described, but some experts believe that it is probably a hybrid between the other two. Both the Common Rustic and the Lesser Common Rustic inhabit open woodland and grassy places. They appear to be widespread in Europe and to occupy the same ground, in many places being equally common. Both occur in Britain.

Rosy Rustic *Hydraecia micacea* Esp.

Des: forewings 1.4–2.0 cm long, light brown, yellowish or reddish, with stigmata, crosslines, and veins darker. Hindwings paler with light band. **H:** damp meadows, farmland, waste ground. **Dis:** Europe to 800 m altitude. In Britain to Shetlands, Ireland. **A:** common. **Fl:** July to October. **LC:** overwinters in egg stage. Caterpillars on roots. **FP:** roots of dock, burdock, etc.

Saltern Ear *Amphipoea fucosa* Freyer

Des: this species is one of another group of moths, the 'ears', which can only be identified with certainty by examining the genitalia. All are medium-sized noctuids with rather narrow, square tipped wings, with several fine, wavy crosslines and a conspicuously ear-shaped reniform stigma. All four species are variable in colour and intensity of markings.

In Europe, *Amphipoea fucosa* occurs in pasture and clearings in pine forests, but *A. fucosa paludis* Tutt, the sub-species which is found in Britain, is chiefly an insect of salt-marshes. The Ear Moth (*Amphipoea oculea* L) is the only other species to occur in south England, but in the north and west of Britain, all four species may occur and the identification problem becomes difficult.

Frosted Orange *Gortyna flavago* Schiff.

Des: forewing length 1.5–1.8 cm. Golden-orange, freckled rust, with dark outer and basal areas of forewing, dark veins and conspicuously outlined stigmata. **H:** marshy places, pastures, clearings, gardens. **Dis:** temperate Europe, to 1,400 m. Britain and Ireland. **A:** locally common. **Fl:** late August to October. **LC:** overwinters as egg. Caterpillars in lower stems of various herbaceous plants. **FP** favours burdock, thistles, foxglove, but occurs in other thick-stemmed herbaceous plants.

Treble-lines *Charanyca trigrammica* Hufn.

Des: forewing length c.1.5 cm. Ochre-brown to greyish-yellow forewings with three, occasionally four, slender crosslines. Dark form occurs in which crosslines paler than ground colour. **H:** widespread, open woodland, grassy places, waste ground. **Dis:** through Europe, to 1,000 m altitude; Britain and Ireland. **A:** common. **Fl:** early May to mid-July. **LC:** caterpillars June to April, feeding slowly through winter. **FP:** polyphagous on herbaceous plants and their roots.

Pale Mottled Willow *Caradrina clavipalpis* Scop.

Des: forewings 1.2–1.4 cm long, light grey-brown to medium-brown. Reniform stigma surrounded by small white dots. Distinguished from related species by reddish-brown outermost line. Hind wings white. **H:** widespread. **Dis:** Europe to 2,000 m. Britain to Shetlands, Ireland. **A:** common. **Fl:** most months of year, commonest in summer, probably two broods. **LC:** caterpillars occur in autumn and spring. **FP:** seeds of plantain, grasses and cereal crops, before and after harvest. Moth used to be resident in coal mines, caterpillar feeding on fodder of pit ponies.

Vine's Rustic
Hoplodrina ambigua Schiff.

Des: forewing length c.1.2 cm. Light brown; orbicular and reniform stigmata always with fine, pale border. Hindwings whitish. **H:** sunny, dry places: wood margins, heathland, field verges, pastures and gardens. **Dis:** widespread in southern Europe. In Britain, well established in southern and south-east England, elsewhere casual migrant. **A:** locally abundant. **Fl:** May to July, and late July to October, in two generations. **LC:** caterpillars from second generation hibernate. **FP:** dandelion, plantain, sorrel, prickly lettuce, and other herbaceous plants.

Hoplodrina respersa Schiff.

Des: forewing length 1.2–1.4 cm. Ground-colour ash-grey, normal markings obscure, but crosslines represented by rows of transverse dots. Hindwings brown. **H:** dry slopes, grassland, heaths, dry fields, woodland, parks and gardens. **Dis:** across Europe, to 1,600 m in Alps. Absent in Britain. **A:** locally common, more so in south. **Fl:** early June to early August. **LC:** caterpillars August to May, hibernating. **FP:** plaintain, sorrel, dandelion, saxifrages.

Pale Pinion *Lithophane socia* Hufn.

Des: long, narrow forewings c.2 cm. When at rest, resembles a piece of wood, light brown to reddish brown in colour. Similar Tawny Pinion (*Lithophane semibrunnea* Haw) has narrower forewings, dark streak in wing angle and dark crests on thorax and abdomen. **H:** open woodland, dry slopes, and hillsides. **Dis:** widespread in central Europe, commoner in south. In Britain, chiefly in western England, Wales and Ireland. In mountains to 1,700 m. **A:** not very common. **Fl:** mid-August to late May, moth hibernating. **LC:** caterpillars April to July. **FP:** sallow and other deciduous trees, including fruit trees.

Conformist *Lithophane furcifera* Hufn.

Des: forewing length 1.8–2.0 cm. Dark grey with reddish tinge; blackish streak at base of wing and another below reniform and orbicular stigmata. Reniform large, reddish-brown in colour. Dark red-brown crests on abdomen (see Non-conformist *Lithophane lamda* F.) **H:** alder carr, river and stream banks, moors. **Dis:** through most of temperate Europe. In Britain, used to occur in south Wales and may still do so. To 1,800 m in mountains. **A:** locally fairly common. **Fl:** late August to mid-June, moth hibernates. **LC:** caterpillars late May to July. **FP:** chiefly alder, sometimes birch.

Non-conformist *Lithophane lamda* F.

Des: forewing length 1.4–1.8 cm. Variable; usually blue- or dark-grey with silky gloss; stigmata variably developed, but always strong, wavy, black basal streak, and two dark blocks in centre of wing. Hindwings brown. Lacks abdominal crests (see Conformist). **H:** carr woodland, boggy moors. **Dis:** mainly upland moors. **A:** very local and not common. **Fl:** end September to early June; moths hibernate. **LC:** caterpillars June and July. **FP:** bog myrtle, bog bilberry (*Vaccinium uliginosum*) and creeping willow.

Green-brindled Crescent
Allophyes oxyacanthae L.

Des: broad forewings 1.8–2.0 cm long, dark brown or grey, lighter along margins, and dusted with green. Orbicular and reniform stigmata large, pale brown; whitish crescent-mark in wing angle. Melanotic *ab. capucina* Mill. is frequent in parts of Britain. **H:** mixed deciduous woodland, pastures, gardens. **Dis:** widespread in temperate Europe; replaced by nearly identical looking *Allophyes alfaroi* Agenjo to south of Pyrenees. **F:** often common. **Fl:** late September to early November. **LC:** overwinters as egg; caterpillars April to June. **FP:** hawthorn and blackthorn, sometimes fruit trees.

189

Cucullia fraudatrix Evers.

Des: forewing length 1.5–1.8 cm. Forewings light grey to brown-grey, with strong pattern; orbicular and reniform stigmata clearly marked. Some specimens have black basal streak and a dark bar from outermost line to reniform stigma. Hindwings ·with darker border. **H:** very dry, warm localities: wasteland, hillsides, especially on sandy soil. **Dis:** an eastern European species which has spread westwards to Denmark. Not recorded in Britain. **A:** local, not common. **Fl:** July to mid-August. **LC:** caterpillars August to September. Pupa hibernates. **FP:** Mugwort (*Artemisia vulgaris*).

Scarce Wormwood Shark
Cucullia artemisiae Hufn.

Des: forewings 1.8–2.0 cm long, of typical shark moth shape, long, narrow and pointed; brown-grey or uniform grey, with clearly marked reniform and orbicular stigmata; series of black interneural spots along outer margin of wing. **H:** dry, sandy heaths, hillsides, wasteland. **Dis:** temperate Europe, with centre of distribution in north-east. Absent from north-western Germany, the Benelux countries and Britain (seven records). **A:** locally quite common. **Fl:** mid-June to end July. **LC:** caterpillars mid-July to September. Pupa hibernates. **FP:** mugwort, also camomile and tansy.

The Shark *Cucullia umbratica* L.

Des: forewings 2.1–2.5 cm long, ash-grey with weak brownish tint. Brown streak in centre of forewing and dark streaks along margin. Hindwings white with darker veins. **H:** waste ground, downs, marshes, shingle and dunes. **Dis:** throughout Europe, including Britain and Ireland. **A:** fairly common. **Fl:** mid-May to mid-August. Often seen at rest on fence posts. **LC:** caterpillars end June to mid-August. Pupa overwinters. **FP:** sow-thistle (*Sonchus* spp.), wild lettuce, hawkweeks, chicory.

Star-wort *Cucullia asteris* Schiff.

Des: forewings light grey or violet-grey, c. 2 cm long. Orbicular and reniform stigmata fairly distinct crescent-mark and dark patch in angle of wing. **H:** woodland rides and clearings, and salt marshes. **Dis:** widespread in Europe, including England and Wales. In Alps to 1,500 m. **A:** moth rather rarely seen, caterpillars often common. **Fl:** June and July. **LC:** two distinct habitats in Britain, open woodland where caterpillars feed on golden-rod, and salt marshes where foodplant is sea aster. Caterpillars July and August. Pupa hibernates.

Mullein Moth *Cucullia verbasci* L.

Des: forewing length 1.8–2.2 cm. Bi-coloured dark and light brown forewing, edges darker than centre. Double crescent-mark midway along trailing edge. Very similar to several other European shark moths. **H:** dry waysides, downs, clearings in woods, gardens. **Dis:** central Europe, to 1,600 m in Alps. Also, England, Wales and south Ireland. **A:** caterpillars seen more often than moth. **Fl:** April to mid-June. **LC:** gaudy blue-green, yellow and black caterpillars May to July. **FP:** flowers and leaves of mullein species.

Sprawler *Brachionycha sphinx* Hufn.

Des: forewings 1.9–2.1 cm long, ash-grey or brown-grey, with distinct black basal streak and other dark streaks. Hindwings grey-white in Continental specimens, brown in British ones. ♂ has feathered antennae, ♀ has not. **H:** deciduous woodland. **Dis:** Europe, including England and Wales; local in Ireland. **A:** locally common. **Fl:** November and December in Britain, earlier on Continent. **LC:** overwinters in egg stage. Caterpillars May – June. **FP:** deciduous trees such as lime, oak, beech, elm, sallow.

Merveille du Jour *Dichonia aprilina* L.

Des: forewing c. 2 cm. Forewings dark moss green, fading to yellowish; stigmata inconspicuous amongst striking black pattern, which may almost cover the wings. Hindwings grey, with darker crosslines and black-and-white patterned border. **H:** dry mixed woodlands, parkland, pastures with isolated trees. **Dis:** widespread in temperate Europe, including Britain and Ireland. **Dis:** locally common; commoner in south Britain. **Fl:** late August to November, not before October in England. **LC:** egg hibernates; caterpillars May and June, rest in bark crevices by day and feed at night. **FP:** mature oaks.

Frosted Green
Dryobotodes eremita F.

Des: forewings c. 1.5 cm; vary in colour from light brown to grey to dark grey-black, with green suffusion. Pattern blurred. Hindwings grey. **H:** dry oak and mixed woodlands, avenues, old gardens and parks. **Dis:** throughout Europe, including Britain and Ireland. **A:** locally fairly common. **Fl** August to October. **LC:** egg overwinters. Caterpillars April to June, at first inside oak bud, later in spun shoots. **FP:** mature oaks.

Dark Brocade *Blepharita adusta* Esp.

Des: forewings 1.8–2.9 cm, grey-brown to dark reddish-brown or nearly black; stigmata variably conspicuous, reniform usually containing some white; dark bar below the two stigmata. Hindwings whitish in ♂, darker in ♀. **H:** woods, heaths and moors, downland. **Dis:** widespread in Europe to 70°N and 2,000 m in Alps; Britain and Ireland. **F:** often common, but has decreased in southern England. **Fl:** May to August in one extended generation. **LC:** caterpillars full-fed August; spend winter in cocoon in which they pupate in April. Difficult to breed successfully. **FP:** polyphagous: bog myrtle, sallow, alder, hawthorn and various herbaceous plants.

Satellite *Eupsilia transversa* Hufn.

Des: forewing 1.8–2.0 cm. Red-brown or grey-brown; in reniform stigma is a round white or yellow spot with two adjacent 'satellites'. **H:** generally distributed, chiefly in woods in southern Britain and moors in north. **Dis:** throughout Europe including Britain and Ireland. **A:** common. **Fl** September to May, hibernating, but active on mild winter nights. Visits sallow bloom in spring. **LC** caterpillars May and June. **FP:** various deciduous trees, also cannibalistic.

Chestnut *Conistra vaccinii* L.

Des: forewing 1.4–1.6 cm. Ochre-yellow, through shades of red-brown to blackish, plain or variegated. Dark spot in reniform stigma frequent feature. Outer margin rounded, not concave near apex as in Dark Chesnut (*Conistra ligula* Esp.). **H:** mixed deciduous woodland. **Dis:** throughout Europe, to 2,000 m in Alps. Britain and Ireland. **A:** common to abundant. **Fl:** September to May, hibernating; moths visit ivy bloom in autumn and sallow in spring. **LC:** caterpillars April to July, remain some weeks in cocoon before pupating. **FP:** buds and catkins of trees at first, later herbaceous plants.

Conistra rubiginosa Scop.

Des: forewing 1.5–1.8 cm. Grey to reddish-brown with characteristic black patches in stigmata (see illustration). Hindwings paler. **H:** mixed woodlands, pastures, hillsides, gardens. **Dis:** warmer parts of Europe; reaches Denmark, but not Britain. **A:** locally fairly common. **Fl:** late August to late April, moth hibernates. **LC:** April to June. **FP** initially buds of deciduous trees, later herbaceous plants.

Red-headed Chestnut
Conistra erythrocephala Schiff.

Des: forewing 1.3–1.8 cm. Two common forms, one reddish-brown with three black dots in reniform stigma, the other variegated (*ab. glabra* Hübn) **H:** mixed woodland of oak and beech, also parks and wooded hillsides. **Dis:** widespread in Europe, but in Britain extremely rare – suspected immigrant which has been established for short periods. **A:** local, but fairly common; numbers said to fluctuate greatly. **Fl:** end September to May, moth hibernates. **LC:** caterpillars May and June. **FP:** oak, beech, elm, and herbaceous plants such as plantain and dandelion.

Dusky-lemon Sallow
Xanthia gilvago Schiff.

Des: forewings 1.6–1.8 cm, ochre-brown, sometimes redder or yellower, mottled darker. Round black spot in reniform stigma. **H:** wooded valleys, mixed deciduous woodland, parks with isolated elms, avenues. **H:** temperate Europe, including England, Wales and southern Scotland. **A:** local. **Fl:** September to November. Moth comes to ivy bloom and berries such as elder and yew. **LC:** eggs overwinter on twigs of foodplant. Caterpillars April to June. **FP:** flowers and seeds of wych elm, sometimes other elm species.

Flounced Chestnut
Agrochola helvola L.

Des: forewing 1.5–2.0 cm, more pointed at apex than in related species. Reddish brown with broad, purplish bands in basal and outer areas, and similarly coloured thorax. **H:** woodland, downs, and moors. **Dis:** Europe to 1,400 m; Britain and Ireland. **A:** usually common. **Fl:** September and October, moth comes to ripe blackberries and other fruit. **LC:** eggs overwinter; caterpillars April to June. **FP:** polyphagous on trees and herbaceous plants.

Brown-spot Pinion *Agrochola litura* L.

Des: forewing c.1.5 cm. Reddish or purplish-brown, sometimes with basal area pale grey. Stigmata with dark centres; conspicuous dark mark or leading edge at junction with outer crossline. **H:** woodland, heaths and commons, parks and gardens. **Dis:** widespread in Europe, including England, Wales and Scotland. **A:** common. **Fl:** August to October. **LC:** caterpillars April to June **FP:** herbaceous plants, also willow, blackthorn, broom, bilberry, and rose.

Red-line Quaker
Agrochola lota Clerck

Des: forewings c.1.5 cm grey to dark grey, often with reddish tint. Dark spot in lower half of reniform stigma, and red, yellow-edged outermost crossline. Hindwings grey-brown with pale fringe. **H:** woods, fens and marshes. **Dis:** widespread in Europe, including Britain and Ireland. **A:** common. **Fl:** September to November. **LC:** eggs overwinter. Caterpillars can be bred from fallen sallow catkins collected in spring. Rests in cocoon for several weeks before pupating. **FP:** willow and sallow.

Panthea coenobita Esp.

Des: forewing 2.0–2.5 cm, ♀ larger than ♂ Black-and-white colouring characteristic. Hindwings grey with dark patches; body blackish. **H:** coniferous woodlands and plantations. **Dis:** central and eastern Europe; not recorded in Britain. Mountains to 1,500 m. **A:** sometimes common. **Fl:** early May to early August. **LC:** caterpillars August to October. Pupa overwinters. **FP:** pine and spruce.

Agrochola macilenta

Pink-barred Sallow
Xanthia togata Esp.

Des: forewings c. 1.5 cm, bright yellow, marked with a broad, irregular, violet or brown-red band across the centre of each wing; several spots of the same colour and varying size along margins and leading edges. Front of thorax also this colour, distinguishing it from otherwise rather similar Sallow (*Xanthia icteritia* Hufn). **H:** damp woodland, fens and marshes. **Dis:** temperate and northern Europe, to 1,700 m in Alps. Britain to Orkneys, and Ireland. **A:** common. **Fl:** September and October, earlier on continent. **LC:** overwinters in egg stage; caterpillars March to early June, occur in sallow catkins. **FP:** sallow catkins and foliage, and herbaceous plants.

Pale-lemon Sallow
Xanthia ocellaris Borkh

Des: forewings c. 1.8 cm, reddish-yellow or reddish-grey; pattern indistinct, with small white dot in reniform stigma and pale veins. Hindwings white. A form, *ab gilvescens* Worsley-Wood, resembles Dusky-lemon Sallow but has more pointed apex of forewing. **H:** damp pastures and meadows with mature poplars. **Dis:** widely-distributed in Europe, occurring especially in larger wetlands. Only in south and east of England. **A:** locally common, especially as caterpillars. **Fl:** September and October. **LC:** egg overwinters; caterpillars can be obtained in numbers from fallen black poplar catkins, in spring. **FP:** black poplar, catkins and foliage, and herbaceous plants.

Bordered Sallow *Pyrrhia umbra* Hufn.

Des: forewings 1.4–1.6 cm, orange-yellow to yellow-brown; outer areas purplish; crosslines and outlines of stigmata reddish-brown. **H:** downs, sea coasts, meadows and lane verges. **Dis:** most of temperate Europe, including Britain and Ireland. **A:** uncommon in north, common south of Alps. **Fl:** June and July. **LC:** caterpillars July and August; pupa hibernates. **FP:** restharrow.

Sallow *Xanthia icteritia* Hufn.

Des: forewings 1.4–1.6 cm, bright yellow mixed with orange or rusty-red. Black spot with white centre in lower half of reniform stigma. Thorax all yellow. Hindwings whitish. **H:** damp woodland, fens and marshes. **Dis:** Europe to 1,800 m in mountains, Britain to Orkneys, Ireland. **A:** common **Fl:** September and October. **LC:** eggs overwinter caterpillars common in sallow catkins, March to May. **FP:** Sallow catkins and foliage, and herbaceous plants.

Xanthia fulvago Clerck

Des: forewing c.1.4 cm. Pale yellow, with narrow reddish-brown band across centre of forewings and similarly coloured outline of reniform stigmata Hindwings white or yellowish. **H:** dry, stony places quarries, cliffs, also parks. **Dis:** a warmth-loving species, more in south of Europe. **A:** local and rare north of Alps. **Fl:** September and October. **LC:** egg overwinters. Caterpillars May to mid-June. **FP** chiefly field maple, willow and birch.

Small Yellow Underwing
Panemeria tenebrata Scop.

Des: small noctuid with forewings c.0.7 cm. These are dark brown with coppery tinge and faint markings. Hindwings black with dark yellow central band. **H:** meadows, downs, dry, open woodland Alpine meadows, wasteland. **Dis:** widespread i Europe to 1,600 m altitude. Britain to south Scotland, western Ireland. **A:** fairly common, easil overlooked. **Fl:** April to June, diurnal. **LC:** caterpillars June and July. **FP:** mouse-ear chickweed.

197

The Flame *Axylia putris* L.

Des: forewings c.1.3 cm; straw-coloured, pattern resembling a piece of wood. Margin darkened, reniform stigma with dark brown centre, orbicular with brown border and centre. **H:** generally distributed, woods, pastures, parks, gardens. **Dis:** common. **Fl:** mid-May to early August. **LC:** caterpillars June to September; pupa overwinters. **FP:** polyphagous on herbaceous plants, including dock, dandelion, plantain, sandwort and grasses.

Poplar Grey
Acronicta megacephala Schiff.

Des: forewings c.2 cm, dark grey with coarse blackish dusting; light-coloured orbicular stigma with dark central area; pale zone beyond reniform stigma. Hindwings white with dark veins. **H:** meadows and pastures, poplar woods and avenues, parks and gardens. **Dis:** throughout Europe, including Britain and Ireland. **A:** common. **Fl:** May to August, partly double-brooded on Continent. **LC:** caterpillars of dagger sub-family unusual among noctuids in being hairy. Those of Poplar Grey occur July to September, and rest by day on leaves, bodies curled in shape of question mark. Pupa overwinters. **FP:** black poplar and aspen.

Scarce Dagger
Acronicta auricoma Schiff.

Des: resembles Knot Grass in size and general form, but forewings slightly paler grey and less coarsely marked, with conspicuous dark streak in angle of each wing. Hindwings paler brown. **H:** open woodland, downs, meadows. **Dis:** through central and southern Europe; resident in England during last century, now extremely scarce presumed immigrant. **A:** fairly common on continent. **Fl:** two generations, first May and June, second late summer. **LC:** caterpillars occur in June and September. **FP:** bramble, birch, oak and bilberry.

Figure of Eight
Diloba caeruleocephala L.

Des: true relationships of this species have alway puzzled entomologists: present views place it i its own family near the prominents. Forewing 1.5–2.0 cm, mottled red-brown, grey-brown an dark grey. Prominent thick, white outlines of ren form and orbicular stigmata make clear 88 mark o each wing. Hindwings whitish, with black apica patch and dark discal spot. **H:** woods, hedgerows orchards. **Dis:** widespread in Europe, includin Britain and Ireland. **A:** common in south, rathe rare in Scotland and Ireland. **Fl:** October and Nov ember. **LC:** gaudy blue and yellow caterpillars i May and June, Pupa in hard cocoon. **FP:** fru trees, blackthorn and hawthorn.

Knot Grass *Acronicta rumicis* L.

Des: forewings 1.4–1.8 cm, dark grey or blackish grey; pattern indistinct, but usually white patche on inner margin of outer crossline show clearl Dark streak in outer angle is absent in this specie distinguishing it from Scarce Dagger (*Acronic auricoma* Schiff). Hindwings brown. **H:** ope country, including cultivated areas, wastelan roadsides, open woodland, gardens. **Dis:** wide spread in Europe, including Britain and Ireland. **A** common. **Fl:** double-brooded on Continent and i southern England, in May and June, and July September. Elsewhere single-brooded, May to Jul **LC:** hairy caterpillars occur during summer ar autumn. **FP:** many low plants including planta and dock, and woody plants such as sallow ar hawthorn.

Miller *Acronicta leporina* L.

Des: forewing c.1.8 cm. Typical Continental for is strikingly pure white, with sparse blackish mar ings including basal streak and prominent ma from leading edge to inner edge of reniform stigm British form is thickly dusted with grey, and mo or less melanic examples occur in some place Hindwings white, with small dark dots round edg **H:** woods, heaths and commons. **Dis:** widesprea in Europe, reaching arctic Finland; through Brita and Ireland. **A:** fairly common. **Fl:** June to Augus **LC:** caterpillars greenish and very hairy, occur Ju – September. Pupate in rotten wood. **FP:** birc alder, sallow, oak and other trees.

Large Dagger *Acronicta cuspis* Hübn.

Des: forewings just under 2 cm. Very similar to Grey Dagger (*Acronicta psi* L) and Dark Dagger (*Acronicta tridens* Schiff.), but slightly more robust. Orbicular and reniform stigmata joined by a dark bar, and there is a black streak on front of thorax. Prominent black basal streak and 'dagger mark' in angle of wing, as in the other two species. **H:** dense, wet alder woods are preferred. **Dis:** local, but probably overlooked because of specialized habitat as well as resemblance to common species. **A:** locally not uncommon. **Fl:** June and July. **LC:** caterpillars resemble those of Grey Dagger, hairy with broad yellow stripe along back; hump near front of body is lower, hair-tuft arising from it is much longer. **FP:** alder.

Grey Dagger *Acronicta psi* L.

Des: forewings c.1.5 cm. Dark Dagger has 'cleaner' look and often faint mauve suffusion, but identification by examination of genitalia only certain means. Hindwings of ♂ Dark Dagger whiter than those of Grey Dagger. **H:** woods, orchards, hedgerows, gardens and parks. **Dis:** Europe, to 1,600 m in Alps. Britain to Hebrides, Ireland. **A:** common. **Fl:** June to August. **LC:** caterpillars characteristic, with broad yellow or whitish stripe along back, and humps on first and eighth abdominal segments, each with a tuft of hair. August to September. Pupa under bark, in rotten wood, or in soil. **FP:** birch, oak, cherry, hawthorn, blackthorn, and many other trees and shrubs.

Silver Barred *Deltote bankiana* F.

Des: forewings c.1 cm, olive brown with two straight, diagonal clear white crosslines. Hindwings pale greyish. Unmistakable. **H:** fens, bogs, damp woodland rides. **Dis:** widespread in Europe, extremely local in England and western Ireland. **A:** locally common. **Fl:** late May to late July. **LC:** caterpillars in August and September. **FP:** sedges and grasses.

Alder Moth *Acronicta alni* L.
Caterpillar – see page 276

Des: forewings 1.5–1.8 cm, typically greyish-brown with black zone across centre of wing and extending from base to angle along trailing half. Frequently, though, ground colour is brown or blackish (melanotic specimens). Hindwings white. **H:** woods and meadows. **Dis:** throughout Europe, commoner in south. Britain to Dumfries, Ireland. **A:** fairly common. **Fl:** mid-May and June. **LC:** young caterpillar resembles a bird dropping, before assuming spectacular black-and-yellow colour in last instar. Pupation in rotten wood.

Coronet *Craniophora ligustri* Schiff.

Des: forewing 1.5–1.8 cm. Very dark, sometimes with green tinge. In most common form, reniform stigma has pale outer border and a distinct white patch next to it, but in melanic forms the white is replaced by dark olive brown. **H:** woodland, fens, down, and commons. **Dis:** temperate Europe, only reaching 800 m in mountains. Britain and Ireland. **A:** common in Europe, local in Britain. **Fl:** June and July; double-brooded on Continent. **LC:** caterpillars thinly covered with short bristles, not densely hairy as in the true daggers. August and September in Britain. **FP:** ash and wild privet.

Chrystoptera c-aureum Knoch

Des: members of the plusia sub-family have variable metallic markings on parts of the forewings, produced not by pigments but by light reflection from specialized scales on the wings. In *Chrysoptera c-aureum* they occur towards the outer margin of the purplish brown wings. A small, golden c-mark on the reniform stigma. **H:** wetlands, fens, marshes, carr. **Dis:** local in Europe to south Scandinavia and Finland. Absent from Britain. **A:** numbers vary considerably. **Fl:** June to August. Caterpillars August to June, hibernating. **FP:** *Thalictrum* and *Aquilegia*.

Earias vernana Hübn.

Des: forewings just under 1 cm, whitish green with faint darker green crosslines. **H:** prefers warm, damp places in riverside woodlands, along banks of streams and isolated groves of white poplar. **H:** widespread but scattered in Europe. Not recorded in Britain. **A:** local and uncommon. **Fl:** two generations, first end April to mid-June, second June and July; Pupa hibernates. **FP:** white poplar.

Cream-bordered Green Pea
Earias clorana L.

Des: forewing length just under 1 cm, uniform bright green with narrow white leading edge and fringe. Hindwings white. **H:** fens and marshes, sallow thickets, even city parks. **Dis:** Europe to 64°N.; England, Clyde Valley in Scotland. One locality in southern Ireland. **A:** locally common. **Fl:** normally single-brooded in Britain, double brooded on Continent, in early and late summer. **LC:** caterpillars in spun shoots, July and August in Britain. **FP:** osier, sallow, and other species of *Salix*.

Green Silver-lines
Pseudoips fagana F.

Des: forewing about 1.5 cm. Green, with oblique silvery crosslines. In male, fringes red and hindwings yellow; in female, fringes yellowish and hindwings white. Antennae red. **H:** deciduous woodland. **Dis:** throughout temperate Europe, to 1,500 m in Alps. Britain and Ireland. **A:** common, but very local in south Scotland and Ireland. **Fl:** May to July, occasional second generation in south England. **LC:** caterpillars in autumn. **FP:** beech, oak and other trees.

Silver Y Autographa gamma L.

Des: forewings 1.6–2.0 cm, grey-brown to violet brown. Most conspicuous feature of complex pattern is gamma-mark in centre of wing, composed of metallic scales. A similar mark in this position is characteristic of several other species of plusia. **H:** chiefly open country. Highly migratory. **Dis:** throughout Europe, reaching tops of highest mountains. **A:** common to abundant, occurring over whole of Britain and Ireland during migrations. **Fl:** spring to late autumn in several generations. Moth easily disturbed by day, visit flowers at dusk and come freely to light. **LC:** caterpillars summer and autumn. Highly polyphagous. **FP:** large variety of wild and cultivated plants; occasionally a pest of peas and cabbages.

Plain Golden Y Autographa jota L.

Des: about same size as Silver Y, but forewings pale brownish purple; rather obscurely marked except for metallic golden Y-mark in centre of wing, which may take form of a 'v' and a dot. **H:** waysides, woods, commons, etc. **Dis:** widespread but rather local in Europe; throughout Britain to Orkneys and Ireland. **A:** locally common. **Fl:** June to August. **LC:** caterpillars August to may, hibernating. **FP:** stinging nettle, honeysuckle; will eat dock, sallow and hawthorn.

Beautiful Golden Y
Autographa pulchrina Haw.

Des: forewings more marbled than similar Plain Golden Y, especially in basal and terminal areas and reniform stigma outlined golden. Extremely similar to two newcomers to Europe which might reach Britain, *Autographa mandarina* Freyer and *A. buraetica* Stdgr., and rather dull-coloured specimens with complete, unbroken Y-mark are worth expert attention. **H:** woodlands, pastures, meadows and gardens. **Dis:** widespread in Europe. Britain to Shetlands, Ireland. **A:** common. **Fl:** June to August. **LC:** caterpillars August to May, hibernating. **FP:** polyphagous on herbaceous plants.

203

Gold Spangle
Autographa bractea Schiff.

Description: forewings c.2 cm, rich golden-brown with violet tinge. Large, lobed golden patch in centre of wing. Hindwings mid-brown, somewhat paler towards base. Can only be confused with Alpine *Autographa aemula* Schiff, which has distinct crosslines and dark patch towards tip of wing.

Habitat: damp areas, pastures, wet meadows, damp margins of mixed woodland, banks of streams and rivers. In Alps to 2,600 m.

Distribution: chiefly montane, but has shown recent spread into lowlands of north-west Europe and is now fairly frequently recorded in southern England. Widespread in Wales, north England, Scotland and Ireland.

Abundance: locally common in northern Britain and Ireland.

Flight: July and early August, double-brooded on Continent.

Life cycle: autumn caterpillars hibernate, and feed up until May. In parts of continental Europe, summer generation feeds up quickly in July and August.

Foodplants: herbaceous plants, including colts-foot, hawkweed, plantain, dock, stinging nettle.

Burnished Brass
Diachrysia chrysitis L.

Description: forewing 1.4–1.8 cm. Most of forewing golden- or greenish metallic, with dark-brown base and oblique band across middle of wing which encloses weakly outlined stigmata. Hindwings brown or brown-grey.

Habitat: wooded valleys, moorland, along rivers and streams, wasteland, lane verges, gardens and parks.

Distribution: throughout Europe to Arctic Circle. Britain to Orkneys, Ireland.

Abundance: common; comes freely to flowers at dusk, and to light.

Flight: two generations, first May to July, second late July to late September.

Life cycle: caterpillars in June and July, and autumn, hibernating and feeding up from spring to May.

Foodplants: stinging nettle, deadnettle, dandelion, plantain, and other herbs.

Dewick's Plusia
Macdunnoughia confusa Steph.

Description: forewing c.1.5 cm; rich olive-brown with darker central area bounded by two fine whitish lines, also containing arched silver-white metallic mark.

Habitat: warm, dry, sunny places along wood margins, hillsides, clearings and burnt areas, wooded valleys, heaths, occasionally in parks and gardens.

Distribution: resident only south of Alps, migrating northwards and sometimes reaching Britain. Small local populations may become established in northern parts of mainland Europe. In Alps up to about 1,200 m.

Abundance: variable, usually rare; fewer than 20 British records.

Flight: two generations, first May to July, second August to October. Moths fly by day as well as at night.

Life cycle: autumn caterpillars hibernate, summer generation feeds up quickly.

Foodplants: camomile, yarrow, bladder campion, field wormwood, and other herbs.

Scarce Burnished Brass
Diachrysia chryson Esp.

Description: forewing c.2 cm, dark to violet-brown, with large square, metallic golden patch in wing apex. Hindwing brown.

Habitat: wooded river valleys, marshes and fens.

Distribution: local in France, Germany, Belgium, Holland, and Denmark; in Alps to 1,200 m. Absent from northern Germany. Very local in Britain, in East Anglia, central southern England and west Wales.

Abundance: locally common.

Flight: June to August, with an occasional second generation on the Continent.

Life cycle: caterpillars hibernate when small. In late spring can be found under leaves of hemp agrimony which they have bitten through the midrib, causing tip to droop.

Foodplants: hemp agrimony, wild clary.

Dark Crimson Underwing *Catocala sponsa* L.

Description: the catocalas are magnificent moths, usually of large size, with intricately patterned procryptic forewings which conceal the brightly coloured hindwings when at rest. They are easily disturbed, and fly off with erratic flight to another settling place, when they 'disappear' – a classic example of the use of flash colouration as a defence. Catocalas occur right across Europe, Asia, and North America. The Dark Crimson Underwing has a forewing of 3.0–3.3 cm. The forewings are dark, rich brown, with black- and cream-coloured jagged crosslines, and usually an irregular pale area which includes the reniform stigma and a rounded patch below it. Hindwings deep crimson, with irregular black transverse band and wide border.

Habitat: oak woods; on Continent, sometimes in woods of quite young trees.
Distribution: throughout Europe, but confined to New Forest, and formerly Kent in Britain, with very occasional immigrants.
Abundance: common in some years.
Flight: mid-July to mid-September, but hardly before early September in England. Like other catocalas, this species comes well to sugar bait, but seldom to light. The sight of several of these fine moths on a sugar-patch is a memorable occasion.
Life cycle: overwinters in egg stage. Caterpillars in May and June; rest on oak twigs and branches by day, and are exceedingly well camouflaged.
Foodplant: oak.

Clifden Nonpareil *Catocala fraxini* L.

Description: the largest European catocala, with forewing length about 4.5 cm. Forewings light grey or grey-brown, with irregular procryptic pattern of jagged crosslines and conspicuous pale spot below reniform stigma. Hindwings mauve, with black-brown base and border. A form with dark-coloured forewings, *ab. moerens* Fuchs, is not uncommon.

Habitat: margins of mixed deciduous woodlands, river banks, avenues, occasionally in old neglected gardens and parks. In mountains, up to deciduous tree line. Breeding population in Britain associated with aspen woods.
Distribution: throughout Europe in mixed woodland. In Britain, bred for a time in Kent and Norfolk; otherwise rare immigrant which has reached Shetland.
Abundance: not rare, but breeding sites have been lost in a number of places since World War I. Now regarded as threatened in several parts of Europe.
Flight: mid-July to late October. This moth is a highly impressive sight at sugar. Also comes to light, though not freely.
Life cycle: egg overwinters. Caterpillars in May and June. After hatching, young caterpillars tend to walk for a long time before settling down to feed; this critical period can be negotiated, they are easy to rear.
Foodplants: chiefly aspen; also other poplar species, oak, birch, alder.

Rosy Underwing *Catocala electa* View.

Description: forewing 3.0–3.5 cm. Forewings rather smooth grey compared to other species, with irregular dark and jagged crosslines. Outer crossline in particular forms a strong 'M' opposite reniform stigma. Hindwings rosy crimson, with angled central band which does not reach right across wing, and black border.

Habitat: pastures, river valleys, banks of streams and rivers with dense vegetation.

Distribution: widespread in Europe, extending across Asia to Korea. Occurs regularly in southern Germany, the Alps and southern Europe, but is rare or absent in north Europe. A mere five reasonably acceptable British records.

Abundance: locally fairly common. Comes t sugar much more freely than to light.

Flight: mid-July to late September; in mountains a shorter period is spent on the wing than at lowe altitudes.

Life cycle: winter spent in egg stage. Caterpillar typical catocala-form (see illustration), and exceed ingly well-camouflaged on twigs and branches foodplants. Occurs in May and June.

Foodplants: chiefly long-leaved species willow, preferring old, pollarded trees.

Red Underwing *Catocala nupta* L.

Description: forewing 3.3–3.8 cm. Distinctly larger and browner-grey than Rosy Under-wing, forewings more coarsely scaled. Very similar to *Catocala elocata* Esp., which occurs in central and south Europe; this species is even larger and distinctly browner in forewing colour. Outer transverse line forms a weaker 'M' than in Rosy Underwing, and there is a pale area just basal to reniform stigma in Red Underwing. Hindwings ochreous red with black, angled crossline which just reaches inner margin, and black border.

Habitat: banks of lakes, rivers and stream, poplar avenues, parkland with mature poplars.

Distribution: widespread in temperate and sou Europe, absent from north. On north side of Alp reaches 1,000 m altitude, while on south sid occurs up to 1,600 m. England to Yorkshire, an Wales.

Abundance: common where it occurs, and ofte seen at rest on trees in suburbs, telegraph poles, even walls of houses. Appears to have declined places.

Flight: mid-July to early October. Comes freely sugar.

Life cycle: overwinters in egg stage. Caterpilla (see illustration) well camouflaged. Hide in crevice of bark during day.

Foodplants: chiefly white willow and cra willow; also weeping willow, black poplar.

Description: forewing 2.8–3.2 cm, the pale and dark-brown pattern forms an excellent camouflage when the moth is at rest on an oak trunk or branch. The pattern, despite its complexity, is remarkably constant. The moth can only be confused with the slightly larger Dark Crimson Underwing, but in the present species the lighter tones on the forewing have a distinctly grey tint, absent in the Dark Crimson Underwing, and the pattern is more variegated. On the hindwing the black crossline is straighter in the Light Crimson Underwing, whereas in the larger species it forms a more definite 'W'.

Habitat: oak woods and mixed deciduous woodland, largish copses, hillsides with bush cover; always in dry, sunny places. In Britain, however, it is confined to mature oak forest.

Distribution: very widespread in the tempera⋅ zone of Europe, extending across Asia Minor ⋅ Armenia. Much more local north of the Alps, ar⋅ not occurring at altitudes above 800 m. In Britai⋅ restricted to the New Forest, Hampshire, and a fe⋅ other large woods in that and adjacent counties.

Abundance: locally common; has brief periods ⋅ abundance between longer periods of comparativ⋅ scarcity.

Flight: July to late August. The first of the larg⋅ catocalas to emerge.

Life cycle: overwinters as an egg. Caterpilla⋅ hatch when the buds burst in spring, and feed up⋅ April and May.

Foodplants: oak, occasionally horse chestnut ⋅ the Continent.

Ephesia fulminea Scop.

Description: in south Europe there are several catocalas, mostly smaller species, with yellow hindwings. *Ephesia fulminea* extends further north than any of the others, and is the most handsome. Forewings 2.2–2.6 cm, grey-brown with heavy dark brown or blackish suffused basal area which contrasts strongly with the paler central area. The black outer crossline strongly and irregularly undulates and forms a double 'W' beyond the reniform stigma. The orbicular stigma is usually invisible. Hindwings are bright brownish-yellow with a black band forming a loop round the basal area, and a broken black marginal band which contains a large yellow spot at the tip.

Habitat: warm, sunny places: hillsides, clearings, woodland margins, valleys with hedges, country roads bordered by trees, old orchards.

Distribution: temperate zone of Europe, extendi⋅ across Asia to Japan. Has a rather eastern dist⋅ bution in Europe, extending into France but abse⋅ from the Netherlands and Britain.

Abundance: locally quite common, but h⋅ become rare in many places and in need of prote⋅ tion.

Flight: end June to late August, earlier than t⋅ larger species.

Life cycle: overwinters in egg stage. Caterpilla⋅ hatch in early spring, when buds break, and fe⋅ from April to June, according to locality.

Foodplants: plum, sloe, pear, oak and hawtho⋅ preferring lower branches of old trees or of coppi⋅

Lunar Double-stripe *Minucia lunaris* Schiff.

Description: forewing 2.2–2.5 cm. Varies in colour from light grey-brown through shades of brown nearly to black. Two gently curved pale cross-lines and conspicuous crescent-shaped reniform stigma give the moth its common name. Orbicular stigma is dot-like. Outermost crossline is jagged and far less conspicuous than the other two crosslines. Hindwings are pale brown with golden sheen and have slightly darker band across centre.

Habitat: sunny, dry hillsides, clearings, wood margins, light mixed deciduous woodlands, especially oak woods. In Britain, occurred as a breeding species in sunny clearings with 'stooled' oaks, on which larvae fed.

Distribution: throughout south Europe, extending to central Europe as a few isolated populations. To 800 m altitude in southern Alpine valleys. Bred in Kent for a few years in 1940s and 50s, now an extremely rare immigrant to Britain.

Abundance: common to very common in south Europe, but declining in many places in central Europe.

Flight: April to June. Easily flushed by day from amongst leaf litter. At night, comes readily to sugar and to light.

Life cycle: caterpillars occur from May to August, according to latitude. Slender and brown, with three narrow stripes along back and a stronger one alongside. Characteristic features are yellow square on first abdominal segment and two small projections at hind end. Winter spent as a pupa in a flimsy cocoon.

Foodplants: in central Europe (and Britain) said to feed exclusively on soft, coppiced shoots of oak, but in south France, found commonly on relatively tough foliage of ilex oak.

Mother Shipton *Callistege mi* Clerck

Description: forewing 1.2–1.5 cm. Forewings grey or grey brown, with elaborate pattern of crosslines bearing a fanciful resemblance to a hag's face, Mother Shipton, in which the dark orbicular stigma is the eye! Hindwings creamy yellow or white, strongly overlaid with wavy crosslines and dark veins. In British specimens, upper and under surfaces of both pairs of wings have a strong yellowish tint, in contrast to continental specimens which are white.

Habitat: meadows, downs, clearings, margins of woods.

Distribution: throughout Europe to 1,700 m in mountains, and including Britain and Ireland.

Abundance: fairly common.

Flight: two generations, first end April to early June, second mid-August to mid-September. Single-broods in Britain, flying in May and June. Diurnal.

Life cycle: in Britain, caterpillars occur from July to September. Pupa overwinters.

Foodplants: clover; other papilionates, sorrel and grasses cited in continental literature.

Ophiusa tirhaca Cramer

Description: forewing c.3 cm. One of the most handsome and exotic-looking of European noctuids; indeed its nearest relatives are tropical. Forewings bright yellowish-green with dark purplish-brown border and conspicuous dark reniform stigma. Hindwings bright yellow with broken black transverse band. Head and thorax green, abdomen yellow.

Habitat: clearings and margins of dry, Mediterranean hardwood forests.

Distribution: a Mediterranean species, also occurring in India and China. Very-rare in central Europe, commoner in south France and Spain. Absent from Britain.

Abundance: a great rarity in central Europe.

Flight: March to October in two overlapping generations. Moths come to light, but particularly well to sugar, on which they are a breathtaking sight.

Life cycle: caterpillars occur during summer and autumn. Pupa overwinters.

Foodplants: cistus, pistachio tree, sumac, tree heath.

Burnet Companion
Euclidia glyphica L.

Des: forewing 1.2–1.4 cm. Rich brown mixed with dark yellow, with two oblique, blackish bands across the wing, outer angled and edged outside with pale yellowish, and a dark patch in wing apex. Hindwings yellow with blackish basal region and incomplete transverse band. **H:** sunny, warm hillsides, dry and damp meadows, clearings and wood margins, preferring calcareous soil. **Dis:** throughout Europe to Arctic Circle, and to 2,000 m in mountains. Britain and Ireland. **A:** generally common. **Fl:** two broods, first May to July, second in August, on Continent; single-brooded in Britain, in May and June. Diurnal. **LC:** caterpillars July to September in Britain, earlier or later on Continent. Pupa overwinters. **FP:** clover and other papilionates.

Herald Scoliopteryx libatrix L.

Des: forewing 2.0–2.2 cm, margins jagged. Grey-brown with yellow-red and scarlet areas, whitish crosslines, outer one double; white speck at base of each forewing and another in orbicular stigma. Hindwings brown. **H:** woodlands, commons and gardens. **Dis:** throughout Europe, to 2,000 m in mountains. Britain and Ireland. **A:** common. **Fl:** single-brooded. Moths emerge from July, hibernate communally in sheds and cellars, and caves, re-emerge in spring and continue on the wing until June. Sluggish. **LC:** lively green caterpillars June to August. **FP:** sallows, willows and poplars.

Straw Dot Rivula sericealis Scop.

Des: forewing c. 1 cm. Pale yellow with weak darker crosslines and dark reniform stigma containing two black dots. Hindwings whitish. **H:** damp areas in woods and on commons, marshes, fens and bogs. **Dis:** widespread in temperate Europe to 1,600 m, including Britain and Ireland. **A:** locally common. **Fl:** May to September, in two or three generations. Easily disturbed by day. **LC:** caterpillars August to May, hibernating. **FP:** grasses.

Blackneck Lygephila pastinum Treits.

Des: forewings 1.8–2.0 cm, light grey with slightly darker outer area; fine transverse streaks. Reniform stigma black, broadly V-shaped. Hindwings light brown. Several other similar species in Europe, but only one in Britain, the Scarce Blackneck (Lygephila craccae Schiff.) which has several dark dots along leading edge of wing. **H:** commons, edges of woods, downs, meadows and marshes. **Dis:** widespread in Europe, including England and Wales. **A:** local and fairly common. **Fl:** June to August. **LC:** caterpillars from late August to June hibernating when small. **FP:** tufted vetch.

Small Purple-barred
Phytometra viridaria Clerck.

Des: forewing 0.8–1.0 cm. Pale olive-brown or greenish, with purple crossline and purplish wash in outer area of forewings. Hindwings pale greyish-brown, sometimes with reddish tint in outer area **H:** meadows, moors, hillsides and clearings depending on presence of milkwort. **Dis:** scattered populations in Europe up to 2,000 m; Britain and Ireland. **A:** locally common. **Fl:** April to July, and August, in two generations; single-brooded in north of its range. **LC:** caterpillars June and July, August and September. Overwinters as pupa. **FP:** milkwort.

Beautiful Hook-tip
Laspeyria flexula Schiff.

Des: forewing 1.2–1.3 cm. Forewings grey with red-brown flush in outer area and angled, pale crosslines edged red-brown. Inconspicuous reniform stigma contains two black dots. Grey hindwings crossed by dark, pale-edged line. **H:** woodland, parks and old orchards. **Dis:** temperate Europe, up to 1,500 m; southern half of England, Wales. **A:** fairly common but local. **Fl:** July and August. **LC:** caterpillars September to May, hibernating small. **FP:** lichens on coniferous and deciduous trees, including larch, spruce, yew, hawthorn and apple.

Lesser Belle
Colobochyla salicalis Schiff.

Des: forewing 1.0–1.3 cm. Forewings grey with three red-brown crosslines edged yellow, outermost reaching apex. **H:** damp woodland and pasture. **Dis:** widespread in Europe, in isolated pockets. In Britain, only in Kent. **A:** Locally fairly common **Fl:** mid-May to early July, sometimes partial second generaton. **LC:** caterpillars July and August. Pupa hibernates. **FP:** chiefly young aspen, also tender shoots of willow and poplar.

Common Fan-foot
Pechipogo strigilata L.

Des: forewing 1.2–1.3 cm. Forewings grey-brown with three faint crosslines, one of which curves sharply outside discal mark in reniform stigma. Hindwings whitish, with two incomplete crosslines. Foreleg of ♂ has large, reversible hair-tufts from which common name is derived. **H:** mixed deciduous woodland. **Dis:** widespread in Europe, commoner in north; mountains to 1,500 m. England, Wales and Ireland. **A:** much decreased in Britain, now extremely local in south England. **Fl:** late May to July. **LC:** caterpillars occur from July to April, and hibernate nearly full-fed. **FP:** withered leaves of oak, beech, hornbeam, etc.

Shaded Fan-foot
Herminia tarsicrinalis Knoch.

Des: forewing 1.1–1.3 cm. Brownish-grey to light brown. In addition to the three fine crosslines, the middle one of which curves round the discal mark, there is a dark shade traversing the centre of the wing which distinguishes this from related species. Outer line reaches the leading edge a short distance before apex (c.f. Small Fan-foot, *Herminia nemoralis* F). Antennae of ♂ do not have thickened knot of scales near base (c.f. males of Fan-foot, *Herminia tarsipennalis* Treits). **H:** pastures and carr woodlands, woodland meadows; bramble thickets. **Dis:** throughout mainland Europe to 1,600 m. Recently discovered breeding in Suffolk, England. **A:** locally common. **Fl:** June to August.

Clay Fan-foot
Paracolax glaucinalis Schiff.

Des: forewing 1.2–1.4 cm. All wings ochre-yellow to brownish, hindwings slightly paler towards leading edge. Forewings with two fine, dark crosslines and crescent-shaped discal mark, hindwings with one crossline and discal mark. **H:** warm, open deciduous woodland, carr woodland, clearings, heaths. **Dis:** scattered through Europe, absent from cooler areas. In south-east England only. **A:** usually common where it occurs. Easily disturbed from clumps of brushwood by day. **Fl:** June to August. **LC:** caterpillars from end August to early June, hibernate when small. **FP:** dry and decaying leaves of oak, bramble and willow.

Buttoned Snout *Hypena rostralis* L.

Des: forewings c. 1.4 cm. Colour varies from grey-brown to dark brown or yellow-brown and the pattern from plain to strongly variegated. Apex with dark, diagonal bar, and another between small orbicular and reniform stigmata. **H:** hedgerows, edges of woods and marshes, sometimes gardens in villages and town. **Dis:** throughout Europe, to 1,600 m in mountains. South-east England and south Wales. **A:** usually common, but range and frequency both reduced in Britain. **Fl:** end July to June; moth hibernates in caves and buildings. **LC:** caterpillars June and July. **FP:** hop.

The Snout *Hypena proboscidalis* L.

Des: forewing 1.3–1.9 cm. Forewings grey-brown or light brown with reddish-brown crosslines. The snout moths are so-called because of their unusually long palps, which show clearly in illustrations of both Snout and Buttoned Snout. **H:** clearings and margins of woods, pastures and river banks, gardens. **Dis:** throughout Europe to 1,600 m. Britain to Orkneys, Ireland. **A:** common. **Fl:** two generations, first May to July, second August to end September. **LC:** caterpillars of second generation hibernate. **FP:** stinging nettle.

Winter Moth *Operophtera brumata* L.

Description: forewing of male 1.2–1.4 cm; female virtually wingless. Forewings of male light brown, with a number of faint, wavy crosslines. Hindwings a little paler. Resembles male of Northern Winter Moth (*Operophtera fagata* Scharf), but this species is slightly larger, the wings are paler and more shiny, and hindwings are almost white. The female Winter Moth is considerably plumper-bodied than the male; the wings are minute, whereas in the Northern Winter Moth they are about half the length of the body.

Habitat: mixed deciduous woodlands, orchards, scrub, even on moors, parks and gardens.

Distribution: central and northern Europe, extending across Asia. Britain to the Shetlands, Ireland.

Abundance: common to abundant through most of its range.

Flight: mid-October to end of December. The moths begin to emerge after the first frosts. Males fly lazily from dusk onwards, and can often be found in numbers resting head upwards, with wings held over their backs, butterfly-like, on tree trunks after dark. During the day they rest in the normal moth posture with wings flat. When the females emerge they run up the trees and the males pair with them. Mated pairs can be spotted from a distance because the male is invariably head downwards. In orchards and gardens containing fruit trees, grease bands may have been put around the trunks of trees. They are covered with a sticky substance, which has been put there with the purpose of trapping the females of this species, which is practically wingless, as they crawl up the tree after emerging from their chrysalises.

In spite of such devices and other precautionary measures taken to safeguard trees from attack, the foliage of such trees as apple and pear will probably be affected in some way by the caterpillars in their season.

Life cycle: the eggs are laid on buds of various trees and bushes during the winter. They hatch when the buds burst, and the green caterpillars feed up in April and May, resting during the day in a shelter made by loosely spinning some leaves together. The abundance of these and other defoliating caterpillars in spring coincides with the breeding season of insectivorous birds such as tits whose young are fed principally on this source.

Foodplants: a great many deciduous trees and shrubs including cultivated species. Oak, birch apple, elm, lime, hawthorn, hazel, hornbeam are among the favourites. On moors, caterpillars have been reported on heather and bog myrtle.

General: the winter moths are the first of the next large family to be dealt with, the geometers. These are often slender, thin-bodied moths which rest with their wings flat. The caterpillars have only one pair of abdominal prolegs, and progress by looping: hence the name of the family, and the familiar names 'loopers' (Britain), 'Spanner' (Germany), 'measuring worms' (America). Several species emerge during the depths of winter and have females that are wingless, or nearly so. Evidently it is an efficient strategy at low temperatures for the egg bags that are the females not to expend energy by flying.

Geometers

Orange Underwing *Archiearis parthenias* L.

Description: forewing 1.5–1.8 cm. Forewings reddish-brown, with whitish markings on the leading edge and across the central field especially in the females; narrow, blackish, jagged inner and outer crosslines and wavy outermost line; discal spot dark-outlined. Hindwings bright orange with black basal patch, discal spot and border.

Habitat: birch woodland, heathy areas with clumps of birches.

Distribution: widespread, but dependent on presence of birch. Occurs in England, Wales and Scotland.

Abundance: locally common.

Flight: March and April. Fly in sunshine from about midday, high around birch trees. The females rest on the twigs, as do the males when the sun is obscured. Can be knocked off high branches in the morning, and sometimes rest on ground in late afternoon.

Life cycle: caterpillars May to July. The caterpillars are green, with six white lines along the back and white stripes along the side. The Orange Underwings are considered to be primitive geometers because the caterpillars have all four pairs of abdominal prolegs, though they show signs of being degenerate. When young, the caterpillars feed on birch catkins and afterwards on the foliage. Pupa overwinters.

Light Orange Underwing *Archiearis notha* Hübn.

Description: forewing 1.4–1.6 cm. Very similar to the Orange Underwing, but slightly smaller, forewings of males are more uniformly coloured, pattern of underside of hindwings is different, forewings are much less variegated and male has feathered antennae.

Habitat: aspen woods.

Distribution: local in Europe, Asia and North Africa. Very local in southern England.

Abundance: usually common where it occurs.

Flight: emerges a little later in the season than the Orange Underwing, usually not before late March. Flies by day round aspens; visits sallow bloom in afternoon.

Life cycle: caterpillars May to July between spun leaves of foodplant. The head is greenish-brown with three conspicuous black spots. Body green, olive green or reddish, line along the middle of the back darker green edged with white; two thin white lines on each side, and a whitish stripe along the spiracles. When mature it burrows into decayed bark or wood, and before changing into a reddish-brown chrysalis, it spins a thin covering of wood and silk over the mouth of the chamber. Pupa overwinters, sometimes twice or even three times.

Foodplant: aspen.

Northern Spinach *Eulithis populata* L.

Des: forewing 1.4–1.7 cm. Forewings yellowish; central area, which is demarcated by two angled, dark crosslines, is often darker than rest of wing; basal area also darker. The outer crossline has a shallow V-shaped angle in the upper half, which distinguishes Northern Spinach from similar Chevron, in which this part of line is straight. Melanotic (all dark) specimens occur in some localities. Hindwings pale yellowish. **H:** moorland and mountain woodland. **Dis:** central and northern Europe to Arctic; west and north Britain, Ireland. **A:** common where it occurs. **Fl:** June to September. **LC:** overwinters in egg stage. Caterpillars April to June. **FP:** bilberry.

The Spinach *Eulithis mellinata* L.

Des: forewing 1.4–1.7 cm. Forewings clear yellow, inner crossline much more strongly angled than in Northern Spinach, upper part of outer line nearly straight, fringes chequered. Hindwings pale yellow. **H:** chiefly gardens, also open woodland where foodplant grows. **Dis:** scattered through temperate Europe. England and Wales, local Scotland, very rare Ireland. **A:** locally fairly common. **Fl:** June and July. **LC:** overwinters in egg stage. Caterpillars May – June. **FP:** currant, gooseberry.

Mottled Umber
Erannis defoliaria Clerck

Des: forewing 1.8–2.2 cm. Winged ♂ very variable in colour, from pale and strongly patterned (see illustration) to dark-rusty or smoky-brown, with pattern less contrasting or obscured. ♀ wingless, body and legs yellow with black spots. **H:** deciduous woodland, copses, gardens. **Dis:** temperate Europe, UK. **A:** common/abundant, larva sometimes serious pest. **Fl:** September–December; rarely in new year. **LC:** eggs hatch when ♀ buds break; caterpillars April to July, conspicuously patterned brown and cream. **FP:** many deciduous trees and shrubs.

March Moth
Alsophila aescularia Schiff.

Des: ♂ forewings 1.7–1.9 cm, grey to brownish with two pale, jagged crosslines, each point on the line with a dark tip; vein dots along the outer margins and a brown discal spot in both forewings and hindwings. ♀ wingless, brown, ovoid with tuft of scales at tip of abdomen. **H:** deciduous woodland, hedgerows, gardens. **Dis:** central Europe, Britain and Ireland. **F:** common. **Fl:** February to April. **LC:** caterpillars in May and June. **FP:** many deciduous trees and bushes.

Drab Looper *Minoa murinata* Scop.

Des: forewing 0.8–1.1 cm. Easy to identify by its uniformly grey or light brown, patternless fore- and hindwings. **H:** open woodland, pastures, mountain meadows. **Dis:** throughout Europe, prefers hilly and mountainous regions. Southern half of England and south-east Wales. **A:** locally common. **Fl:** late May to July, in some places a second generation in late summer. **LC:** caterpillars July to early September. Pupa overwinters. **FP:** wood spurge (in Britain) and cypress spurge.

Autumnal Moth
Epirrita autumnata Borkh.

Des: members of the genus *Epirrita* are difficult to distinguish from one another, but easily recognizable as 'November moths'. Ample-winged, grey moths with forewings up to 2 cm, traversed by several fine, wavy or angled crosslines. When these lines are well developed, they give good guide to the species' identity. With the Autumnal Moth, the line immediately outside the discal dot is nearly straight, and leaves the trailing edge at right angle before turning sharply towards the base of wing just before leading edge. In poorly marked or melanotic specimens, accurate identification only by examination of genitalia. **H:** deciduous woods and heaths. **Dis:** Europe to Arctic Circle. **A:** common.

223

Small Phoenix *Ecliptopera silaceata* Schiff.

Description: forewing 1.3–1.6 cm. Forewings brown to blackish-brown, with broad black band across centre of wings, which is divided by a complex of pale lines, where branches outline the two main divisions of the band. Further pale crosslines occur in the basal and outer areas of the forewings, and there is a pattern of lines and dark blotches within the median area. Hindwings paler, weakly marked.

Habitat: pastures, banks of streams and rivers, clearings and rides in damp, mixed woodland.

Distribution: Europe, Asia and North America Britain to Orkney, Ireland.

Abundance: fairly common to common.

Flight: two generations, first mid-April to mid-June, second July to end August.

Life cycle: caterpillars occur in June and July, the second generation in early autumn. Pupa over-winters.

Food plants: species of willowherb, including rosebay, and enchanter's nightshade.

Scallop Shell
Rheumaptera undulata L.

Des: forewing 1.4–1.7 cm. Immediately recognizable by the presence of many fine, zigzag lines which cross both fore- and hindwings. Ground colour light brown, sometimes with reddish tint. **H:** damp pastures and carr, and open woodland with bilberry. **Dis:** temperate Europe, scarcer in south. Britain to southern Scotland, Ireland. **A:** local, fairly common. **Fl:** June and July. **LC:** caterpillars occur from August to October. Pupa overwinters. **FP:** two quite different foodplants, associated with two habitats – sallow and bilberry.

Small Argent-and-Sable
Epirrhoe tristata L.

Des: forewing 1.1–1.2 cm. Ground colour of wings white, with irregular blackish-brown basal patch, median band and outer areas; a series of fine dots in white areas of fore- and hindwings between central band and outer dark zone. Fringes chequered. **H:** Alpine meadows, hillsides, pastures, clearings, copses, lane verges. **Dis:** temperate Europe; occurs high up in mountains. Western distribution in Britain, and Ireland. **A:** locally frequent. **Fl:** double-brooded (only partially so in Britain), in May and June, and July and August. **LC:** caterpillars from June to September. Pupa overwinters. **FP:** heath bedstraw.

Green Pug
Chloroclystis rectangulata L.

Des: forewings up to 1 cm. Similar to the pug moths belonging to the large genus *Eupithecia*, but *Chloroclystis* species are green. In the Green Pug, the crosslines are rather faint; in industrial areas, a black form is common. **H:** woodlands, orchards, gardens, city parks. **Dis:** through Europe, including Britain and Ireland. **A:** common. **Fl:** June and July. **LC:** caterpillars occur in April and May. Pupal stage brief. Overwinters in egg stage. **FP:** flowers of apple, pear, cherry and blackthorn.

V-Pug *Chloroclystis v-ata* Haw.

Des: resembles Green Pug, but lighter green and pattern stronger, especially towards leading edges of forewings in central areas, where dark-coloured inner crossline forms a distinct V. Hindwings weakly marked. **H:** woods, meadows, parks, gardens. **Dis:** widespread in Europe. In Britain, to southern Scotland, Ireland. **A:** fairly common. **Fl:** double-brooded except in north, flying in May and in late summer. **LC:** caterpillars in summer and autumn. Overwinters as pupa. **FP:** flowers of many plants, including hemp agrimony, traveller's joy, elder and bramble.

225

Dark-barred Twin-spot Carpet
Xanthorhoe ferrugata Clerck

Des: forewing 1.0–1.2 cm. Grey-brown or reddish grey-brown with broad, dark central band. Very similar to forms of Red Twin-spot Carpet (*X. Spadicearea* Schiff.), which differ in having central band edged white on outer side, and inner edge of band not forming a notch as it reaches leading edge of wing. Both species have black double spot near apex of each forewing. **H:** wooded valleys, beside streams and rivers, meadows, parks and gardens. **Dis:** throughout Europe to Lapland; Britain and Ireland. **A:** common. **Fl:** double-brooded in south Britain and on Continent, May and June, then July and August. **LC:** caterpillars in July and September. Pupa overwinters. **FP:** various herbaceous plants: sandwort, bedstraw, bellflower cited.

Garden Carpet
Xanthorhoe fluctuata L.

Des: forewing 1.2–1.4 cm. Greyish-white with blackish basal patch and a large one between middle of forewing and leading edge, with a much smaller one near tip. Hindwings with several weak crosslines. Dark grey specimens occur in north Britain and in industrial areas. **H:** commonest in suburbs, less so in countryside. **Dis:** Europe, including Britain to Shetlands, Ireland. **A:** common. **Fl:** two or three broods from April to October. Rests by day on fences and buildings. **LC:** caterpillars in summer and autumn on various *Cruciferae*, such as bittercress, horseradish, and perennial wall rocket.

Chimney Sweeper *Odezia atrata* L.

Des: forewing 1.2–1.4 cm. Sooty black with white apical fringes; unmistakable. **H:** meadows and downs. **Dis:** central and northern Europe, and chiefly northern and western in Britain, Ireland. **A:** locally common. **Fl:** late May to late July. Diurnal, resting on grass stems between flights. **LC:** overwinters in egg stage. Caterpillars May and June. **FP:** pignut (*Conopodium majus*).

Balsam Carpet
Xanthorhoe biriviatea BORKH

Des: forewing 1.1–1.3 cm. Rustier-brown tha previous species, with narrower, more contrastin transverse band, whiter zone outside it and blurre dark patches in apical region of wing instead clearly defined black spots. Summer brood spec mens smaller and darker. **H:** damp, open woodlar beside rivers and canals. **Dis:** central Europe Siberia; only in south-east England, where appa ently spreading. **A:** local. **Fl:** two generations, Apr to June, then late summer. **LC:** caterpillars Jur and September. Pupa overwinters. **FP:** balsar species: touch-me-not in Europe, and orang balsam in England.

Shaded Broad-bar
Scotopteryx chenopodiata L.

Des: forewing 1.6–1.9 cm. Ground colour of fore wings yellow to reddish- or purplish-brown. Dark central zone which contains a dark discal spc and oblique dark streak in apex. Both fore- an hindwings traversed by numerous fine, reddish brown lines. **H:** downland, dunes, waste groun meadows. **Dis:** widespread in Europe from low lands to mountains. Britain to Orkney, Ireland. **A** locally common, though apparently less so Britain than in the past, when it was known as 'Th Aurelian's Plague' because of its abundance. **Fl** July and August, easily disturbed by day. **LC** caterpillars September to June, hibernating. **FP** vetches and clovers.

Treble-bar *Aplocera plagiata* L.

Des: forewing 1.8–2.2 cm. Forewings grey to blue grey or brownish-grey, traversed by three fasciate lines and other less conspicuous ones. Dis tinguished from Lesser Treble-bar (*A. efforma* Guen) by shape of first fascia which is bent, ne sharply angled, near leading edge; by slightly large size; and by much longer claspers in ♂, whic give elongated look to abdomen (specimen illus trated is ♀). **H:** downs, moors and open woodlanc **Dis:** Europe, including Britain and Ireland. **A** common. **Fl:** May–June and autumn. **LC:** caterpi lars in summer, and from October to April. **FP:** S John's wort species.

Birch Mocha
Cyclophora albipunctata Hufn.

Des: forewings 1.2–1.3 cm, greyish white, more or less flushed pink. Brownish-rimmed circular spot in centre of fore- and hindwings; crosslines consisting of series of dark dots. **H:** birch woods and thickets. **Dis:** throughout Europe in suitable habitat, including Britain and Ireland. **A:** common in birch woods. **Fl:** two generations, in May and June, and August. **LC:** caterpillars in summer and autumn. Pupa butterfly-like, strapped to a leaf by a silk girdle; second generation overwinters. **FP:** birch.

Single-dotted Wave
Idaea dimidiata Hufn.

Des: forewings 0.8–0.9 cm, pale straw-coloured with conspicuous brown mark in angle of wing which make this one of the easiest species of the large genus *Idaea* to identify. Small dark discal dot on all four wings, and faint crosslines often reduced to dots. **H:** damp woods, marshes, gardens. **Dis:** most of Europe; Britain to south-west Scotland, Ireland. **A:** fairly common. **Fl:** June to September. **LC:** caterpillars September to May, hibernating. **FP:** cow parsley, withered leaves including those of dandelion.

Blood-vein *Timandra griseata* Petersen

Des: forewings 1.4–1.6 cm, yellowish-grey to reddish brown. From pointed apex of each forewing extends a straight, oblique dark-red line which is continuous with a similar line on the hindwings; margin and fringes also red on both pairs of wings. Hindwing margin strongly angled. **H:** weedy places in gardens, waste ground, edges of woods, etc. **Dis:** Europe; Britain to southern Scotland, Ireland. **A:** common. **Fl:** double-brooded, in early summer and autumn. **LC:** caterpillars in summer, and from August to May, hibernating. **FP:** dock, sorrel, knotgrass and goosefoot.

Lewes Wave *Scopula immorata* L.

Des: forewings 1.1–1.5 cm. All wings whitish heavily irrorated greyish- or olive-brown, leaving fairly distinct, broken, whitish outermost crossline and a streaky, blackish terminal line adjacent to the fringes. Each wing with a small dark discal spot. Fringes chequered white and brown. European specimens of first generation larger than British specimens. **H:** Alpine meadows, woodland edges and ridges, heathy ground. **Dis:** widespread in Europe, but apparently extinct in England. **A:** locally common. **Fl:** two generations between May and August. **LC:** caterpillars in summer and August to May, those of second generation hibernating. **FP:** heather; knotgrass and plantain in captivity.

Lace Border *Scopula ornata* Scop.

Des: forewings 1.0–1.2 cm. Wings gleaming silver-white. Next to the dotted, thick black outer transverse line are crescent-shaped brown marks on both fore- and hindwings. In Europe, can only be confused with more strongly marked *Scopula decorata* Schiff. **H:** downland, sunny hillsides. **Dis:** Europe and Asia; south-east England. **A:** fairly common locally. **Fl:** double-brooded, in May and June, and later summer. Easily disturbed by day. **LC:** caterpillars in summer and from August to May, hibernating. **FP:** thyme and marjoram.

Tawny Wave
Scopula rubiginata Hufn.

Des: forewings 0.8–1.0 cm. All wings rich, dark red when fresh, with fine, dark crosslines, three on forewings, two on hindwings. Fringes light brown. **H:** dry, warm fallow fields, heaths, downs and meadows. **Dis:** central and southern Europe; in Britain, only resident in East Anglia. **A:** locally common. **Fl:** two generations between May and September. Easily disturbed by day. **LC:** caterpillars in summer, and September and May, hibernating. **FP:** birdsfoot trefoil; in captivity on dandelion and knotgrass.

Magpie Moth *Abraxas grossulariata* L.

Pupa – see page 230

Description: large geometer with forewings up to 2.3 cm, having striking orange and black pattern on white background. Hindwings white with transverse band of dark spots across middle of wings and a row of larger ones along borders. Thorax and abdomen also yellow with black markings. The great majority of specimens seen in the wild are similar to the one illustrated, but this is a species that has been studied intensively in the laboratory, where many extraordinary forms have been bred and their genetics worked out. In extreme forms the wings are almost entirely black, or the black markings are almost entirely wanting.

Habitat: gardens with fruit bushes, hedgerows, damp woodlands.

Distribution: widespread in Europe; Britain t Hebrides, Ireland.

Abundance: very variable. Diminished in gardens but still common in many places.

Flight: mid-June to late August. Flies from jus before dusk, well into the night.

Life cycle: the typically looping caterpillars hav the same pattern of white, black and yellow as th adults. Live from September to June, hibernating Pupa, which is dark brown with narrow yellow bands, in a loose silk web amongst the foodplant.

Foodplants: in gardens, associated with goose berry and blackcurrant. In wild, on hawthorn, black thorn, hazel, spindle. In Hebrides, local populatio on heather.

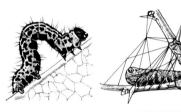

Clouded Magpie *Abraxas sylvata* Scop.

Description: slightly smaller than Magpie Moth, wing forewings 2.0–2.2 cm. Pattern also is distinctive, consisting of rounded brown basal patch marked with blue-grey, and a row of variously sized spots of similar colour across the outer areas of both fore- and hindwings. Several pale blue-grey spots on the wings, the largest of which occupies the middle of the forewing. Thorax dark, abdomen yellow with black spots. Minor variations in this pattern are frequent, but extremes, in which the extent of the dark markings is greatly increased, are rare.

Habitat: deciduous woodland and large, wooded parks.

Distribution: central Europe to central Asia. Britain to Dumfries, Ireland.

Abundance: locally common. Occasional wan derers turn up far from known breeding grounds.

Flight: late May to July. Moths rest by day o upper surface of woodland herbaceous plants especially dog's mercury, where they resembl large, splash-type bird droppings.

Life cycle: fine olive-green and yellow stripe caterpillars feed from August to October. Winte spent in pupal stage.

Foodplants: chiefly wych elm; also bird cherr beech and hazel.

G: A third species of Magpie Moth, *A. panter* occurs in southern Europe. It is like a pale Clouded Magpie, with dark markings much reduced, and i locally common.

Geometers

231

Peppered Moth *Biston betularia* L.

Des: one of the most robust of *Geometridae*, with plump body and forewing up to 2.8 cm. ♀ larger than ♂. Antennae of ♂ feathered except towards tip. Typically, all wings white with scattering of small black dots and patches, the more concentrated patches along the leading edges of the forewings. Body is similarly coloured. The appearance, establishment, subsequent spread and genetics of the black industrial mela notic form *carbonaria* Jordan have been studie extensively. **H:** deciduous woodlands, parks an gardens. **Dis:** Europe to southern Scandinavia an Finland. Britain to southern Scotland, Ireland. **A** common. **Fl:** mid-May to late July. **LC:** stick-lik caterpillars with two pointed ear-like structures a front known to hop pickers as 'hop cats'. Occu from July to September. Pupa overwinters. **FP** many trees and shrubs, including birch, oak, ash elm, blackthorn, hop.

Scorched Carpet
Ligdia adustata Schiff.

Des: forewings c.1.2 cm. Ground colour cream-white, with basal area of forewing and outer zone beyond outer crossline dark brown with darker markings, giving 'scorched' appearance. Hindwings white, weakly banded. **H:** light woodland, hedgerows, gardens. **Dis:** throughout Europe, including England, Wales and Ireland. **A:** fairly common. **Fl:** double-brooded, flying between April and August. **LC:** caterpillars early summer and autumn. Pupa overwinters. **FP:** spindle.

Tawny-barred Angle
Semiothisa liturata Clerck

Des: forewings 1.4–1.6 cm grey mixed with red dish-brown; three distinct crosslines on forewing and two on hindwings. **H:** pine woods, gardens an parks with pine. **Dis:** widespread in coniferou woodland, including Britain and Ireland. **A** common in suitable habitat. **Fl:** double-brooded i southern part of range, including southern Englanc elsewhere one emergence in June and July. **LC** caterpillars in summer and autumn. **FP:** pine Norway spruce.

V-Moth *Semiothisa wauaria* L.

Des: forewing c.1.5 cm. Ground colour brown to violet-grey, sometimes with whitish dusting. Conspicuous black V-mark in centre of each forewing, from leading edge, and three other dark spots alongside. **H:** dry lane verges with hedgerows and thick bush cover, clearings and pastures, gardens and parks. **Dis:** widespread in Europe. Britain and Ireland. **A:** thinly distributed and evidently decreased in Britain. **Fl:** June and July. **LC:** overwinters in egg stage. Caterpillars from April to June. **FP:** black currant, red currant, gooseberry.

Rannoch Looper
Semiothisa brunneata Thunb.

Des: forewings 1.0–1.3 cm, ♂ with longer wing but more slender bodies than ♀. All wings dar fulvous yellow, browner in ♂, with narrow dar crosslines. ♀ have stronger pattern than ♂. **H** clearings in ancient pine and birch woodland. **Dis** northern Europe. Resident Scotland, rare migrant t southern England. **A:** locally common. **Fl:** June t August. **LC:** overwinters as small larva; caterpillar April to June. Pupa may then overwinter from on to four years. **FP:** bilberry.

233

Brimstone Moth
Opisthograptis luteolata L.

Des: forewings 1.4–1.9 cm, specimens of second brood smaller. Wings bright lemon yellow with reddish-brown patches along leading edges of forewings and dark-outlined, whitish discal mark. Hindwings also with small discal spot. An unmistakable species. **H:** woods, lanes, gardens. **Dis:** widespread, but does not reach high altitudes. Britain to Orkney and Ireland. **A:** common. **Fl:** up to three broods between April and October. **LC:** may overwinter as caterpillar or pupa. Caterpillar very like a gnarled stick: remains perfectly still during day and feeds at night. **FP:** hawthorn, blackthorn, plum, mountain ash, honeysuckle.

Little Thorn Cepphis advenaria Hübn.

Des: forewings 1.1–1.3 cm. Wings light yellowish-brown or greyish-brown; central field of forewings a little darker. Weak crossline and discal spot on hindwings. Chequered fringes. Outline of wings rather angular. **H:** open woodland with bramble or bilberry undergrowth. **Dis:** scattered throughout Europe, including England, south Wales and western Ireland. **A:** local. **Fl:** May to July. **LC:** caterpillars July and August. Overwinters as pupa. **FP:** bilberry, bramble.

Bordered Beauty
Epione repandaria Hufn.

Des: forewing 1.2–1.5 cm. Ochre yellow with purplish brown terminal area, strongly angled inner line on forewings. Hindwings also with dark outer area. All wings speckled with small, streak-like dots. ♂ has feathered antennae. **H:** damp woodlands, carr, moorland, gardens. **Dis:** temperate Europe, including Britain and Ireland. **A:** fairly common. **Fl:** July and August. **LC:** overwinters in egg stage. Caterpillars May and June. **FP:** sallow.

Scorched Wing Plagodis dolabraria L.

Des: forewing c.1.7 cm. Wings yellow, with fine, dark-brown crosslines and dark golden-brown shading on forewings and patch of purplish brown in angles of hindwings, producing 'scorched' appearance. ♂ has feathered antennae. **H:** mixed deciduous woodland, copses and gardens. **Dis:** throughout Europe, including Britain and Ireland. **A:** common. **Fl:** May and June, earlier on Continent. **LC:** caterpillars July to September. Pupa overwinters. **FP:** oak, birch, sallow, lime.

Pale Brindled Beauty
Apocheima pilosaria Schiff.

Des: forewings c.2 cm in ♂ wingless. Forewings of ♂ yellowish-green with darker mottling and indistinct crosslines, hindwings paler. A dark blackish-green melanotic form occurs in industrial areas. **H:** mixed deciduous woodlands, parks and gardens. **Dis:** Europe, particularly in central and northern areas, including Britain and Ireland. **A:** common. **Fl:** emerges in response to first mild days of new year, January to March. **LC:** stick-like caterpillars occur April to June. Pupa overwinters. **FP:** various trees and shrubs, including oak, birch, hawthorn, lime, sallow.

Dark Bordered Beauty
Epione parallelaria Schiff.

Des: forewing 1.2–1.4 cm. ♂ and ♀ quite different. ♂ resembles Bordered Beauty, but basal crossline is rounded, not pointed, and inner margin of dark terminal area more wavy; ground colour a richer orange. ♀ is thicker bodied, narrower winged; wings pale yellow without reddish speckling and terminal areas of wings purple. **H:** boggy moorland. **Dis:** widespread in Europe, but extremely local in England and Scotland. **A:** fairly common where it occurs. **Fl:** June to August. **LC:** overwinters in egg stage. Caterpillars May and June. **FP:** creeping willow in Britain; also aspen and birch.

Dusky Thorn
Ennomos fuscantaria Haw.

Des: forewings 1.8–2.0 cm. Golden yellow to dark ochre with very jagged wing margins. Inner and outer crosslines of forewings curve towards base and sometimes meet on trailing edge. Marginal area darker. Hindwings uniformly coloured. **H:** mixed deciduous woodland, pastures, avenues, parks and gardens. **Dis:** central Europe to south Scandinavia. England and Wales. **A:** locally common. **Fl:** July to October, earlier in southern part of range. **LC:** overwinters as an egg. Caterpillars May to July. **FP:** ash.

September Thorn
Ennomos erosaria Schiff.

Des: forewing 1.5–1.8 cm. Wings smoothly ochreous with jagged margins, hindwing with square projection near middle of margin. This angle and smooth appearance distinguish from related species. **H:** mixed deciduous woodland, parks and gardens. **Dis:** widespread in wooded areas, including Britain. Two Irish records. **A:** fairly common. **Fl:** July to October, earlier in southern part of range. **LC:** overwinters in egg stage. Caterpillars May to July. **FP:** oak, lime, birch.

Canary-shouldered Thorn
Ennomos alniaria L.

Des: forewings 1.8–2.0 cm. Wings and body orange-yellow, with sulphur-yellow thorax which, together with brownish speckling on wings, distinguishes it from September Thorn. **H:** woods, fens and marshes, damp valleys, etc. **Dis:** temperate Europe to 64°N; Britain and Ireland. **A:** locally common. **Fl:** July to October. **LC:** overwinters in egg stage. Caterpillars May to July. **FP:** various tree species including alder, birch, lime and willow.

Purple Thorn
Selenia tetralunaria Hufn.

Des: forewing of spring individuals 2.0–2.2 cm; second generation moths much smaller. Wings violet-brown, basal half of fore- and hindwings much darker; dark crescent in tip of each forewing and round dark spot in outer area of each hindwing. Whitish crescent-mark in centre of all four wings. Second-brood individuals more uniformly coloured and more rusty brown. **H:** Woodlands and gardens. **Dis:** Europe; England, Wales and Scotland. **A:** Fairly common. **Fl:** two generations, spring and summer. **LC:** caterpillars in summer and autumn. Overwinters as pupa. **FP:** oak, alder, willow, birch, and other trees.

Early Thorn *Selenia dentaria* F.
Caterpillar – see page 277

Des: forewings 1.9–2.3 cm, brown-yellow to reddish-brown, occasionally melanotic. Three dark crosslines on forewings and dark crescent-shaped mark in each tip; small white crescent on middle crossline, and also on hindwing. **H:** mixed deciduous woodland, parks and gardens. **Dis:** European woodlands; Britain to Orkney, Ireland. **A:** common. **Fl:** two generations, first April and May, second July and August; the latter are smaller and redder. **LC:** caterpillars in summer and autumn; like those of other thorn moths, extremely twig-like in appearance, and rely on camouflage for survival. Winter as pupa. **FP:** deciduous trees and shrubs.

Lunar Thorn *Selenia lunularia* Hübn.

Des: forewings of spring generation 2.0–2.2 cm. Moths of summer generation (not in Britain), much smaller. Wings more golden-brown and margins more jagged than in other *Selenia* species. Like Purple Thorn, basal half of wings darker than outer half. **H:** deciduous woodland, copses, gardens. **Dis:** temperate Europe, including Britain, Ireland. **Fl:** only one generation in Britain, May and June, but summer generation regular in Europe. **LC:** caterpillars (in Britain) July to September. Overwinters as pupa.

Lilac Beauty *Apeira syringaria* L.

Description: forewings 1.7–2.2 cm. Wings yellow-brown, reddish-brown or violet-grey, with orange area near apex of each forewing; whitish patches along leading edges and fine dark line across fore- and hindwings, that on forewing are sharply angled near leading edge. At rest, the forewings are characteristically pleated. Females larger and paler than males.
Habitat: deciduous woodlands.
Distribution: scattered populations all over Europe, including England, Wales and Ireland.

Abundance: locally common.
Flight: June and July; in mainland Europe, sometimes a second generation in August and September.
Life cycle: caterpillars from September to May, hibernating when small.
Foodplants: honeysuckle species, lilac, wild privet, ash.

Scalloped Oak *Crocallis elinguaria* L.

Des: forewing 1.6–2.0 cm. Pale yellow with darker central zone on each forewing between converging crosslines; dark spot in centre. Hindwings paler, with dark central spot and weak crossline. Many Scottish specimens darker and uniformly coloured. **H:** woods, moors, pastures and gardens. **Dis:** Europe to Arctic Circle and in mountains to 1,500 cm. Britain to north of Scotland, Ireland. **A:** common. **Fl:** July and August, earlier on Continent. **LC:** overwinters in egg stage. Caterpillars in spring on many deciduous trees and shrubs.

Swallow-tailed Moth *Ourapteryx sambucaria* L.

Des: forewing 2.5–2.8 cm. Hindwings with conspicuous tail; forewings with two straight, almost parallel crosslines and linear discal spot, hindwings with single crossline. Ground-colour of all wings pale yellow. **H:** gardens, pastures, deciduous woods. **Dis:** temperate Europe, including Britain and Ireland. **A:** common. **Fl:** June and July. **LC:** caterpillar August to June, hibernates. **FP:** ivy elder, clematis, and other trees and shrubs.

Orange Moth *Angerona prunaria* L.

Des: forewing 2.0–2.6 cm. ♂ orange, smaller than pale yellow ♀, wings of each sex freckled with brown and with dark discal streak on all four wings. A common form has basal and outer areas of all wings brown. **H:** open woodland. **Dis:** Europe; England, south Wales, south Ireland. **A:** locally common. **Fl:** late May to July. **LC:** caterpillars August to May, hibernating. **FP:** various trees and shrubs, including birch, lilac, heather.

Spring Usher *Agriopis leucophaearia* Schiff.

Des: forewing in ♂ 1.4–1.8 cm. ♀ flightless, with extremely short wing-stumps. ♂ very variable, often with basal and outer areas of forewings black, sometimes with whole of wings darkened. Hind wings paler, lacking pattern. **H:** deciduous woodlands, large gardens and parks. **Dis:** temperate and warmer parts of Europe including Britain, but only one record from Ireland. **A:** common. **Fl:** February and March. **LC:** caterpillars April to early June. Pupa overwinters. **FP:** oak.

Belted Beauty *Lycia zonaria* Schiff.

Description: forewings of male c. 1.4 cm. Females wingless. Males whitish, with broad oblique, brownish crosslines on fore- and hindwings; veins blackish.
Habitat: coastal sandhills in Britain; on Continent, roadsides, fields, heathland, sandy hillsides.
Distribution: central Europe to central Asia. In Britain, extremely local in north Wales, north-west England, west Scotland and Ireland.
Abundance: locally common.

Flight: end of March to end May. Both sexes rest by day low down on sandhill grasses; males fly at night.
Life cycle: caterpillars appear to be gregarious, occur May to July. Pupa overwinters, for up to four years.
Foodplants: birdsfoot trefoil, plantain, yellow iris, creeping willow, yarrow, heather, knapweed, and other low plants.

Brindled Beauty *Lycia hirtaria* Clerck

Des: forewings 1.8–2.3 cm, yellowish-brown brindled with blackish scales. Dark crosslines usually rather unconspicuous; pale outermost line on forewings. ♀ heavier bodied and more thinly scaled than ♂, sluggish, but perfectly capable of flight. **H:** woods, parks, avenues of trees, common in suburbs of towns. **Dis:** temperate Europe. Britain, but rare and local in Ireland. **A:** often common. **Fl:** March and April. **LC:** caterpillars May to August. Pupa overwinters, sometimes for several years. **FP:** various deciduous trees.

Oak Beauty *Biston strataria* Hufn.

Des: very similar in size and build to Peppered Moth, but antennae of ♂ feathered to tip and with prominent brown bands across forewings, edged by very jagged, blackish crosslines. Fully melanotic specimens occur rarely. **H:** deciduous woods and parkland. **Dis:** temperate Europe; Britain to south Scotland, Ireland. **A:** common. **Fl:** March to May. **LC:** caterpillars May to July. Pupa overwinters. **FP:** oak; also elm, hazel, lime, poplars, and sometimes fruit trees.

Common Heath *Ematurga atomaria* L.

Des: forewing 1.1–1.4 cm. ♂ have feathered antennae, more ample wings, more slender bodies and are darker in colour (♀ illustrated). ♂ ochre-yellow with irregular brown freckling and crosslines, ♀ whiter. Fringes chequered in both sexes. **H:** heaths and moors, downs, open woodland. **Dis:** widespread in Europe to east Asia. Britain and Ireland. **A:** common. **Fl:** April to September in two broods. Dirunal. **LC:** caterpillars in early summer and autumn. Overwinters as pupa. **FP:** heather, clovers, and trefoils.

Bordered White *Bupalus piniarius* L.

Des: forewing 1.4–1.9 cm. ♂ with strongly feathered antennae and wings dark brown to blackish with extensive white or yellowish areas in basal two-thirds; ♀ with simple, thread-like antennae and similar wing pattern, but orange-brown with less contrast between basal and outer areas. **H:** pine forests. **Dis:** temperate Europe including much of Britain and Ireland. **A:** varies considerably, but sometimes a serious pest of pine forests. **Fl:** May and June, later in north. **LC:** caterpillars July to September. Overwinters as pupa. **FP:** pine.

241

Great Oak Beauty *Boarmia roboraria* Schiff.

Description: forewing 2.5–3.3 cm. Distinguished from similar Pale Oak Beauty (*Serraca punctinalis* Scop.) by larger size, more extensive dark patch where central crossline meets trailing edge of forewing, and by presence of square pale patch in tip of forewing on underside. Wings grey with dusting of dark scales and rather indistinct dark crosslines. ♂ has strongly feathered antennae.

Habitat: oak woodland.

Distribution: throughout the extensive deciduous woods of Europe. In Britain, chiefly in south England and south-east Wales.

Abundance: fairly common; decreased and now more local in Britain.

Flight: June and July in Britain; partial second generation in places on Continent.

Life cycle: caterpillars August to May, hibernating.

Foodplants: oak; stated to feed on elm, ash and sometimes fruit trees on Continent.

Willow Beauty
Peribatodes rhomboidaria Schiff.

Des: forewing 1.8–2.2 cm. Considerably smaller and browner than previous species. Pattern of crosslines similar to several other related species, one of which, the Feathered Beauty (*Peribatodes secundaria* Esp.) occurs in south England. This lacks pale square patch in tip of forewing on underside, present in Willow Beauty, and pectinations of ♂ antennae longer and reach nearer tip. **H:** fairly generally distributed in woods, parks, gardens, bushy places. **Dis:** almost throughout Europe, including Britain and Ireland. **A:** common. **Fl:** June to August, sometimes a second generation in autumn. **LC:** caterpillars August to May, hibernating when young. **FP:** numerous deciduous and evergreen trees and shrubs, including fruit trees, birch, hawthorn, garden privet, yew and ivy.

Pale Oak Beauty
Serraca punctinalis Scop.

Des: forewing 2.2–2.5 cm. Differences from larger Great Oak Beauty described under that species. Pale, serrated, outermost crossline usually conspicuous and persists even in melanic specimens. **H:** deciduous woodland, young plantations, pastures, parks and gardens. **Dis:** widespread in temperate Europe including southern England and Wales. Twice recorded in Ireland. **A:** usually common where it occurs. **Fl:** May to July. As with similar species, rests by day, well camouflaged, on tree trunks, sometimes fences. **LC:** caterpillars July and August. Overwinters as pupa. **FP:** oak, beech, birch, sallow.

Mottled Beauty *Alcis repandata* L.

Des: forewing 1.8–2.3 cm. Bears a general resemblance to Willow Beauty, but crosslines on forewing sinuous rather than toothed, outermost usually pale. Extremely variable, within and between populations, e.g. melanotics in both industrial areas and northern pine forest (different genes), proportion of banded forms in populations in west Britain, small grey form often given sub-specific status in Outer Hebrides. **H:** deciduous and coniferous woodland with undergrowth, parks and gardens, rocky moorland. **Dis:** throughout Europe, including Britain and Ireland. **A:** common. **Fl:** end May to mid August. **LC:** caterpillars August to June, hibernating when young. **FP:** birch, bramble, honeysuckle, hawthorn, bilberry, heather, dock, and many other plants.

Grey Birch *Aethalura punctulata* Schiff.

Des: distinctly smaller than near relatives, with forewing just under 1.5 cm. On forewings, three dark crosslines complete only on leading edge, where they form conspicuous spots; outermost line pale, wavy. Fringe chequered. **H:** birch woodland and mixed woods with birch. **Dis:** widespread Europe; Britain to south Scotland, rare in Ireland. **A:** locally common. **Fl:** May and June, earlier on Continent, where occasional second generation occurs. **LC:** caterpillars July and August. Pupa overwinters. **FP:** birch, sometimes alder.

Clouded Border *Lomaspilis marginata* L.

Description: forewings 1.1–1.3 cm, white, with large dark-brown patches along leading edge and outer border. Hindwings white with spots along border. Extent of dark markings extremely variable.
Habitat: widespread in woodland, carr, and fen woodlands, marshy places.
Distribution: widespread in the deciduous woodland zone of Europe and Asia, including Britain and Ireland.

Abundance: locally common.
Flight: single-brooded in Britain, in June and July, but regularly double-brooded further south on Continent, in spring and summer.
Life cycle: caterpillars in August and September. Overwinters as pupa, and sometimes remains in this state for more than one year.
Foodplants: chiefly sallow and aspen; birch, hazel and poplar also recorded.

Common White Wave
Cabera pusaria L.

Des: forewings 1.2–1.5 cm. Wings fine-scaled, white, forewings with three, hindwings with two, brownish crosslines which form continuous lines when moth is at rest (see illustration). ♂ has feathered antennae. **H:** deciduous woodland, meadows. **Dis:** temperate Europe from lowlands to mountains. Britain and Ireland. **A:** common. **Fl:** double-brooded in south, including south England, May to August. **LC:** caterpillars June to September. Pupa overwinters. **FP:** sallow, birch, alder, oak, elm, and other trees.

Common Wave
Cabera exanthemata Scop.

Des: resembles Common White Wave, but coarser-scaled, wings dusted with brown scales and outer crossline curved. Often more obscurely marked than Common White Wave. **H:** damp woodland, carr, fens, bogs and marshes. **Dis:** Europe, including Britain and Ireland. **A:** fairly common, but more local than previous species. **Fl:** May to August, later emergences being a partial second generation. **LC:** caterpillars July to September. **FP:** sallow, aspen, preferring small bushes.

White-pinion Spotted
Bapta bimaculata F.

Des: forewings 1.2–1.4 cm, white, with two conspicuous blackish spots on each leading edge. Hindwings white. **H:** deciduous woodland, hedgerows, parks and gardens. **Dis:** widespread in temperate Europe from lowlands to mountains. England, south Wales, Ireland. **A:** fairly common. **Fl:** May and June. **LC:** caterpillars June and July. Pupa overwinters. **FP:** wild cherry, bird cherry, blackthorn, plum, hawthorn.

Light Emerald
Campaea margaritata L.

Des: forewing 1.8–2.4 cm. When fresh, elegantly-shaped wings are delicate blue-green, but quickly fade to whitish. Two almost straight dark, white-edged crosslines on forewings, outer ones continuing on hindwings. **H:** woodlands, large gardens and parks. **Dis:** deciduous woodland zone of Europe, through Britain and Ireland. **A:** common. **Fl:** May to September, in two generations. **LC:** caterpillars late summer, and September to May. Overwinters as caterpillar. **FP:** beech, oak, birch, hawthorn, and other deciduous trees.

245

Sussex Emerald
Thalera fimbrialis Scop.

Des: forewings 1.4–1.8 cm. Ground colour of wings grey-green to yellow-green. Hindwing characteristically notched on margin. Forewing with two, hindwing one, fine white transverse lines. Fringes chequered red and white. **H:** shingle in Britain. On Continent, much more catholic; heaths, waste ground, dry fields. **Dis:** temperate Europe; south-east England. **A:** fairly common. **Fl:** mid-June to mid-August. **LC:** caterpillars late August to June, hibernating. **FP:** yarrow, thyme, mugwort, golden-rod, probably other herbs.

Large Emerald
Geometra papilionaria L.

Des: largest green geometer of area, with forewing length of over 2.5 cm. Wings rich bluish-green when fresh, marked with fine, jagged, broken crosslines. **H:** woods and heaths. **Dis:** deciduous woodland zone of Europe, including Britain and Ireland. **A:** fairly common. **Fl:** May to August, emerging later in Britain. **LC:** caterpillars September to May, hibernating. **FP:** birch, sometimes alder, hazel.

Common Emerald
Hemithea aestivaria Hübn.

Des: forewings 1.3–1.5 cm, dark grey-green when fresh. Hindwings distinctly angled, but not notched (cf. Sussex Emerald). Wings with fine, white crosslines, fringes chequered. **H:** deciduous woodland, hedgerows, parks, gardens. **Dis:** temperate Europe, including England, Wales and Ireland. **A:** common. **Fl:** June to August. **LC:** caterpillars August to late April, hibernating. **FP:** hawthorn, blackthorn, birch, oak, sallow.

Small Emerald
Hemistola chrysoprasaria Esp.

Des: forewings 1.3–1.5 cm. Wings rich green when fresh, but pigment seems particularly unstable in this species and quickly fades, often in unsightly blotches, to yellow. Hindwings angled. Wings with fine white crosslines. **H:** woods on basic soils, hedgerows, chalk downland. **Dis:** central and southern Europe, England. **A:** local. **Fl:** June to August. **LC:** caterpillars August to June, hibernating. **FP:** wild clematis.

Barred Red *Ellopia fasciaria* L.

Des: forewing 1.8–2.1 cm. Common form in Britain has greyish-red wings, but on Continent there is a form with green wings, *ab. prasinaria* Schiff. Both have two white crosslines on forewings and one on hindwings. **H:** coniferous woodland. Red form associated with lowland pine forest, green form with upland pine and spruce forest. **Dis:** Europe, including Britain and Ireland. **A:** common in suitable habitat. **Fl:** June to August. **LC:** caterpillars August to June, hibernating when small. **FP:** pine, Douglas fir, Norway spruce.

Grass Emerald
Pseudoterpna pruinata Hufn.

Des: forewing 1.5–1.7 cm. Ground colour of wings grey-green to pale bluish-green. Forewings each with two jagged dark crosslines and a pale outermost line. Hindwings with one dark line and one pale line. **H:** heathland, shingle, road embankments. **Dis:** central, western and south Europe, including Britain and Ireland. **A:** locally common. **Fl:** June to August. **LC:** caterpillars August to May, hibernating. **FP:** needle whin, gorse, broom.

247

Full-spotted Ermel *Yponomeuta evonymella* L.

Description: forewing 1.0–1.3 cm. Forewings silver white with five longitudinal rows of black dots, innermost row consisting of 9–11 dots. Hindwings smoky brown with dark margin, broader and shorter than forewings. Antennae long, fine, almost two-thirds length of forewings. When at rest, the wings are rolled round the body so that the moth appears tube-like. If disturbed, it hops quickly away and drops to the ground.

Habitat: Full-spotted Ermels are found in valley woodlands, banks of streams with bushes and trees, also in gardens and parks.

Distribution: found almost throughout Europe, from river valleys up to deciduous tree line. Includes Britain and Ireland.

Abundance: this fluctuates from year to year, but usually they are common to abundant.

Flight: early July to mid-August.

Life cycle: the young caterpillars hibernate on the buds of foodplant and become active in spring when these buds break. They are highly gregarious, living in a communal silk web. They feed until late May or early June, then pupate in dense cocoons *en masse* in the larval web, or in a web amongst debris at the base of the foodplant.

Foodplants: almost exclusively bird cherry, *Prunus padus.* This is a northern species in Britain, and presumably another foodplant is used in southern Britain.

General: Several other species of *Yponomeuta* occur in Britain. Members of the genus are easily recognized: all have elongated wings with rather rounded tips. The forewings are white or greyish with numerous small black dots, and the hindwings are dark greyish-brown. Most of the species can be distinguished from one another by paying attention to the number and distribution of the black dots on the forewings, and also on the tegulae of the thorax, and the amount of grey on the wings. In *Y. sedella* Treits., (Twenty-spot Ermel) the forewings are entirely grey and there are no spots in the terminal area. *Y. plumbella* D. & S. (Kent Ermel) has a considerable amount of grey shading, but is best distinguished by the presence of a larger black blotch near the dorsum and another in the tip of the wing. *Y. rorrella* Hübn. (Few-spotted Ermel) and *Y. irrorella* Hübn (Surrey Ermel) also have grey shading on the forewings, in the former extending from base to tip in the leading half of the wing, and in the latter forming a conspicuous dark blotch near the centre of each wing, and a dark terminal band. Opinions remain divided concerning the validity of three other 'species' comprising what is known as the '*padella* complex'. Moths in this group are variable in colour and structurally so similar that it is considered unsafe to try to assign caught specimens to a species within the group. However, the foodplants and larval habits are evidently different. *Y. padella* Linn. (Common Hawthorn Ermel) feeds gregariously in a dense web on various rosaceous trees, blackthorn, hawthorn, cherry or plum, and the cocoons are often formed *en masse* within the web. *Y. malinellus* Zell. (Adkin's Apple Ermel) has similar habits, but appears to be restricted to apple, and the cocoons are formed in neat rows in the bottom of the web. *Y cagnagella* Hübn (Allied Ermel) occurs on spindle and cultivated *Euonymus japonica*, and the larvae of this species also make their cocoons in neat rows. The three are perhaps best regarded as biological races of one species on the way to becoming truly separate. Spindle is also the foodplant of *Y. irrorella* (Surrey Ermel) and *Y. plumbella*, (Kent Ermel) but few larvae occur in each web, and they pupate alone. *Y. sedella* (Twenty-spot Ermel) may also feed on spindle, but in Britain is found characteristically on orpine (*Sedum telephium*). *Y. rorrella* (Few-spotted Ermel) is found on white willow (*Salix alba*)

Dark-inlaid Grass-veneer
Crambus lathoniellus Zinck.

Des: forewing 1.0–1.1 cm. Forewings pale brown with long, gleaming white, pointed streak from base of each wing well past middle, and angled outer line which cuts off triangular tip containing a white patch. Hindwings ample, brown with pale fringes. **H:** meadows, wood edges, parks, gardens. **Dis:** almost throughout Europe. Britain to Shetlands, Ireland. **A:** abundant. **Fl:** May to August. **LC:** summer to April in silk gallery amongst roots. **FP:** roots of grasses. **G:** numerous species of crambid or grass-veneer. Many rest on grass stems by day with wings closed round body and are easily disturbed. Look larger in flight because of large hindwings.

Common Grass-veneer
Agriphila tristella Schiff.

Des: forewing 1.1–1.3 cm. Rusty brownish, with narrow, pale longitudinal streak reaching wing margin. Hindwings pale grey. Long, narrow forewings and broad hindwings typical of crambids show well in set specimen illustrated. **H:** grassy places, **Dis:** throughout Europe; Britain to Orkney, Ireland. **A:** abundant. **Fl:** July to September. **LC:** caterpillars September to June in silk galleries among grass roots. **FP:** roots of grasses in dry areas.

Yellow Satin Grass-veneer
Crambus perlella Scop.

Description: forewings 1.1–1.3 cm. Typical crambid shape with long, narrow forewings and broad hindwings. In one form, forewings bright, glossy white or yellowish; in *ab. warringtoniellus* Staint. (illustrated), veins and part of ground colour streaked dusky grey. Hindwings whitish.
Habitat: dry calcareous grassland, meadows bogs.
Distribution: throughout most of Europe from lowlands to tops of mountains, including Britain and Ireland.
Abundance: common to very common.
Flight: end of June to mid-August. Easily disturbed by day, when moth flies a few metres before settling again on a grass stem, becoming difficult to see. Presumably alert behaviour combined with trick of 'disappearing' on settling has survival value.
Life cycle: caterpillars from September to June in silk gallery among bases of stems of grasses.
Foodplants: grasses, eating stem bases.

Allied Ermel
Yponomeuta cagnagella Hübn.

Des: forewing 1.2–1.3 cm. Forewings silvery white with three row of black dots, innermost with four to seven dots; fringes white. Hindwings grey-brown. **H:** wood edges, gardens. **Dis:** temperate and cool regions of Europe, including Britain and Ireland. **A:** common. **Fl:** July and August. **LC:** gregarious caterpillars live in communal web on foodplant in May and June, said to have hibernated when young. Pupae in cocoons in larval web. **FP:** spindle, including *Euonymus japonicus* in gardens.

Adkin's Apple Ermel
Yponomeuta malinellus Zell.

Des: forewing up to 1.0 cm. Wings similar to those of Allied Ermel, with inner line of dots numbering four to six, but fringes pale grey. **H:** orchards, edges of woods. **Dis:** temperate Europe to Mediterranean. Britain. Introduced to North America. **A:** sometimes a pest of apple orchards. **Fl:** July. **LC:** young caterpillars said to hibernate; feed in communal web in spring to late May. **FP:** apple. **G:** status of these two *Yponomeuta* is uncertain; some believe they are mere races of another species *Yponomeuta padella* L.

Wax Moth *Galleria mellonella* L.

Des: forewing 1.3–1.7 cm. One of the most robust of European pyralid moths; ♀ usually larger than ♂. Forewings ochreous brown mixed with lead grey in ♀ more purplish-brown. A few black longitudinal streaks in outer half of wing. Hindwings grey. **H:** bee-hives. **Dis:** Europe, including Britain and Ireland. **A:** local; decreased. **Fl:** June to October, two or more broods. Moths scuttle about in hives, occasionally flying abroad. **LC:** caterpillars occur through much of year; winter larvae hibernate. Live in galleries amongst honeycombs. Cocoons often in masses. **Food:** wax in bees' nests and hives.

Pine Knot-horn
Dioryctria abietella Schiff.

Des: forewing 1.2–1.5 cm. Ground colour of fore wings grey, speckled with dark scales, and with two to three whitish, black-edged crosslines and wh discal crescent. Hindwings greyish-white. coniferous woodland and parks. **Dis:** Europ including Britain. **A:** common. **Fl:** July and Augu **LC:** details of life cycle of very similar *Dioryc* species have to be worked out; larvae found cones, shoots, and bark of pines.

Mediterranean Flour Moth
Ehestia kuehniella Zell.

Des: forewing 0.8–1.1 cm; narrow, grey, with indistinct irregular crosslines. Hindwings white with dark veins. **H:** flour mills, bakeries, larders, seldom out-of-doors. **Dis:** worldwide in areas of human habitation. **A:** sometimes abundant. **Fl:** April to October in three overlapping broods. **LC:** caterpillars make silk galleries in flour and other stored food. Can be a serious pest in mills.

Translucent Straw Pearl
Microstega hyalinalis Hübn.

Des: forewing c.1.3 cm. Forewings glossy li yellow with greyish-yellow clouding on leadi edge; inner line forming rounded curve, outer c curved strongly in upper half; two dark-yell discal spots. Hindwings paler with wavy crossli **H:** chalk downland, clearings in beech woods. **D** Europe, including England. **A:** local. **Fl:** June a July. Easily disturbed by day. **LC:** caterpill August to May, hibernating when young. Pupa June in a cocoon among leaves of foodplant. **F** black knapweed.

Meal Moth *Pyralis farinalis* L.

Des: forewing 1.0–1.5 cm. Very characteristic markings on light brown ground colour, with reddish-brown basal patch and outer area on each forewing, former edged and latter crossed by a white line; outer line wide at leading edge then snaking across dark area. **H:** barns. **Dis:** worldwide. **A:** often common inside buildings. **Fl:** June to August. Moth rests on inside walls of barns with tip of abdomen turned up and wings spread. Occasionally flies at night and comes to light. **LC:** caterpillars in silk gallery amongst stored grain; rate of development variable. **Food:** stored grain.

Small Magpie *Eurrhypara hortulata* L

Des: forewing 1.3–1.6 cm. Unmistakable bla spotted, white wings and orange-yellow head a thorax and tip of abdomen. **H:** open, shady woc land, parks, gardens. **Dis:** across Europe and As Britain to south Scotland, Ireland. **A:** comm **Fl:** June and July. **LC:** caterpillars August a September in rolled or spun leaves; spend winter cocoon under bark or in hollow stem and pupate spring, a common strategy among pyralids. **F** stinging nettle.

Wainscot Grass-veneer
Chilo phragmitella Hübn.

Description: forewings 1.3–1.8 cm; wing-profile of female narrower and more pointed than that of male, and wings longer and paler. Male usually reddish-brown with weak dark longitudinal streak through dark discal spot; hindwings brown. Female almost unmarked except for discal spot, pale yellowish-brown, hindwings white. Conspicuously long palps in both sexes.
Habitat: reed beds, banks of slow-flowing rivers and streams, lakes with marginal vegetation.
Distribution: central Europe extending into eastern Europe to central Sweden, England, Wales and south Scotland.
Abundance: locally very common.
Flight: June to August. Moths rest on lower stems and dead leaves of reed during day and are well camouflaged. Fly gently at night.
Life cycle: caterpillars live from September to June in lower stems and rootstocks; pupate in stem below an exit 'window' made by caterpillar.
Foodplants: pith inside stems of common reed and reed sweet-grass.

False-caddis Water-veneer
Acentria ephemerella Schiff.

Des: narrow forewings 0.6–0.9 cm. ♀ usua wingless, but fully winged form larger than ♂. A wings narrow, whitish, unmarked. **H:** shallow lak with plenty of water plants. **Dis**: through Europ including Britain and Ireland. **A:** locally commo ♂ sometimes swarm at light far from water. F summer. **LC:** wingless females fully aquatic. Cate pillars adapted for life under water, in loose spi nings among water weeds to 2 m depth. Coco also under water. **FP:** Chiefly Canadian pondwee and pondweeds (*Potomogeton* species).

Gold-fringed Tabby
Hypsopygia costalis F.

Des: forewing 0.8–1.0 cm. Unmistakable: win purplish-red with two yellow crosslines, whic commence as club-shaped spots on leading edg of each forewing and continue across hindwing **H:** hedgerows, thatch, haystacks; sometimes insi barns. **Dis:** Europe, western Asia and parts North America. England. **A:** locally common. F chiefly July and August. **LC:** caterpillars Septemb to May. **FP:** stored clover and hay, can be comm enough to be a pest. Also squirrels' dreys.

Brown China-mark *Elophila nymphaeata* L.

Description: forewing 1.1–1.4 cm. Females slightly larger than males, but less strongly marked. Wings white, with elaborate pattern of brown outlines and bands, and clear golden-brown margins to fore- and hindwings before pale fringes. Of the several other china-mark species in Europe, this is largest. Beautiful China-mark (*Nymphula stagnata* Don.) is most like Brown China-mark, but is smaller and whiter, without extensive brown areas on wings.
Habitat: margins of ponds, lakes and canals with abundant aquatic vegetation.
Distribution: Europe, including Britain and Ireland.

Abundance: usually common where it occu and readily colonizes newly available habitat, su as gravel pits.
Flight: June to August or September; two gene ations on Continent, one in Britain.
Life cycle: caterpillars July and August, and Se tember to May; fully aquatic, first mining a lea then living in a floating case made of pieces water plant leaf. Pupa in an underwater cocoon.
Foodplants: pondweeds (*Potomogeton* specie bur-reed, frogbit, fringed water lily.

March Day *Diurnea fagella* Schiff.

Des: forewing 0.9–1.2 cm. Strong difference between ♂ (illustrated) with fully developed wings, and flightless ♀ with short, pointed wings. Pattern varies, and wings sometimes almost entirely black. **H:** deciduous woodland and tree-steppe zones. **Dis:** Europe to central Asia; Britain and Ireland. **A:** common; ♂ on tree trunks by day. **Fl:** March and April. **LC:** caterpillars June to October, in loose spinning or folded leaf. Pupa overwinters. **FP:** oak, beech, birch, sallow.

Oak Long-horned Flat-body *Carcina quercana* F.

Des: forewing 0.8–0.9 cm, characteristically angled leading edge and pointed tip. Ground colour orange-red with fine brown dusting; clear yellow, triangular patch on leading edge, with dark spot below. Hindwings whitish. Antennae very long, white. **H:** woods and gardens. **Dis:** Europe including Britain, North America. **A:** common. **Fl:** July and August. **LC:** caterpillars in spring in white webs under leaves of foodplants. **FP:** oak, beech, sycamore, apple, etc.

Common Clothes Moth *Tineola bisselliella* Hum.

Des: forewing 0.5–0.7 cm. Small, inconspicuous moth with yellowish sheen on wings and slow whirring flight. Wings without pattern. **H:** hedges bushes, but mainly in houses and store rooms with fabrics and furs. **Dis:** world-wide. Probably originally inhabitant of birds' nests and lairs of mammals, now a domestic pest. **A:** rare in open countryside, but can become very common in houses; much decreased in Britain. **Fl:** May to September; in houses throughout year. **LC:** continuous succession of generations; caterpillars in silk tubes among food material. **Food:** woollen fabrics, furs, other animal material.

Funereal Ermel *Ethmia funerella* F.

Des: forewings 0.8–0.9 cm with striking pattern of blackish-brown blotches and spots on white ground. Hindwings brown with white fringes. **H:** gardens, shady deciduous woods, reaching high into mountains. **Dis:** deciduous tree zone of Europe to Caucasus; England. **A:** widespread; local in England. **Fl:** June to September. **LC:** caterpillars August to October, in slight web under leaves of foodplant. Pupa overwinters. **FP:** comfrey, lungwort, gromwell.

Bordered Echium Ermel *Ethmia bipunctella* F.

Description: forewing length 1.0–1.5 cm. Upper half of forewings dark brown, contiguous with three spots of same colour in middle of wing; lower half of wings white. Two black spots on white thorax. Abdomen yellow. Hindwings light brown.
Habitat: warmth-loving species of dry fields and hillsides, and shingle, dependent on presence of viper's bugloss (*Echium vulgare*).
Distribution: central and southern Europe to Asia Minor; England, only in south-east.

Abundance: moderately common.
Flight: two generations, first April to June, second August to October. Moths rest on posts during day strongly resembling bird-droppings.
Life cycle: caterpillars June and July, and autumn, under slight web on leaves and amongst flowers of foodplant. Pupa overwinters in dead stem or rotten wood.
Foodplant: viper's bugloss.

Cnephasia stephensiana Doubl.

Des: forewing length 0.9–1.1 cm. Very variable pattern: the grey forewings are traversed by broad, dark-brown-grey bands, of which usually only the middle one reaches the inner margin. **H:** gardens, wasteland, light woodlands. **Dis:** widespread in Europe, including Britain and Ireland. A: common in some regions, nowhere rare. Several very similar species. **Fl:** end May to August. **LC:** April to June after hibernation. **FP:** In spun shoots of various herbaceous plants.

Codlin Moth *Cydia pomonella* L.

Des: forewing length 0.7–0.8 cm. The brownish ground colour is covered by numerous fine, grey transverse lines around the base and the central field. The outer third of the forewing is marked by a brown, round patch which is crossed by golden lines. Hindwings dark. **H:** gardens and orchards. **Dis:** Europe. From here it has spread throughout the world wherever apple trees are cultivated. **A:** common; this species is often a pest. **Fl:** May to August in one or two generations. **LC:** during development of apples. **FP:** apples (apple maggot).

Hedya nubiferana Hw.

Des: forewing 0.8–1 cm; with dark basal half of forewing marked with fine lively pattern made up of bluish, red-brown, whitish and blackish spots. Outer half predominantly pale to whitish, but with dark apex. Hindwings smoky-grey. **H:** gardens, parks and deciduous woodlands. **Dis:** Europe to Asia Minor, including Britain and Ireland. **A:** usually common. **Fl:** June to August. **LC:** April to May. **FP:** buds and young shoots of deciduous trees; the caterpillar may occasionally cause damage to fruit trees. **G:** at rest the moth resembles a bird dropping.

Green Oak Tortrix *Tortrix viridana* L.

Des: forewings 0.9–1.2 cm; uniform light green with grey hindwings and white fringes. **H:** oak woods, parkland and large gardens containing oak. **Dis:** deciduous woodland zone of Europe, North Africa and Asia Minor. Britain and Ireland. **A:** abundant. **Fl:** June and July, sometimes disturbed in clouds from oak branches. **LC:** caterpillars serious defoliators of oaks; live among spun shoots. Black pupa in spinning. **FP:** oak. **G:** young of many insectivorous woodland birds nourished largely on these caterpillars.

Dark Oblique-barred Twist
Pandemis heparana Schiff.

Des: forewings 0.8–1.2 cm, ♀ larger than ♂, and with tips of forewings more produced at apex. Forewings deep reddish ochreous, with weak reticulations and oblique dark bars. Hindwing dark brownish-grey. Specimen illustrated is either unusually pale or another, related species. **H:** deciduous woodland, parks and gardens. **Dis:** Europe and Asia. Britain and Ireland. **A:** common. **Fl:** June to August. Double-brooded on Continent. **LC:** young caterpillars hibernate and feed up in spring in rolled leaves. Pupa in larval habitation. **FP:** polyphagous on deciduous trees.

Currant Twist
Pandemis cerasana Hübn.

Des: forewing 0.8–1.1 cm. Wing shape similar to others of genus, commonly called 'bell moths' because of outline of resting insect. This species has rather rounded dark basal patch, oblique dark cross band and dark spot on leading edge near apex; but ground colour and blackness of marking varies. **H:** woodland, gardens. **Dis:** deciduous tree zone throughout Europe and Asia, including Britain and Ireland. **A:** common. **Fl:** June to September. **LC:** overwinters as egg or young caterpillar. Caterpillars live in folded or rolled leaves. **FP:** polyphagous on many trees and shrubs.

Pine-shoot Moth
Rhyacionia buoliana Schiff.

Des: forewings 0.8–0.9 cm; orange-brown with whitish longitudinal streaks, fine white dots along leading edge and an incomplete white line before apical area. Hindwings dark. **H:** pine forests and plantations. **Dis:** Europe to Far East. Britain and Ireland. **A:** common. **Fl:** June to August. **LC:** caterpillars overwinter in hollowed-out buds and feed on shoots and buds in spring. Serious pests; when terminal shoot is attacked, permanent 'post-horn' bend is formed in growing tree. Pupa in silk cocoon in larval habitation.

Small Brown-barred Conch
Eupoecilia ambiguella Hübn.

Des: forewings c.0.7 cm, narrow, light brown, with oblique, dark median band. Dark dots in marginal area. Hindwings dark. **H:** wine-growing areas of Europe, but in Britain on moist heaths and lime-stone scrub. **Dis:** Europe, extending to North Africa and Far East. South England and south Wales. **A:** local and scarce in Britain, but can be a pest of viniculture. **Fl:** May and late summer in two generations; only one generation in Britain. **LC:** on Continent, first generation of larvae in flower-heads of vines, second in the grapes. In Britain, caterpillars in late summer in fruits of alder buckthorn. **FP:** grape vine, alder buckthorn, honeysuckle, ivy, possibly other fruits.

Degeer's Longhorn
Nemophora degeerella L.

Des: forewings c.1 cm, ♂ larger than ♀. Metallic golden-brown with oblique yellow cross band clearly delineated in black. Veins dark. ♂ has enormously long, white-tipped antennae, ♀ has shorter antennae. **H:** wood margins and rides, with some shade. **Dis:** Europe to Asia Minor; England, Wales and Ireland. **A:** locally common. **Fl:** May and June. Moths easily disturbed by day, and at dusk ♂ fly in dancing swarms. **LC:** caterpillars live in a flat case made of bits of dead leaf. Pupation inside case. **FP:** probably leaf litter.

Metallic Long-horn Nemophora metallica Poda (= scabiosella Scop.)

Des: forewings 0.8–0.9 cm, uniform golden-brown colour with strong metallic sheen. Hindwings similar to forewings but with long fringes. Very long antennae. **H:** downland, meadows, margins of wooded valleys. **Dis:** Europe, but only in southern England to Norfolk. **A:** locally fairly common. **Fl:** June to August; flies during daytime. **LC:** caterpillars August to April, first in a seed, then in a case made from a seed, finally in a flat case made of leaf pieces. **FP:** scabious, knapweed, and other composites.

Common Plume Moth
Emmelina monodactyla L.

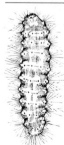

Des: plume moths have feather-like wings in which the forewings are usually divided into two lobes, and hindwings more deeply so into three lobes. They rest with wings outstretched. Legs long, slender and brittle. In the Common Plume, forewings 1.1–1.3 cm. Wings greyish-white to reddish-yellow, forewing with conspicuous dark dot in centre. **H:** woodlands, gardens. **Dis:** temperate Europe; Britain and Ireland. **A:** common. **Fl:** from June, moth hibernates. **FP:** convolvulus.

Large White Plume Moth
Pterophorus pentadactyla L.

Des: forewing 1.2–1.4 cm. Pure white, lobes of wings broadly fringed. **H:** fields and meadows, gardens, hedgerows. **Dis:** Europe, including Britain and Ireland. **A:** common. **Fl:** June and July. **LC:** caterpillars hibernate when small, and full-grown in May. **FP:** convolvulus.

Grey Fruit-tree Case
Coleophora hemerobiella Scop.

Des: the case-moths are a large and difficult genus; very narrow hindwings with extremely wide fringes. This species has forewings 0.5–0.6 cm, grey-brown, finely speckled with black dots. **H:** orchards and deciduous woodlands. **Dis:** Europe to Asia Minor, southern England. **A:** common in warmer areas. **Fl:** July. **LC:** caterpillar stage lasts two years; young caterpillar lives in a curved case made from leaf-cuticle; later, in a straight case cut from leaf margin. Similar cases are made by the other *Coleophora* species. **FP:** fruit trees, hawthorn.

Larch-mining Case
Coleophora laricella Hübn.

Des: forewing barely 0–5 cm; wings brownish, with usual wide fringes. **H:** larch woods. **Dis:** Europe to Japan; Britain and Ireland. **A:** locally very common; in places, can be a pest, causing complete defoliation of larches. **Fl:** June and July. **LC:** young caterpillars mine larch needles; autumn case made from part of a needle. After hibernation, caterpillar in a stumpy, white case. **FP:** larch.

Goose-feather Case
Coleophora anatipennella Hübn.

Des: forewing 1.2–1.5 cm. Forewings whitish, with scattering of blackish scales. Hindwings uniformly brown, as are fringes of forewings. **H:** light deciduous woods, orchards. **Dis:** deciduous woodland zone of Europe to near East; Britain and western Ireland. **A:** common. **Fl:** June and July. **LC:** full-grown case, in spring, black and pistol-shaped. **FP:** undersides of leaves of apple, hawthorn or blackthorn.

Argyresthia bonnetella L.

Des: small species with wingspan of c.1 cm. Wings narrow, with broad fringes, especially on hindwings. Forewings creamy white with oblique brown band curving into apex and white streak at base of each wing. Hindwings dark grey. **H:** hedgerows and scrub. **Dis:** Europe including whole of Britain and Ireland. **Fl:** June to August. **A:** very common. **LC:** caterpillars hibernate when young, and in spring mine shoots. **FP:** hawthorn.

Argyresthia conjugella Zell.

Des: 1.0–1.4 cm. Forewings whitish suffused with purplish towards leading edge. Brown streak from base of each wing, and brown cross-band angled towards tip. Hindwings grey. **H.** decidous woodland, gardens, also high in mountains. **Dis:** Europe, Asia, North America. Britain and Ireland. **A:** common. **Fl:** May to July. **LC:** caterpillar June to August in rowan berries, on Continent attacks apples and can cause damage. Hibernates in cocoon as pupa or full-grown caterpillar. **FP:** apple, whitebeam, rowan.

Lyonetia clerkella L.

Des: wingspan 0.7–0.8 cm. Forewings narrow, silvery-white with dark patch at tip and long, brown fringe in outer half. Hindwings very narrow with long fringes, grey. **H:** deciduous woodlands, hedgerows, gardens. **Dis:** Europe, North Africa, from lowlands to mountains. Britain and Ireland. **A:** common. **Fl:** throughout year, last generation hibernates. **LC:** continuous generations through year. Caterpillars make sinuous mines in leaves. **FP:** cherry, apple.

Classification

While almost any insect that is a butterfly or moth can be recognized immediately as such (the exceptions being some of the clearwings), it soon becomes clear that there are different categories of lepidopteron. Most people are able to distinguish a butterfly from a moth, and it is but a step to discover that the butterflies themselves fall into several clear-cut categories, as do the moths. It is interesting to observe that in the majority of instances the superficial features – what bird-watchers would call 'jizz' – of different groups of butterfly and moth are amply reinforced by the more formal characters that the taxonomist demands when constructing a classification scheme. There is persuasive evidence that the differences between species and species-groups exist because they have evolved from a common ancestral stock, as a result of the interaction between heritable variability and environmental pressure; it is the taxonomist's task to point out inter-relationships as well as to catalogue similarities and differences.

In classifying the Lepidoptera, the scientist makes use of a variety of structural features which are regarded as important. They include: structure of the head appendages, particularly the mouthparts, palps and antennae; the pattern of the veins of the wings and the way the fore- and hindwings are coupled together; and structure of the male and female genitalia. Conclusions drawn from the study of adult structures are further reinforced by comparison of the early stages in the life cycle, and increasingly by genetic and biochemical studies. Some of the techniques involved are, of course, inaccessible to the amateur naturalist, but it is useful to know on what broad principle an expert will agree with one's own differentiation of, say, a hawkmoth and a prominent. Broadly, the Lepidoptera can be grouped into the following categories:

Butterflies (*Rhopalocera*). Nearly 300 species in central and western Europe, between Portugal and Arctic Norway. Recognizable by clubbed antennae; by having fore- and hindwings locked together without using a 'bristle and catch' mechanism; and by sleeping with their wings held together above their backs. Diurnal. The modern view is that skippers are so different from other butterflies that they should be regarded as a separate group.

Hawkmoths (*Sphingidae*). Large tropical family with about 25 species in central and western Europe. Usually large moths, with streamlined bodies, thickened antennae, hindwings much smaller than forewings, and fast, powerful flight. Caterpillars usually with curved horn on hind end of body.

'Bombyces'. This 'flag of convenience' includes a heterogenous group of somewhat unrelated families broadly connected by being large, males having strongly feathered antennae and caterpillars which are hairy and which make silken cocoons. The group includes lackeys and eggars (*Lasiocampidae*), silkmoths (*Attacidae*), tiger moths and footmen (*Arctiidae*), and tussocks

(*Lymantriidae*). The prominents (*Notodontidae*) can also be placed here.

Noctuids or owlet moths (*Noctuidae*). Over 700 species in central and western Europe. Mostly thick-bodied, nocturnal moths with a forewing pattern consisting of variations on a theme of three cross-lines and three stigmata near the middle of the wing – orbicular (round), reniform (kidney-shaped), and claviform (dart-shaped) stigmata.

Geometers or inch-worms (*Geometridae*). Approximately 700 species in central and western Europe. Mostly slim-bodied and ample-winged, having slow, fluttering flight. Forewings variously marked. Rest with wings held flat and spread. 'Looper' caterpillars.

'Micro-moths'. Another term which is falling into disuse because of the heterogenous nature of the groups included. As implied, included here are the majority of small to extremely small moths, most of which occur in Europe. Most have not been referred to in this book. A few examples of pyrales (*Pyralidae*), plume moths (*Pterophoridae*), tortricids or bell moths (*Tortricidae*), and case-moths (*Coleophoridae*) have been included.

Swifts (*Hepialidae*). About 10 species in central and western Europe. Very primitive moths with peculiar device for connecting the pairs of wings and vein-structure which shows affinity with more ancient insects. Rather less primitive are the goats and leopard moths (*Cossidae*).

It is believed that the Lepidoptera shared a common ancestry with the caddis-flies (*Trichoptera*), and that the hair-like structures that clothe the wings of these insects were the precursors of the scales characteristic of butterflies and moths.

Variation with species

Populations of a species that became isolated from one another, for example on mountain tops or islands, have often produced recognizably different local forms or races, a result of the selective influence by the environment on the natural variation which occurs in all species. When the differences are considered to be significant, the different populations are termed sub-species and given names. Britain, a group of offshore islands, is poor on species compared to mainland Europe, but remarkably rich in local forms and sub-species, as entomological forays to south England, the Highlands, Shetlands, Orkney, the Hebrides and Scilly Isles will quickly show.

Changes within populations, observable within a human lifetime, are extremely rare; the classic example is the spread of dark forms of moth that rest in exposed places in industrial areas of Britain and the Ruhr. The best-known and most intensively studied example is the Peppered Moth (*Biston betularia*). The late Dr. H. B. D. Kettlewell proved,

antennae shapes

by field experiment, that the original pale form of the species was at an advantage in rural areas where the trees remained lichen-covered, but was easily seen and devoured by insect-eating birds in soot-blackened industrial areas, where the melanotic *ab carbonaria* was overlooked. The converse effect was demonstrated with *ab carbonaria* in rural sites.

Metamorphosis

The bodies of insects are covered by a tough, waterproof exoskeleton of a material called chitin. This poses a problem during growth which has been solved by periodically shedding the old exoskeleton: beneath is a new one which is soft and flexible at first, and stretches before hardening. So as an insect grows, its body length increases.

In the more primitive insects like locusts, the young resemble adults in general form except that they are smaller, lack wings, and have undeveloped sexual organs. These early stages are called nymphs; each skin-shedding is an ecdysis, and the periods between ecdyses are termed instars. In the Lepidoptera and other advanced insects, there are four stages to the life cycle. In the caterpillar stage, which is the feeding and growing stage, there are often five instars.

The caterpillars are quite unlike the adult insect, and give no clue to what they will turn into, unless the life history is already known. Between the caterpillar and adult stages, a chrysalis or pupa is formed, in which the tissues of the caterpillars are reorganized into the adult structure, from groups of cells floating in an energy-rich fluid. According to the species, the time spent as a pupa varies greatly. When the time approaches for the adult to emerge, one sees first the dark eyes, and later the pattern of the wings beginning to appear beneath the pupal shell. When the insect emerges, the wings are initially limp and unexpanded. A suitable resting place is found, then the insect pumps blood into the wing veins, causing the wings to expand. The fluid is withdrawn and the wings become hard enough to support the animal in flight. The whole process may take several hours, during which the insect is particularly vulnerable.

It has long been known that each species of butterfly or moth has its particular season for growth, pupal period and adulthood, and studies have shown that the changes involved are controlled by the interaction of hormones in response to changes in day-length. Changing levels of moulting hormone (ecdyson) lead up to each ecdysis, while another hormone – juvenile hormone – decides whether the result of an ecdysis will produce another caterpillar stage, or a pupa. It also triggers the behavioural change which causes a full-grown caterpillar to leave the foodplant, seek a pupation site, and perhaps spin a cocoon. The situation is a little more complex in species that are double-brooded, with one generation maturing quickly during the summer months and the other entering a period of dormancy during the winter. Again, the prime environmental factor is day-length, which governs the hormonal response. Adults of the two generations are often visibly different. Not only is the summer generation usually smaller than the earlier one, may differ in colour or pattern. This is particularly noticable in the case of the Map Butterfly (*Araschnia levana*), but is also true of the common white butterlies: a phenomenon called seasonal dimorphism.

It is impossible to generalize about he seasonal pattern of butterfly and moth life cycles. For instance in British butterflies, the winter may be spent in he egg stage (Purple Hairstreak), as a caterpillar (Meadow Brown), as a pupa Large White), or as an adult (Small Tortoiseshell). All strategies are successful, and are ways of avoiding competition between species.

Conservation of Butterflies and Moths

Studies of the abundance and distribution of butterflies and moths in Britain reveal that some species are undergoing increases and others are declining. Annual fluctuations are normal in population size in response to weather but there are longer-term changes taking place.

Changes in the countryside can be seen by comparing aerial survey photographs and maps from the period around the Second World War with those taken recently. Woods and copses have been removed, miles of hedgerows have been pulled up to increase the size of fields, neglected field corners have been ploughed and sprayed, lanes have been widened for motor vehicles and flowery grass verges have been lost, reseeded or sprayed with herbicides.

All this has removed the wild, flowering plants on which the caterpillars of so many butterflies and moths feed. There have been major losses of heathland to agriculture, forestry and building development, salt-marshes have been reclaimed, fens, marshes and water-meadows have been drained and peat bogs have been mechanically stripped for peat on a vast scale compared with the days when they were worked by hand for fuel. All of these habitats support species of butterflies and moths which live nowhere else.

In a typical lowland broadleaved wood there can be over 200 species of larger moth dependent upon the native trees and shrubs, but alien conifers will support less than twenty species.

Only three per cent of the traditional hay meadows present at the end of the Second World War survive today. Many special habitats now exist only as small fragments, sliced up by new roads, affected by spray drift and drainage of the surrounding land. Because butterflies and moths generally have annual life cycles and cannot survive like plants do, for example, as seed, they need the right quantity of foodplant in the right situation every year to breed. If they fail to breed in any one year they will disappear from the site, and for many species other suitable breeding habitats are now too widely scattered for these butterflies and moths to find and to colonize them.

Several bodies in Britain, which are dedicated to the conservation of different forms of wildlife and their habitats, manage nature reserves and Sites of Special Scientific Interest (SSSIs). This way representative habitats are protected in which creatures such as butterflies and moths can breed.

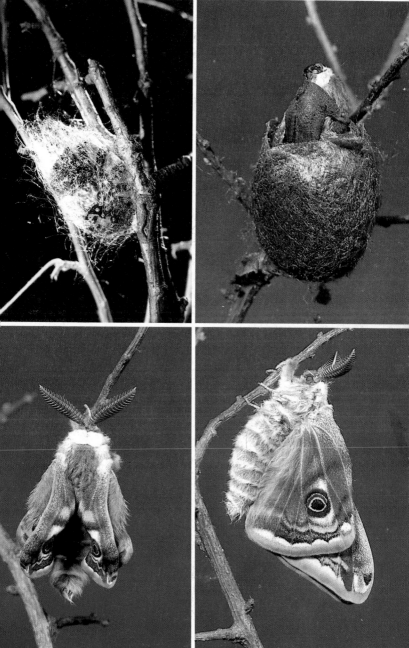

Pale Clouded Yellow, p 30

Dark Green Fritillary, p 46

Scarce Fritillary, p 48

Black V Moth, p 74

274

The Dragon, p 104

Oleander Hawkmoth, p 126

Willowherb Hawkmoth, p 124

Pine Hawkmoth, p 118

275

Elephant Hawkmoth, p 122

Small Elephant Hawkmoth, p 122

Alder Moth, p 200

Grey Dagger, p 200

Light Crimson Underwing, p 210

Early Thorn, p 236

Swallow-tailed Moth, p 238

Light Emerald, p 244

Large White, p 22

Orange-tip, p 30

Pale Clouded Yellow, p 30

Magpie Moth, p 230

Poplar Admiral, p 42

Silver-washed Fritillary, p 46

pupa in cocoon, Burnet Moth, p 106

pupa in cocoon, Burnet Moth, cut open, p 106

Further Information

A wide range of societies, journals, field courses, museum collections, butterfly houses and trade fairs exist for those with an interest in moths and butterflies and there are many local recording schemes to which new contributors are always welcome. An excellent guide to all of these is provided by: Reavey, D. and Colvin, M., *A Directory for Entomologists* (Amateur Entomologists' Society, 1981).

(1) Legislation and codes of conduct for entomologists

(a) The Wildlife and Countryside Act 1981, amended 1988.

Three species of butterfly and six species of moth are protected by law in England, Scotland and Wales and it is illegal to collect, disturb or trade in them in any of their stages. The species are:

Swallowtail *Papilio machaon* L.

Large Blue *Maculinea arion* (L.)

Heath Fritillary *Mellicta athalia* (Rott.)

New Forest Burnet *Zygaena viciae* D. & S.

Essex Emerald *Thetidia smargdaria* Fabr.

Barbery Carpet *Pareulype berberata* D. & S.

Black-veined Moth *Siona lineata* Scop.

Viper's Bugloss Moth *Hadena irregularis* Hufn.

Reddish Buff *Acosmetia caliginosa* Hn.

In addition it is illegal to trade in twenty-two species of British butterfly without a licence issued by the Department of the Environment:

Argus, Northern Brown *Aricia artaxerxes*

Blue, Adonis *Lysandra bellargus*

Blue, Chalkhill *Lysandra coridon*

Blue, Silver-studded *Plebejus argus*

Blue, Small *Cupido minimus*

Copper, Large *Lycaena dispar*

Emperor, Purple *Apatura iris*

Fritillary, Duke of Burgundy *Hamearis lucina*

Fritillary, Glanville *Melitaea cinxia*

Fritillary, High Brown *Argynnis adippe*

Fritillary, Marsh *Eurodryas aurinia*

Fritillary, Pearl-bordered *Boloria euphrosyne*

Hairstreak, Black *Strymonidia pruni*

Hairstreak, Brown *Thecla betulae*

Hairstreak, White-letter *Strymonidia w-album*

Heath, Large *Coenonympha tu¹lia*

Ringlet, Mountain *Erebia epiphron*

Skipper, Chequered *Carterocephalus palaemon*

Skipper, Lulworth *Thymelicus acteon*

Skipper, Silver-spotted *Hesperia comma*

Tortoiseshell, Large *Nymphalis polychloros*

White, Wood *Leptidea sinapis*

(b) *A Code for Insect Collecting.*

This is a leaflet produced by the Joint Committee for the Conservation of British Insects (JCCBI) and is available by sending an S.A.E. c/o Royal Entomological Society of London (RESL; see address below).

(c) *Insect Re-establishment – A Code of Conservation Practice.*
Also produced by the JCCBI, published in full in *Antenna* 10:13–18, summarized in *Bulletin of the Amateur Entomological Society.*
(d) *Legislation to Conserve Insects in Europe.*
This review by Collins, N.M. (1987) covers the legal position regarding collecting insects in Europe up to 1987. It costs £3.45 including postage and is available from AES publications, The Hawthorns, Frating Road, Great Bromley, Colchester CO7 7JN.

(2) **Societies**

Amateur Entomologists Society (AES). Registrar: Mrs N. Cribb, 22 Salisbury Road, Feltham, Middlesex TW13 5DP. Publishes the *Bulletin of the Amateur Entomologists Society.*
British Butterfly Conservation Society (BBCS). Membership secretary: Mrs C. Harper, 31 Romany Way, Norton Stourbridge, West Midlands DY8 3JR. Publishes the *BBCS News.*
British Entomological and Natural History Society (BENHS). Contact: J. Muggleton, 30 Penton Road, Staines, Middlesex TW18 2LD. Publishes the *British Journal of Entomology and Natural History.*
Royal Entomological Society of London (RESL). Contact: The Registrar, 41 Queen's Gate, London SW7 5HU. Publishes *Antenna, Ecological Entomology, Physiological Entomology, Systematic Entomology, Medical and Veterinary Entomology* and handbooks for the identification of British insects.
Societas Europea Lepidopterologica (SEL). Contact: SEL, Hemdener Weg 19, D–4290 Bacholt (Westf), West Germany. Publishes *Nota Lepidopterologica.*

(3) **National Journals** (other than those of the above societies)
Entomologists Record and *Journal of Variation.* (Contact: Publicity Director, 4 Steep Close, Orpington, Kent BR6 6DS.
Entomologists Gazette. Contact: E. W. Classey Ltd, PO Box 93, Faringdon, Oxon SN7 7DR.

Photographic Acknowledgements

a = above, b = below, r = right, l = left, m = middle.

T. Angermayer: Pfletschinger: 23 br, 33 bl, 35 al, 51 b, 57 bl, 71 al, 71 bl, 73 a, 73 b, 75 al, 77 ar, 79, 83 ar, 99 br, 103 ar, 123 a, 127 b, 131 b, 143 b, 149 b, 163 ar, 167 bl, 179 ala, 215 ar, 219 br, 241 bl, 247 ar, 247 ml, 259 mr, 261 bl, 270 a, 270 m, 270 b, 271 al, 271 ar, 271 bl, 271 br, 274 al, 274 ar, 274 bl, 274 br, 275 al, 275 ar, 275 bl, 275 br, 279 br, 282 al, 282 ar, 283 bl, 283 br; **K. Geigl:** 71 ar, 87 a, 105 mm, 117 a, 129 ar, 153 b, 161 br, 173 br, 175 mr, 183 ml, 191 ml, 199 ala, 199 mr, 199 bl, 199 br, 235 ar, 237 mr, 245 ml; **B. Geiges:** 53 a, 53 b, 55 al, 55 ar, 55 mr, 57 mr, 59 ar, 65 al, 65 mr, 75 mr, 75 br, 85 ml, 85 mr, 85 bl, 91 al, 91 ar, 91 ml, 91 mr, 91 bl, 91 br, 93 al, 93 ar, 93 ml, 93 mr, 93 br, 95 ar, 97 b, 101 mr, 103 br, 105 al, 105 ml, 105 bl, 105 mr, 109 ml, 133 b, 141 al, 147 a, 155 a 161 al, 161 ar, 163 ml, 163 mr, 163 bl, 165 ar, 165 ml, 165 mr, 167 ar, 167 ml, 167 mr, 167 br, 169 al, 169 ml, 171 al, 171 ar, 171 mr, 173 ar, 175 ar, 175 bl, 175 br, 177 ar, 177 ml, 177 mr, 177 bl, 179 al, 179 ar, 179 ml, 179 mr, 179 bl, 183 al, 183 ar, 183 mr, 183 bl, 185 ar, 185 ml, 185 bl, 185 br, 187 br, 189 al, 189 ar, 189 ml, 189 mr, 189 bl, 191 al, 191 ar, 191 mr, 191 br, 193 ar, 193 ml, 193 br, 195 al, 195 ml, 195 bl, 197 ml, 197 mr, 197 bl, 197 br, 199 al, 201 al, 201 bl, 201 br, 203 al, 203 bl, 205 al, 211 a, 215 mr, 215 bl, 215 br, 217 al, 217 ar, 217 ml, 217 mr, 217 bl, 219 al, 221 a, 221 b, 223 ar, 223 mr, 223 bl, 223 br, 225 ar, 225 mr, 225 bl, 225 br, 227 al, 227 ar, 227 ml, 227 mr, 227 br, 229 al, 229 ar, 229 mr, 233 a, 233 ar, 233 br, 235 ml, 235 mr, 237 al, 237 ml, 239 a, 239 br, 241 ml, 241 br, 243 a, 243 ml, 243 mr, 243 bl, 243 ar, 245 mr, 245 bl, 247 al, 247 bl, 247 br, 251 a, 251 ml, 251 bl, 251 br, 253 ml, 253 mr, 255 ar, 255 b, 257 al, 257 ar, 257 ml, 257 mr, 257 b, 259 al, 259 ml, 259 bl, 261 al, 261 ar, 261 mr, 263 al, 263 ar, 263 ml, 263 mr, 263 bl, 263 br; **H. Heppner:** 109 mr; **Natural History Photographic:** Dalton: 71 bl, 163 al, Fotheringham: 165 br, Tweedie: 67 al, 71 mr, 75 ar, 103 ml, 105 ar, 109 ar, 133 a, 155 b, 169 br, 171 ml, 171 bl, 173 al, 173 ml, 175 ml, 185 mr, 187 al, 187 ml, 189 bl, 193 mr, 193 bl, 195 ml, 197 al, 197 ar, 199 ar, 203 br, 225 al, 225 ml, 299 br, 233 ml, 235 bl, 239 ml, 251 al, 253 al, 253 bl, 255 ml, 255 mr, 259 ar, Zepf: 63 ar, P. Sterry 101 bl, 133a; **Nature Photographers:** P. Sterry 101 bl, 133 a; **A. Limbrunner:** 17 b, 101 ml, 151

al, 191 bl; **J. Lindenburger:** 17 al, Bellmann: 41 bl, 83 al, 171 br, 249 a, Da Costa-nature: 25 a, Höfels: 43 ar, Jacana-Chaumeton: 59 al, 227 bl, Jacana 249 b, Jacana-Hervy: 125 b, Jacana-Lorne: 55 al, Jacana-Moiton: 21 bl, 27 b, 31 ar, 45 b, 49 bl, 57 al, 59 br, 85 ar 89 al, 107 al, 113 bl, 121 b, Jacana-Nardin: 95 al, Jacana-Winner: 95 bl, König: 69 a, Löffler: 67 bl, Maas: 219 bl, Skibe: 203 mr; **K.-H. Löhr:** 77 b, 85 br, 87 b, 103 bl, 131 a, 141 ml, 159 a, 159 b, 161 ml, 163 br, 167 al, 173 mr, 173 bl, 175 al, 187 mr, 201 ml, 219 ar, 233 bl, 259 br; **T. Marktanner:** 55 br, 69 b; **R. Siegel:** 23 a, 33 a; **G. Synatzschke:** 107 b; **H. Partsch:** 29 a; **Bildagentur Prenzel:** Moosrainer: 113 a, 115 a; **M. Pforr:** 17 ar, 23 bl, 25 b, 33 br, 35 br, 39 a, 51 al, 55 ml, 57 bl, 65 br, 71 ml, 75 bl, 77 al, 81 al, 83 bl, 89 ar, 89 b, 95 bl, 99 al, 99 bl, 101 br, 105 br, 127 a, 129 a, 135 b, 151 b, 153 a, 157 a, 157 b, 169 mr, 169 bl, 183 br, 185 al, 187 ar, 187 bl, 195 ar, 201 mr, 203 ar, 205 ar, 205 bl, 215 al, 217 br, 223 al, 237 ar, 245 a, 253 ar, 261 ml; **J. Porter:** 165 bl; **Dr. E. Pott:** 19 a, 51 ar; **O. Willner:** 247 mr; **K. Wothe:** 141 ar; **W. Zepf:** 6, 19 bl, 19 br, 21 al, 21 ar, 21 br, 27 al, 27 ar, 29 bl, 29 br, 31 al, 31 ml, 31 mr, 31 bl, 31 br, 35 al, 35 bl, 37 a, 37 bl, 37 br, 39 b, 41, 41 al, 41 ar, 41 br, 43 al, 43 bl, 43 br, 45 al, 45 ar, 47 a, 47 bl, 47 br, 49 al, 49 ml, 49 mr, 49 br, 57 ar, 57 br, 59 ml, 59 mr, 59 bl, 61 al, 61 ar, 61 bl, 61 br, 63 al, 63 ml, 63 mr, 63 bl, 63 ar, 65 ml, 65 mr, 65 bl, 67 ar, 67 ml, 67 bl, 67 br, 75 ml, 81 ar, 81 bl, 81 br, 83 br, 85 al, 93 bl, 97 al, 97 ar, 99 ar, 101 al, 101 ar, 103 al, 103 mr, 105 am, 107 ar, 109 al, 109 bl, 109 br, 111 a, 111 bl, 111 br, 113 br, 115 b 117 bl, 117 br, 119 al, 119 ar, 119 bl, 119 br, 121 al, 121 ar, 123 b, 125 a, 129 al, 137, 139, 141 mr, 141 bl, 141 br, 143 al, 143 ar, 145 al, 145 ar, 147 bl, 147 br, 149 a, 151 ar, 161 mr, 161 bl, 165 al. 169 ar, 177 al, 177 br, 179 br, 181 a, 181 b, 193 al, 195 br, 199 ml, 201 ar, 203 ml, 205 br, 207 al, 207 ar, 207 bl, 207 br, 209 al, 209 ar, 209 bl, 209 br, 211 b, 213 a, 213 bl, 213 br, 215 ml, 223 ml, 229 ml, 229 bl, 231 a, 231 b, 235 al, 235 br, 237 bl, 237 br, 239 mr, 239 bl, 241 mr, 245 br, 253 bl, 261 br, 266 al, 266 ar, 266 bl, 266 br, 267 al, 267 ar 267 bl, 267 br, 278 al, 278 ar, 278, bl, 278 br, 279 al, 279 ar 279 bl, 280 al, 280 ar, 280 bl, 280 br, 281 al, 281 ar, 281 bl, 281 br, 282 bl, 282 br, 283 al, 283 ar

Bibliography

Bradley, J. D. & Fletcher, D. S. *A Recorder's Log Book or Label List of British Butterflies and Moths* (Curwen, London, 1979)

Bradley, J. D. & Tremewan, W. G. *British Tortricoid Moths, Cochylidae and Tortricidae: Tortricinae* (Ray Society, London. 1973)
— *British Tortricoid Moths, Tortricidae: Olethreutinae* (Ray Society, London. 1979)

Ford, E. B. *Butterflies. New Naturalist series. No: 1* (Collins, London. 197)
— *Moths. New Naturalist series. No: 30* (Collins, London. 1977)

Forster, W. & Wohlfahrt, T. A. *Die Schmetterlinge Mitteleuropas Band I, Biologie der Schmetterlinge* (Franckh'sche Verlagshandlung. Stuttgart. 1977)
— *Die Schmetterlinge Mitteleuropas Band II, Tagfalter* (Franckh'sche Verlagshandlung. Stuttgart. 1976)
— *Die Schmetterlinge Mitteleuropas Band III, Spinner und Schwärmer* (Franckh'sche Verlagshandlung. Stuttgart. 1960)
— *Die Schmetterlinge Mitteleuropas Band IV, Eulen* (Franckh'sche Verlagshandlung. Stuttgart, 1971)
— *Die Schmetterlinge Mitteleuropas Band V, Spanner* (Franckh'sche Verlagshandlung. Stuttgart, 1981)

Friedrich, E. *Breeding Butterflies and Moths. A Practical Handbook for British and European Species* Translated by Steven Whitebread. (Harley Books, Colchester. 1986,

Goater, B. *British Pyralid Moths. A Guide to their Identification* (Harley Books, Colchester. 1986)

Heath, J. et al (Eds) *The Moths and Butterflies of Great Britain and Ireland Volume 1, Micropterigidae – Heliozelidae* (Blackwell Curwen, Oxford. 1976)
— *Volume 2, Coddidae – Heliodinidae* (Harley Books, Colchester. 1985)
— *Volume 7, part 1, Hesperiidae – Nymphalidae* (Harley Books, Colchester. 1989)
— *Volume 9, Sphingidae – Noctuidae (Part 1)* (Curwen Books, London. 1979)
— *Volume 10, Noctuidae (Part II) and Agaristidae* (Harley Book, Colchester. 1983)

Heslop, I. R. P. *Indexed Check-List of the British Lepidoptera with the English Name of each of the 2323 Species* (Watkins and Doncaster, London. 1947)

Higgins, L. G. & Riley, N. D. *A Field Guide to the Butterflies of Britain and Europe* (Collins, London. 1970)

Kettlewell, H. B. D. *The Evolution of Melanism* (Clarendon Press, Oxford. 1973)

Leraut, P. *Liste Systématique et Synonymique des Lépidoptères de France, Belgique et Corse* (Alexanor, Paris. 1980)

Skinner, B. & Wilson, D. *Colour Identification Guide to Moths of the British Isles* (Viking, London. 1984)

Tweedie, M. *Pleasure from Insects* (David & Charles, Newton Abbot. 1968)

Whalley, P. *Butterfly Watching* (Severn House Naturalist's Library, London. 1980)

Index of English Names

Index of Scientific Names